# Subjectivity and Being Somebody

# ST ANDREWS STUDIES IN PHILOSOPHY AND PUBLIC AFFAIRS

Founding and General Editor:
John Haldane, University of St Andrews

*Values, Education and the Human World*
edited by John Haldane

*Philosophy and its Public Role*
edited by William Aiken and John Haldane

*Relativism and the Foundations of Liberalism*
by Graham Long

*Human Life, Action and Ethics:*
*Essays by G.E.M. Anscombe*
edited by Mary Geach and Luke Gormally

*The Institution of Intellectual Values:*
*Realism and Idealism in Higher Education*
by Gordon Graham

*Life, Liberty and the Pursuit of Utility*
by Anthony Kenny and Charles Kenny

*Distributing Healthcare:*
*Principles, Practices and Politics*
edited by Niall Maclean

*Liberalism, Education and Schooling:*
*Essays by T.M. Mclaughlin*
edited by David Carr, Mark Halstead and Richard Pring

*The Landscape of Humanity: Art, Culture & Society*
by Anthony O'Hear

*Faith in a Hard Ground:*
*Essays on Religion, Philosophy and Ethics by G.E.M. Anscombe*
edited by Mary Geach and Luke Gormally

*Subjectivity and Being Somebody*
by Grant Gillett

*Understanding Faith:*
*Religious Belief and Its Place in Society*
by Stephen R.L. Clark

*Profit, Prudence and Virtue:*
*Essays in Ethics, Business and Management*
edited by Samuel Gregg and James Stoner

# Subjectivity and Being Somebody

Human Identity and Neuroethics

Grant Gillett

St Andrews Studies in Philosophy and Public Affairs

*ia*

IMPRINT ACADEMIC

*Copyright © Grant Gillett, 2008*

The moral rights of the authors have been asserted.
No part of this publication may be reproduced in any form
without permission, except for the quotation of brief passages
in criticism and discussion.

Published in the UK by Imprint Academic
PO Box 200, Exeter EX5 5YX, UK

Published in the USA by Imprint Academic
Philosophy Documentation Center
PO Box 7147, Charlottesville, VA 22906-7147, USA

ISBN 9781845401160 paperback
ISBN 9781845401467 cloth

A CIP catalogue record for this book is available from the
British Library and US Library of Congress

Cover Photograph:
St Salvator's Quadrangle, St Andrews by Peter Adamson
from the University of St Andrews collection

# Contents

Preface . . . . . . . . . . . . . . . . . . . . . . . . . . . . . . . . . . vii
1. Introduction . . . . . . . . . . . . . . . . . . . . . . . . . . . . . 1
2. Origins . . . . . . . . . . . . . . . . . . . . . . . . . . . . . . . . 7
3. What I Am Not . . . . . . . . . . . . . . . . . . . . . . . . . . . 32
4. Metaphysical Subjectivity . . . . . . . . . . . . . . . . . . . . . 62
5. The Moral Subject . . . . . . . . . . . . . . . . . . . . . . . . . 84
6. The Sins of the Fathers . . . . . . . . . . . . . . . . . . . . . . 107
7. Deep Play In the Mechanics of the Mind . . . . . . . . . . . . 137
8. Names and Narratives . . . . . . . . . . . . . . . . . . . . . . . 170
9. Care of the Soul . . . . . . . . . . . . . . . . . . . . . . . . . . 194
10. The Expulsion of Humanity . . . . . . . . . . . . . . . . . . . 222
11. Retrospective and Conclusion . . . . . . . . . . . . . . . . . . 248
Appendices . . . . . . . . . . . . . . . . . . . . . . . . . . . . . . . . 253
   A. On method in moral science . . . . . . . . . 253
   B. Essence and identity . . . . . . . . . . . . . . 256
   C. On possible worlds and metaphysics . . . . 259
   D. Kant's I and the refutation of idealism . . . 261
   E. On natural kinds . . . . . . . . . . . . . . . . 269
   F. The problem of reference . . . . . . . . . . . 270
Bibliography . . . . . . . . . . . . . . . . . . . . . . . . . . . . . . . 273
Index . . . . . . . . . . . . . . . . . . . . . . . . . . . . . . . . . . . 283

To Matthew,

a relentless questioner who has stimulated
some of my deepest thinking

Preface

# *Subjectivity and Being Somebody*

## Human Identity and Neuroethics

I have been doing neuroethics for thirty-five years, though inadvertently, you could say. Inadvertently not only because of a coincidence between what I have been doing in philosophy and bioethics and what is now known as neuroethics but also because the questions that inspired me to get serious about philosophy were exactly those central in neuroethics — human identity, consciousness and moral responsibility or the problem of the will. This book therefore is a kind of report on that thirty-five years of work.

I remember that when I actually began to do philosophy seriously (in Oxford in 1983) I thought that I knew at least one area of philosophy I need take no interest in — the philosophy of language. My book *Representation, Meaning and Thought* (1992) was a commentary on that determination. In the process I have traversed some fascinating territories of the mind — philosophical logic, linguistics, psycholinguistics, psychology, neuroscience (and, in particular, neurosurgery), neuropsychology, anthropology, theology, ethics, metaphysics, phenomenology, existentialism, structuralism, post-structuralism, and, most recently, post-colonial studies (therefore Jack of many intellectual trades even if master of none). Along that journey there have been wonderful encounters with a cast of characters too varied and interesting to do more than mention.

My family have been constantly encouraging and Matthew, to whom this book is dedicated, has (as a young man on his own intellectual journey) asked all the hard questions in the interface between neuroscience and ethics addressed in this book. He has never been satisfied with pseudo-answers and therefore provoked me to think very deeply into what I have gestured at here. Other younger inquirers have also played significant parts such as the wonderful students in the Otago Bioethics Centre and those whom I have had the privilege of teaching in the Otago University Philosophy Department. Certain individuals stand out such as Doug McConnell, Gilbert May, John McMillan (himself now an accomplished bioethicist and philosopher in his own right), Simon Walker and Claire Gallop.

Colleagues in Bioethics and Philosophy have often forced me to think things through to the point where I have had to sort out for myself a knotty problem that refused any easy resolution. Particular thanks are due to Alan Musgrave, Neil Pickering, Andrew Moore, Paul Snowdon, Jim Nelson, Donald Evans, David Zimmerman, Stan and Glenys Godlovitch, Dewey Ducharme, Ngaire Naffine, Rebecca Dresser and Derek Bolton. I owe a huge and continuing debt to Kathy Wilkes and Don Webster, both of whom were always supportive and encouraging and challenged my ideas at crucial phases in my career.

This book attacks the issues of neuroethics at their intellectual heart by offering an account of human identity that is robust enough to inform a variety of work in philosophy, bioethics, and other areas of related thought. I hope that people will find it stimulating and I hope it will lead some to look at old issues in new ways. Most of all I hope that those who read it enjoy it and are provoked to think by it.

I have dedicated the book to Matthew because in the process of his own intellectual development in jurisprudence and political philosophy he has, as I have said, always made me search my mind to relate ethical and political thinking to the fundamentals of human natural history (in so far as we can speak of such a thing). The ways of thought that he has provoked have therefore both been spurred on by and ultimately grounded in very practical and human intellectual challenges.

# Chapter 1

# *Introduction*

## Subjectivity and Being Somebody

> How can a body *have* a soul?
> (Wittgenstein, *Philosophical Investigations*)
> The soul is to the body as sight is to the eye. (Aristotle, *De Anim*a)

Being *somebody* is not just a matter of being some *body*. But what is the difference? The human subject is, as Russell points out (1988, 125), a queer thing, an inhabitant of the space of reasons[1] who is also a natural creature, a lump of protoplasm operating according to the causal regularities of biochemistry and physiology. But how can our thinking about a human being as having a "community of nature" with other objects in the natural world accommodate the difference between the philosophical self and other objects?[2] It is evident to anyone with a realistic attitude (not the same as philosophical realism)[3] that the subject who exercises reason and obeys the laws of logic is a human being, "warts and all".

Kant, in fact, confronts the contrast between nature and (what Frege and Wittgenstein call) "logic" as follows:

> Everything in nature works in accordance with laws. Only a rational being has the power to act in accordance with his idea of laws — that is, in accordance with principles — and only so has he a will (1948, 76).

He notes two standpoints delivering two different understandings of the human being: that of the essential engagement of human

---
[1] To use Sellars' term (1997).
[2] See Wittgenstein, *Tractatus Logico-Philosophicus* [henceforth *Tractatus*], 5.641.
[3] This distinction is made by Cora Diamond (1995). I discuss it briefly in Appendix A.

beings in the domain of reason; and that of their engagement in the world of nature where the former obeys "oughts" and the dictates of rational argument and the latter only causes.[4]

I will use the terms "subject", "soul", "self" to refer to the being who exhibits subjectivity, whose function is the organising, animating, and dynamic principle that gradually develops, sustains and lives through, a human life. The various ways of indicating this have their own specificity but I will argue that the human being can only adequately be understood as also responding to or belonging in a domain of reason and argument and not mere causal transactions. The two (apparently competing) conceptions each reflect the fundamental structures of the type of thinking involved – rational persuasion on the one hand and causal compulsion on the other. The account embodies a kind of naturalism but does not equate human thought with processes in psychology, biology or any other natural science structured according to laws of causality.[5] Naturalism of this type retains the logical and conceptual distinctions preventing immodest and ultimately mistaken metaphysical conclusions (particularly about persons). Throughout the (Kantian) ethos of an analytic of our understanding and the many discourses which inform it underpins a robust conception of humanity and the human spirit.

A neo-Aristotelian framework for human subjectivity begins with embodiment and, since Hippocratic times, we have known that our subjectivity is intimately tied to neurological function. But subjectivity is also the source of the value that guides our actions and the meaning we invest in each other and in what is around us. That meaning arises from what we might call, after Kant and Frege, the "logical subject", the being who inhabits the space of reasons (or argument/discourse).[6] Wittgenstein notes that the relevant inquiry can be mistaken for a kind of psychology (as a scientific study of a natural phenomenon) when he addresses the riddle of "one of the simplest and most pervading aspects of experience" (Russell, 1988, 127). Subjectivity requires, I argue, a radical approach; "The solution of the riddle of life in space and time lies *outside* space and time." I will investigate how the identity of a subject, deriving in an essential way from the subject's constitution within the space of reason

---

[4] A point subsequently picked up by Davidson (1980).

[5] The views railed against by Kant, Frege and Husserl were psychologism or biologism and their philosophical odium was extended by Wittgenstein to any other form of reductionism that aims to provide a complete understanding of the being of things in scientific terms.

[6] Thus argument is therapy for the soul as medicine is for the body.

("logic") is also and essentially entwined with embodiment and, in particular, neurological aspects of embodiment.

The fact that we are human beings directs us first towards our origins as individuals and the varieties of reductionism that affect philosophical writing about origins and identity. We can then examine rational subjectivity as emergent from our (neuro-)biological constitution as beings-in-the-world-among-others so as to examine the relationship between identity, subjectivity, and experience through the work of Heidegger, Levinas, Foucault and Lacan. This allows us to determine the significance of the many neurological interventions undertaken by contemporary biomedicine. Such interventions include psychosurgery, neuroimplantation, and the promise of cyborgs.

Further puzzles arise in relation to the psyche as psyche, especially from Multiple Personality Disorder (Dissociative Identity Disorder) and its implications for narrative theories of the self and memory based theories of identity (neo-Lockean theories). These must be explored in relation to *Dasein* and the care of the self – Foucault's *cura sui*. The post-structuralism of Foucault and Lacan generates a conception of human spirituality as an essential aspect of human subjectivity. In a final "applied" discussion I will consider the interaction between human identities and the kinds of social context we fashion for ourselves to inhabit.

The further chapters elaborate on the many philosophical issues raised by neuroethics in relation to our understanding of human identity.

*Chapter 2. Origins: The natural genesis of the human subject*

Metaphysics in a post-structuralist vein is a way of attending to all our dealings with a thing (including our moral discourse), which is problematic for Locke's distinction between the nominal and real essence of any given type of thing (where the latter reflects what it is, in nature, that goes into the ongoing persistence of the thing being the thing it is). The human embryo reflects the co-production of a human being by genetics and formative factors both contextual and emergent. That view reinstates a robust notion of Aristotle's formal cause and a neo-Aristotelian account of the soul as necessarily embodied with a developmentally shaped form. Each of us is always already engaged within a world of others so that a narrative account of human identity should reflect our existence within an ethical context of mutual care and regard. In fact we are so profoundly relational in our being that an adequate understanding of human identity must go beyond "the facts of our natural existence" and draw on a richer nexus of meaning.

*Chapter 3. What I am not: Narrative metaphysics and identity*

In this chapter I will examine austere specifications of metaphysical essence such as the origin view and the metaphysical reductions based on them (a conceptualisation that confines our gaze to a narrow version of "the natural facts"). Arguments built on that foundation are often taken to have wide-reaching consequences for our thought about human lives and their value. A holistic conception of identity problematizes those conclusions in relation to issues surrounding pregnancy, birth and genetic diagnosis, because of the ungrounded and under-developed intuitions justifying them. The moral dilemmas of bipolar disorder, and other genetically influenced conditions, support the view that a realistic view of human identity (and the associated theory of individual health) give ethical arguments some substance by situating them in real contexts of social and personal life.

*Chapter 4. Metaphysical subjectivity: The genesis of the logical subject*

Kant's postulation of the noumenal self often serves as a reason to dismiss his views as irrelevant to a naturalistic account of personal identity. However if we take Kant to espouse a form of transcendental naturalism as the basis of our logical being, then the more "spooky" or spiritualist "noumenal self" can be set aside and an understanding of the human being as an embodied subject inhabiting the domain of reason (Kant, Sellars, Husserl) and of will (Wittgenstein, Nietzsche, Sartre) can be explored and developed. That account of the noumenal subject also illuminates the difference between actuality (*ding-an-sich* or *Dasein*) and our representation/signification of it (or phenomenon), and deepens our understanding of embodiment as a transcendental ground for the exercise of thought and reason.

*Chapter 5. The Moral subject: Memory identity and the human soul*

The traditional neo-Lockean views concentrate on memory and the span of conscious understanding of one's psychic life as definitive of the identity of an individual, but that focus is unduly superficial and restricted, especially in the light of Locke's own remarks about real essence. The defects are laid bare by a robust understanding of the contribution of the unconscious to the human psyche; and when we look seriously at memory and identity (in a way indebted to Marya Schechtman, among others) we derive a richer analysis of the human subject more in keeping with Lacan and post-structuralism than the standard neo-Lockean views. A rationale for the care of the remembering and narrating self emerges from that analysis.

*Chapter 6. The sins of the fathers: Enacted subjectivity*

If the inherited self is significantly formative, both in the character of the individual and the capacities of the will through which the identity of an individual is defined, and the inheritance is configured by the socio-cultural order in which one develops, in what sense is the individual the owner of or responsible for their own actions? The causal model of action and the idea of genetically determined traits are both explored in the light of the Neo-Kantian and Aristotelian considerations intrinsic to the present account. Action explanation is then recast in an account (heavily indebted to Kant, Nietzsche, and Sartre) exhibiting contested freedom and moral responsibility.

*Chapter 7. Deep play in the mechanics of mind: Locked in syndrome, psychosurgery, and cyborgs*

Embodied subjectivity is vulnerable to physical insults and interventions and in particular instances is radically affected by natural contingencies. Neural interventions and technologies are used to alter human psychology, and pose questions about how our understanding of these phenomena should inform our conception of the human subject. A neo-structuralist (broadly Wittgensteinian) discussion of such techniques and the moral challenges posed by profound changes in character or manipulations of the physical body allows us to re-examine the neuroethics of human subjectivity.

*Chapter 8. Names and narratives: Multiple personality and other disorders*

If subjective identity is significantly formed as a narrative with its own structures of meaning and value then a Cartesian (or even Cartesian materialist) conclusion seems to follow in the case of multiple personality disorder (MPD) or dissociative identity disorder. The thought that each "alter" personality is a person in its own right is, however, alarming in the light of clinical and psychiatric ethics (giving rise to the "It was him not me" and "therapeutic murder" problems). The Cartesian view is, however, not sustainable in the light of a careful examination of the related topics of subjectivity, of an individual trajectory in the human world, and of the constitution of identity. That examination, according to a sustainable (neo-Kantian) account of the *psyche*, provides us with reasons to resist radical conclusions about the fragmented identities of an MPD subject. The therapeutic destruction and forensic autonomy of "alters" both embody mistakes, but those mistakes deepen our understanding of human selves as beings whose identity is (in part) a palimpsest of variously motivated texts.

*Chapter 9. Care of the Soul: Demons, spirits and identity*

How do we give substance to a conception of spirituality compatible with the idea of soul and identity recommended by neuroethics? The substance is found in the many connected words, images, stories and relationships that inform spiritual life. Building on a kind of structuralism that problematizes traditional theological metaphysics, I argue that standard attempts to secure spiritual identity all fail. We are left instead with a view linking each of us spiritually to a place in the world where he or she is rooted, to the ancestors we have sprung from, to the family we help to give shape to, and to the stories and myths that inform our cultural and familial lives. This leads to a rich notion of ethics and an inquiry into the enduring value of the embodied subject.

*Chapter 10. The Expulsion of humanity: The reductive society and its friends*

Any society may have ideological enemies and friends. I take the enemies to be those who undermine or denigrate the ideals and practices on which that society depends for its integrity. Armed with Hacking's seminal idea of the looping effect of human kinds, we can speak of these topics in new ways. To speak of a reductive society is to suggest that certain practices and patterns of thought demean and diminish us by accepting a philosophically reductive view of human beings. The present account of human subjects and their identities reflect a richer understanding of ourselves. The reductive understanding particularly affects our ways of dealing with individuals who have psychological impairments — a thesis that I will explore in relation to Alzheimer's disease.

*Chapter 11. Retrospective and conclusion: Problematising the subject*

Chapter 2

# *Origins*

## The Natural Genesis of the Human Subject

---

The Master said, He who works on a different strand destroys the whole fabric.

(Confucius, *The Analects*)

... sound moral reasoning ... relies on gathering morally relevant considerations and weighing and sorting among multiple and diverse sources of moral knowledge. This latter pattern of reasoning is what I have in mind with the metaphor of a tapestry: a rich collection of images and threads. Out of the threads borrowed from the tapestry we construct webs to support our practical moral judgments. The web is the metaphor I employ for justification in practical moral reasoning. The best webs have many strong strands woven harmoniously together with few gaps. Strong webs provide good support for our practical moral judgments.

(Tom Murray, *The Worth of a Child*)

Confucius' invocation of the "way of morality" reminds us of the commonality that we express when we voice and clarify our moral intuitions, especially about our shared humanity. But these are vulnerable to re-imaging of key concepts through changes in practice or forms of life and particularly in the area of our own origins.

The human subject begins as a scrap of biological tissue, the result of a chance coming together of a sperm and an egg, itself perhaps the result of a chance connection, in the immensity of space and time, between a man and a woman. How does that scrap of tissue give rise to the thinking human subject, who can contemplate timeless truths such as the incalculability of the square root of 1 or the nature of the fundamental particles that were part of the big bang? And why should its fate be of such concern? Applying such a question to the essence of a human subject we soon strike deep complexities.

Confucius and Tom Murray convey two different pictures of morality—one as a tapestry that is spoilt if one weaves in a different strand from that which fits the pattern, and the other as a work that will bear departures and differences at certain points while still conveying the "way of morality" as a "whole fabric" that is made up of our proceedings in general and that yields an evocative picture of our discursive practices of dealing with and responding to human beings (as souls).[1]

The human subject at the centre of this web or tapestry results from a story of biological development, but the present account has in view the development of the human soul and so we need to be aware of two possible paths to trace. One directs us toward the soul as an immaterial substance, a bearer of psychic and spiritual properties that may or may not be attached to a body; the other toward a way of thinking about human creatures captured by the concept of a person as a type of living thing and not as something spooky or other-worldly. Aristotle takes the second path (as does St Thomas Aquinas) according to which the human soul (or psyche) is a holistic conception of a human being as a subject of experience. Notice that, in addition to eternal truths, the soul thinks everyday thoughts such as that its joints hurt. Therefore an understanding of the human subject should tell us about a creature who is part of nature but also capable of "the view from nowhere".[2]

Locke, seeking objective knowledge of the things in the world, distinguishes the nominal essence of any given type of thing from its real essence, where the former is given by our thinking of a thing and the latter concerns what it actually is.[3] The essence of the human subject is often linked to that famous philosophical claim "I think therefore I am." But imagine that you walk into a philosophy class and instead of a lecturer you find a tape recorder. It clicks into life; "I think therefore I am"(*Cogito ergo sum*). Do these words, in and of themselves, establish the existence of a thinking being? If not, why are they sometimes taken to be sufficient to capture the essence of a human subject (as a thinking thing)? What is required for "I think

---

[1] Wittgenstein uses the term "soul" as the ground of one's attitude to another human being (*Philosophical Investigations* [henceforth *PI*], 178).

[2] The phrase is from Thomas Nagel's book *The View from from Nowhere* (1986), which concerns our capacity for objective knowledge of the world.

[3] *An Essay Concerning Human Understanding* [henceforth *Essay*], 4216ff.

therefore I am" to be a statement rather than a clever philosophical trick? What real essence is normally made manifest by the utterance?

Whatever else we might say about the real essence of a creature able to assert the *cogito*, it has reason and reflection that knows itself as itself at different times and places (to echo Locke). But how does a being of flesh and blood come to have that complex capacity, and what is implicit in it? If both Descartes and Locke focus on a nominal or subjective essence, then the real essence of a human subject also requires further elucidation.

Kant latches on to exactly this point when he argues that to know oneself thinking is a phenomenon of a very special sort: it reveals an essential or intelligible feature that is definitive of a human being as a rational creature. But that is only a partial representation of a being whose real nature (as-it-is-in-itself) is not yet fully seen.[4] In itself this being may be physical or natural (even necessarily so), despite Descartes' claim that its essence is contained in the *cogito*. We are owed an account of how the subject of consciousness and moral concern (as a responsible agent) is related to human embodied subjectivity.

The conscious subject is also the ethical subject but when does that conception fit a human being? A human embryo is a human being-in-the-process-of-becoming, a fact with implications for our attitudes to human embryos and fetuses. I argue that the idea of co-production by genetics and epigenetic factors (both contextual and emergent) yields a robust notion of formal cause as part of our metaphysics and supports a neo-Aristotelian account of the moral subject as having a developmentally shaped form. A narrative view of individuation and essence can then be used to ground a set of moral attitudes to the beginnings of human life. So much for the bill of fare.

## 1. Human embryos are distinctive beings

Are human embryos children-to-be or little bits of human tissue? Some regard this as a moral decision rather than something to be decided metaphysically but the thrust of the present work is that the two are not separable, both are aspects of the ways that something is located in our cognitive map (i.e. "in logical space"[Wittgenstein, *Tractatus*, 1.13]). If we take a sufficiently broad view of what goes into that (so that it includes "all that is the case"[*Tractatus*, 1.1]), then to map the cognitive profile is to limn the real essence of something rather than just its nominal essence, because by so doing we maxi-

---

[4] He makes the point in the paralogisms of personal identity and I shall return to it in Chapter 3 below.

mally connect it to our thoughts about and understanding of the world. Our discussion of human embryos should therefore mesh with our intuitions about young human lives.

A good place to begin is with Aristotle's distinction between *form* and *matter*. Substance, we might say "is form and content" (*Tractatus*, 2.025). The *form* (at least for any biological thing) is the living configuration or life principle of that type of thing (for instance, a fox instances the form of a canine of a specific type) and it has a biological or developmental trajectory. For Aristotle, the living human form (or soul/psyche) has "nutritive, perceptive, and intellective faculties and movement [or activity]" and is "the cause and principle of the living body" (*De Anima*, 413b, 415b). Form, conceived thus, is an intrinsic and dynamic feature of a thing and is obscured (for instance by losing its longitudinal integrity) if we reduce individuals to "stacks" of quasi-independent sub-entities that have come to be called "time slices". The form and matter of a thing therefore comprise its "metaphysical essence" in the sense that they encapsulate our understanding of what is proper to their nature and individuation (how we tell when we have a cognitive grip of an identifiable and re-identifiable individual) and unify our understanding of that individual and how it should be treated. Aristotle's view entails that the matter involved does not tell us how we should think of a thing, because a holistic conception of its integrity and telos as a being is part of any adequate conception (or, in Gareth Evans' terms, "fundamental idea", of it).[5] In fact Locke's "real essence" differs from this fundamental idea of a given entity only in so far as the real essence may lie beyond our knowledge at a given time whereas Evans' fundamental idea is a foundational node of our system of knowledge.[6]

The human body turns over all its molecules and a large number of its cells over time and, as Locke notes, these successive collections of matter are organized into a continuous living entity by the form in which they participate. Therefore, I am the same person as the person who married, graduated from medical school, enrolled at Oxford University, and so on, despite the fact that I share virtually no molecules with that person at any one of those times. If we eschew a mystical view of the soul (whereby I have one which is an inner ghostly shadow or core of my being) then I am a human soul

---

[5] Evans (1982, 107ff) discusses fundamental ideas, essence, and individuation.

[6] They can be brought together by the simple expedient of granting that a fundamental idea of something, such as a frog, is whatever will ultimately prove to be essential to its frogginess in a developed understanding of zoology.

which forms the *internal dynamic* (that from which the movement itself arises), the *purpose* (that for the sake of which it exists), and the *pattern* (the formal substance), of the human body. As for any living thing, a person changes over time revealing different aspects of one unfolding reality (hence a biological life — and indeed a soul — has a "narrative" shape).

We might be tempted (perhaps by some residue of the "I have a soul which is the inner essential me" view) to focus on my genetic constitution as defining the essential me. It is true that a guiding pattern encoding elements of the human story interacts with the effects of environment and, for each of us is located in his or her DNA but already, in view of what we are learning about genetics, the genetic story is not reductive or simple.

The trap we can fall into is DNA essentialism. DNA, we could say, is a link in the chain connecting each of us to a characteristic type of life lived by our ancestors and adapted to our ethological context. That fuller reality allows us to make a metaphysical distinction between the embryo of a frog and that of a human being even though they appear physically indistinguishable and to make it on the basis of a DNA test. The test, we could say, (epistemically) marks something that is really important — the membership of a given lineage with a proper place in the biosphere (or, if you prefer, creation). One could say of an embryo with human DNA, "This one carries the mark of a human." A thought experiment (in a nearby possible world) makes the intuition more compelling.[7]

> *Humambas*: In 2017, the human race is faced by an unprecedented microbiological threat resulting in a slowly spreading but lethal viral pandemic affecting not only human beings but also most other creatures. Scientists notice that black mamba snakes are not susceptible to the pandemic. The global crisis leads to a genetic modification of human beings by the insertion of crucial piece of mamba DNA found to confer immunity on pre-embryos. The result is a strange creature. Unfortunately the resulting embryo has an unpredictable dichotomous developmental path (due to epigenetic cell-to-cell interactions and complex intercellular exchanges of nucleic acids). Some embryos become humans and others become *humambas* (so-called because they look vaguely reptilian, show very few human characteristics, have an extreme version of autistic spectrum disorder, do not develop speech,

[7] I will not be using the thought experiment to isolate certain preferred intuitions yielding necessary or sufficient conditions for the moral judgments concerned as is done in writing which aims to define metaphysical essences.

have lives of unremitting pain and violence usually culminating in death through self mutilation, and have a lethal bite due to nests of poison secreting cells in their mouth (leading to horrific experiences in nurseries with a non-discrimination policy).

It would be reasonable, in the imagined scenario, to make an early determination (using DNA or any other cytogenetic measures) of the developmental path that is emerging as the embryo is forming so as to decide whether a given individual is actually human or *humamba*. One could then make rational decisions about the treatment of the embryo concerned based on its underlying nature (or essence as revealed by the measures – including DNA – which indicate its developmental or formative trajectory). We therefore have what we might call a *humamba* argument for the importance of form as a concept.

C: *The Humamba Argument*

C1 Humambas and Humans are genetically indistinguishable.

C2 The real essence of a thing is that in virtue of which it is a distinct type.

C3 Humambas show what they really are as their form unfolds itself.

C4 That (developmental) form grounds the real essence of living individuals.

The *humamba* scenario makes vivid the fact that the early human embryo has an indeterminate status in that its formation is an extended event with significant epigenetic influences rather than a "row-of-dominoes" based on DNA alone. Any given embryo may be a human-being-in-the-process-of-becoming (and therefore potentially a member of our moral community) or something quite other depending on its developmental trajectory. That trajectory distinguishes it by determining a form such that an embryo that does become a person is therefore an early phase of that person (a view close to that of De Grazia [2003] but which does not reify phases of biological lives as metaphysically distinct entities). The (internal)[8] relation between an early phase and what follows is an aspect of its being the type of creature it is (a developmental feature of its essence as an individual). The humanity of a human embryo is internally

---

[8] An internal relation is secured by the logic or conceptual requirements rather than being a matter of causality or contingency.

related to the humanity of an adult (where that is a complex attribute — in part moral — created through human interactions).[9]

Why not, as some do, regard the early embryo as a human being *sans phrase*? There are four reasons, all related to the role of development in determining form.

*First*, the embryo in part forms through epigenetic interactions progressively determining its nature so that it becomes a distinctive thing (Copland & Gillett, 2003).

*Second*, the dynamic formation of the embryo may result in more than one human being (e.g. identical twins or triplets) or even in something not a human being (e.g. a malignant uterine tumour, nothing at all — a discarded or profoundly defective embryo, or, in some possible worlds, a *humamba*).[10] Because an early embryo could have any one of these alternative forms, at a given stage, its nature is indeterminate until events determine it.

*Third*, an early developmental stage is not the same as a later stage (see the painting analogy below).

*Fourth*, the early embryo-like thing may not be a developing organism of any kind but actually part of a therapeutic process (a point relevant to stem cells).

Each of these links moral attributes to form as revealed by development as in the present (neo-Aristotelian) view of metaphysical nature. Imagine a cluster of embryonic cells. Some (molecular biological) tests reveal that it is an embryonic stage of a *humamba* not a human being. We can now treat it in accordance with the form that it is progressively instancing as a *humamba* and in so doing appeal to its real nature to justify our decision.

The question "What kind of thing is a human being and what makes a given human being the being that he or she is?" is profoundly important for ethics and metaphysics. I have begun where Locke did, regarding a human being as a creature of a certain kind such that the principled basis (or *principia individuationis*) for its being the creature it is justifies our thinking of it as a creature of that kind. Locke, as we have seen, follows Aristotle in regarding this categorical basis to be a matter of *form* rather than mere matter so that a human being is essentially an animal with a unity of conscious autobiographical life as "a thinking intelligent being, that has reason and reflection and consider itself as itself, the same thinking thing in dif-

---

[9] A view derived in part from a paper by David Wiggins.

[10] Possible worlds talk is, arguably, a way of trying out an idea to see whether it is conceivable that things could be as envisaged; it is, therefore, a modal device.

ferent times and places" (*Essay*, Bk XXVII #9). But Locke is cautious about treating this claim reductively: "'tis not the Idea of a thinking or rational being alone, that makes the idea of a Man in most people's sense; but of a Body so and so shaped joined to it; and if that be the Idea of man, the same successive body ... as well as the same immaterial Spirit go to the making of the same Man"(p. 335). His holism follows from his remarks about real essence in that he recognises that there may be an important (internal or conceptual) connection between embodiment and the rational or metaphysical subject as the bearer of mental and moral (and even spiritual) properties.

Locke himself links the mental qualities of the same human thinker to a unified conscious life but it is not clear that he means to detach that from its underpinning in the same animal. We may be able to conceptually entwine the two by asking "What is the basis or necessary condition for a human conscious life? Thinking rightly about this may turn out to be difficult, but even asking the question blocks an easy acceptance of a reductive view until more is said about the real essence of human subjectivity.

In fact the antireductive caution cuts against both a "mentalist" or "psychological criterion" of identity and also an "animal body" or (reductive/biologistic) physical view. Both fail to acknowledge the intuition that being a person with a distinctive and individual conscious life is what makes me *me*. And both misrepresent the facts of human psychology as a psychosomatic creature paired with others (to use Husserl's phrase).[11] A human being is dependent on human interactions in a formative historico-cultural context to develop as a person with an identity and is, in that sense, deeply relational. Our view of human subjectivity should therefore reflect the many discourses (biological, social, personal, and moral) that articulate our understanding of human identity yielding a situated, holistic, indeed almost textual, view of what it is to be a person whereby the narrative structure of human life grounds the individuation of the human subject (more on this below).[12]

## 2. Holistic Longitudinally-extended Form

The moral value of a human being is an aspect of being-in-the-world-with-others, a type of being shaped by human interaction

---

[11] Husserl, in his Fifth Cartesian Meditation uses a term translated as psychophysical to describe the beings with whom we pair ourselves to apprehend what we are like.

[12] I will critique reductive views in Chapter 3.

within groups that have individually focused relationships and reactive attitudes.[13] It arises in this context as part of a longitudinally extended form in which characteristically human features develop, mature, and decline.[14] Given that the relevant moral attributes of a human life include character, relationships, behaviour, and situated identity there is also a changing profile of the reactions, attitudes, and relationships that inform moral attitudes. On this basis, the moral value of the human being attaches to all phases of human life as phases of a single being but has different implications at different points (as reflected in laws indexed to age or stage in life — concerning infancy, childhood, or adolescence, for instance). The resulting Holistic Longitudinally-extended Form (HLeF) view of a human life is represented in a figure capturing the dynamic of development (see Figure 1).

Figure 1
The Holistic Longitudinally-extended Form of a human life

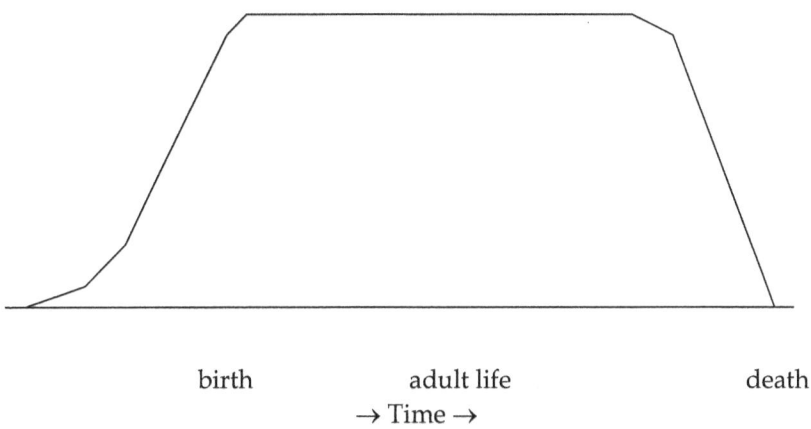

birth　　　　　　　adult life　　　　　　　death
→ Time →

The vertical axis represents the developing capacities of a human individual which come to their fullness and then decline during the terminal phase of life.

---

[13] Strawson (1974). Thus the progressive and formative influences on us continue beyond embryonic and foetal life.
[14] Gillett (2004), especially Appendix C.

The HLeF view underpins many ethical judgments (about life-preserving treatment, entitlement to health resources, propriety of health interventions, and so on) all of which are contestably indexed to the individual's position on the HLeF curve. For instance, many share the intuition that we should not use the same heroic measures on the elderly or irredeemably infirm as on others. In fact, we have a set of expressons to mark the context of decisions for the seriously inform or elderly ("I've had a good life"; "She would not have wanted to be a burden"; "He would have hated all this fuss, and for what, to keep him alive in hospital for another week or so?"; "You shouldn't spend all this money on me—use it for a young person with their life in front of them!" and so on.)

The distinct (and tentative) place of embryos (who may be young human beings-in-the-process-of-becoming) on the HLeF curve is reflected in our thinking about the ethics of reproductive technologies, controls on infertility treatments, and embryo research. The arguments about embryos reveal conceptual continuities and discontinuities between the human form in embryos, foetuses, infants, and morally engaged human beings among us.

The human form comprises characteristic functions showing the integrity proper to human creatures. This gives rise to norms grounding functions (she runs well; he has a hearty appetite) that are not merely statistical but intrinsically *normative* and exemplify a sense of *natural goodness*, because they reflect adaptations which suit us to our mode of living and make life go well for us. Just as a gazelle *should* be swift and vigilant, a beaver *should* be good at making lodges, a lion *should* have strength, agility, and sharp teeth and claws so as to kill its prey, and any creature *should*—at some point in life—be capable of procreation, a human individual should exhibit certain "natural" functions (relationality, self-control, reason, or whatever)[15] that flow from our life as self-forming (or co-creating) creatures living in an increasingly humanized world.

The sense of *normal* in play here has implications for what can be said to be good and what could be said to be a defect for a creature of the type in question and gives us the link that Aristotle outlined between human form and human well-being (or *eudaimonia*—a harmony of lively forces). It has profound implications for our think-

---

[15] This basis for judgments about illness is contested because construed in narrowly biological terms it does not reflect the profound influence of culture and history on what counts as adequate functioning in a human group (a topic to which I shall return in Chapters 6, 7 and 9).

ing about young human beings and our moral attitudes toward them.[16]

One further point deserves reiterating. I have argued that the human form operates as a formal cause of certain properties exhibited by a human being. Thus the matter incorporated by the thing takes on, as part of its assimilation (and through metabolic work), the form it needs to contribute to the functioning of the human body. For that reason, an answer to the question "Why does the heart operate like that?" or "Why does the heart look like that?" can properly be given in terms of Aristotle's conception of a formal cause. The answer, "That's what it is to be a human heart" does not identify an efficient or material cause — the things that explain the process of bringing something about and those that account for what it is made from (the normal terms within which we discuss causes in current philosophy) — but rather directs us to the form in which the thing in question participates. It is therefore an explanation according to which the whole is the explanation for the particular trajectory of development of a part, a lesson with profound implications for human identity as a body as a historico-socio-cultural artifact inscribed and in-formed to produce a distinctive human person.

## 3. Human life follows a developmental story

I have argued that Aristotle's view of the human form as that of a rational, social, and animal being introduces a complex tapestry of discourse and practices centred on the thought that each human being instances an integrated and dynamic set of processes. The complex developmental trajectory entailed by that form links the early embryo (a being-in-the-process-of-becoming) and the adult member of the moral community. The unifying (diachronic) form also grounds (and is in part constituted by) pervasive moral judgements informing our treatment of one another as beings-in-relation and we are morally entitled beings because we are engaged in this milieu. Young human beings are beings-in-the-process-of-becoming of a special kind but their specialness (of type) steadily gives way to individual significance as they take on a formed identity.[17]

In fact, interpersonal recognition, evident in all our dealings with each other, can have an echo very early on in a given life because of

---

[16] I have discussed these in Gillett (2004).

[17] They are, we could say, beings with potential; but note that their potentiality is differently related to their actuality than that shown by, for instance, a sleeping person or one in extended, but reversible, coma (of which more later).

the engagement concerned in that an embryo regarded by the mother (or both parents) as an eagerly anticipated child is arguably different (in moral significance) from a similar embryo who is not. For some parents, particularly prospective mothers in infertile couples or those hoping desperately for a child, every menstrual period signals the loss of yet another potential child and the first missed period indicates an embryo implanted successfully (call this "the desperate mother's view"). For such a mother, and those close to her, a morally significant interaction with the potential child occurs much earlier in the gestational process than in other cases. This particular child has, as it were, an "early entrance" into the community of discourse that intensifies its moral value. As a result of that "entrance" the loss of the embryo is a significant human tragedy inadequately captured by "She has had a miscarriage." Thus, even though their interaction does not fit our normal conception of an interpersonal moral exchange, the relation between this embryo and the prospective mother has properties that are deeply morally relevant (and inform/reflect our view of early human life in general). But the possibility and plausibility of such a maternal intuition is clearly not sufficient to ground a metaphysical claim that at conception an embryo has all the moral properties of a distinct human being. This is not a sufficiently entrenched part of our fabric of knowledge to be a constant presence in relevant discourses, rituals, and other practices of grief and loss. If metaphysics as a guide to morals aims to do justice to the crystallized or prominent features of our discourse (particularly those aspects of it which inform our most general and widely accepted, i.e., scientific and/or reflectively endorsed understandings of things), then individual or peripheral usages of this kind do not have the conceptual weight to do what is sometimes demanded of them (a flaw that also affects the problematic and arcane counterexamples found in some brands of metaphysics).[18]

---

[18] We are not well served here by arguments deriving from some fixed logically defined essence (a "God's eye" view) to a set of preferred metaphysical concepts, to the loss of any humility associated with our (interest driven and provisional or restricted) concepts and the thought that our intuitions, or some preferred set of them, fully reveal a Leibnizian world where unchanging and logically rigorous claims can rule on the fundamental nature of every particular thing independent of the vicissitudes of our cognition and its shortcomings (which were evident, for instance, to Spinoza, Kant, Wittgenstein, or Heidegger), and the contingencies of the world.

Notice that the recognition that the embryo has a human and moral value, even in the normal case, is a relational rather than an "intrinsic" property of the embryo (according to traditional metaphysics)[19] but there is a fairly straightforward argument that it should not be discounted on that basis.

D: *The Engagement Argument*

D1  That a creature is justifiably a focus of moral attitudes depends on its being engaged in the right way with the source of moral value as we know it—the human world.

D2  Such engagement depends on human interactions (which may be asymmetrical).

D3  Recognition of a human-being-in-the-process-of-becoming-a-morally-engaged-being is one variety of such engagement.

D4  Embryos are recognised in that way at varying points in gestation.

D5  Different embryos are morally engaged with us at different points in gestation.[20]

Because (i) "the desperate mother's view" is understandable but not central to our thought about the very early phases of human life and (ii) metaphysics aims to do justice to the most significant and central aspects of our shared conceptions of types of thing,[21] that view should not weigh disproportionately in our metaphysics. We know that almost every fertile woman loses a number of early pregnancies so it is understandable that the boundaries of the concept "young human being" reflect not only the gradual determination of form but also a tentative membership of the human moral community.

Embryos, foetuses, and infants are all examples of human beings-in-the-process-of-becoming—with whom we have some commonal-

---

[19] One might worry about the distinction as it applies to colours, Global Positioning, parentage, cladistic affiliation, ethnicity, etc.

[20] If some find this dependence on the judgments of others somewhat counterintuitive (it seems to substitute a relational view for the intrinsic properties we normally take as the metaphysical basis of our thinking) they would do well to consider the parallel arguments for cyborgs. Arguably cyborgs (human technology composites) are morally significant depending on the quality and nature of their experience with the moral community—or at least the more open-minded and perceptive members of it; see Gillett (2006) or Chapter 6 below.

[21] A significant contributor to our metaphysics is the conception found in canonical science of the kind applicable to things of that type, so that the metaphysics of water would include the fact that it is $H_2O$ (hence critical scientific realism about natural kinds).

ity. One hears and understands the Chinese mother (or any mother who has lost her foetus) when she says, years later, "At times like this I think what s/he would have been doing this year." But if this involvement in each others' life stories does engage us with one another and ground our values, and it can happen at various times for various human beings, then fixing a point of beginning for the moral life of a human being is deeply problematic. Does morally significant life only begin when relationships are actually developed or can it begin before there is any reciprocity at the level of animate, intellective, and social functions? The *Engagement Argument* and the *Humamba Argument* combine to support the claim that we are attuned to the potential of an expected child in a way that depends both on relational factors and projected trajectory rather than the intrinsic physical qualities of the embryo itself at a given point in time. But they also reinforce the fact that there must be some individual for our attitudes to attach to rather than the austere view of potential whereby a mixture of eggs and sperm qualifies as an aggregate being with potential (however much that may be the focus of a set of earnest expectations).

Thus the desperate mother cannot skew our metaphysics beyond the point where the idea of a determinate thing collapses under the weight of critical scrutiny. The arguments about form, and a sufficiency of structure to realise the formal cause animating and organising the embryo so that it is on the path of development into a human being, suggest that the individual, as a being of a given type, is not present until a certain point but thereafter its nature is clear enough for our thoughts to be well-grounded.[22]

The naturalness of this gradualist way of thinking is further supported by two scenarios. The first is an *Adequacy Requirement* on a conception and the second I would call a *"Work-in-progress" Intuition*.

The *Adequacy Requirement* demands that our conception of any substance (or object) should not overlook its most significant features in favour of a sparse (e.g. purely physical) characterisation.

Imagine that I purchase a ticket to the world cup final and put it in my pocket. I arrive home and my clothes have been laundered. I realise my ticket is missing. I make enquiries and it turns out my wife has

---

[22] Even if their metaphysical connections do not determine our moral judgments about what ought to be done in a given case, they do determine what we are doing in any case.

thrown it out. I suffer near apoplexy but she says, "What is all the fuss about, it was only a small piece of paper?"

Now my wife is right but also very wrong. Her conception of what she has destroyed is patently inadequate. Similarly, a metaphysician focusing on intrinsic physical properties seems committed to a view that is inadequate to the thought of most people (from diverse cultures) when he says of a human embryo, "Why all the fuss, it is only a scrap of tissue?"

The *Adequacy Requirement* therefore supports the following argument.

E: *The Adequacy of Characterisation Argument*

E1  Our dealings with something should be rationally based on an adequate conception.

E2  An adequate conception of the embryo notices that it is an early human life.

E3  Conceiving of a human embryo as a scrap of tissue neglects that fact.

E4  A conception based on present physical properties is inadequate.

The significance of the embryo, its morally relevant nature, therefore seems to rest on considerations other than current physical properties (as in the HLeF view).[23]

The *Work in progress* intuition supplements the adequacy requirement in its metaphysical characterisation of embryos.

Imagine a work of art in process of composition. Quite possibly some works are indeterminate in form until they are finished and others "flow" from the first brushstroke; some realise a preformed conception while others are vitally shaped by what appears on the canvas. Intuitively, the loss of a few brush strokes on the canvas is a lesser thing than when the painting is complete even though an essential even unique promise or moment of genius, that cannot easily be recaptured, may be present in the early brush stroke.

Some balance of these features mark the definition of tissues and organs in an embryo/foetus such that similar intuitions are appropriate to our thinking about the unique production that is a human being-in-the-process-of-becoming.

---

[23] I will look at the time-slice view of the current metaphysics of substances in the context of other reductive views in the next chapter.

The human embryo, like the painting, develops from almost nothing (a gleam in the father's eye, a combination of sperm and ovum, or a presence that may be unsuspected) to a living, loving, and loved child. Therefore the human organism accrues value as it takes shape and appears among us (as is reflected in the law of most countries) in such a way that our responsibilities — to pay due regard to each other and nurture and protect the young and vulnerable — also progressively come into play. The human subject with its cognitive, emotional, and spiritual functions is, on this view, produced through mortal human life into something that is of unique value (and exhibits subjectivity). The embryo is precious in a certain way but not in quite the same way as one already among us — a manifest human *relatum*. The argument has the following form.

W: *The Work in Progress Argument*

W1 Any valued object with a form which is gradually realized approximates that value as it reaches completeness of form.

W2 A developing human being is valued and gradually realizes its form.

W3 A human being progressively approximates its moral value as it develops.

One might object that a human embryo is of a type where the form is fully present at conception (or *ab initio*) but that objection is defeated by the *humamba argument* (some things apparently of the same type as an early embryo do not have that form because of the contribution of formal biological causes to development), and the fact that treating embryos as a type reveals that many beings of that type are not of great value (they are discarded through natural attrition, an event without any great moral significance).[24]

I have argued that a conglomerate of cells forming a biological entity draws moral significance from its typical form, that has a developmental trajectory embodying a *telos* (proper end or dynamic organizing principle). For a human embryo the *telos* is becoming a human being among us, but others (physically identical) may become two human beings, or a malignant tumour, or a "humamba". The moral properties of any entity are, therefore, determined and in part developed in a set of interactions with the world. The moral value of a human being-in-the-process-of-becoming is not that of a human being-manifestly-among-us, even though

---

[24] Or at least not an event regarded by most as having great moral significance.

it has a special status reflecting the moral values associated with it as part of the broader thinking that characterizes many of our beliefs and attitudes about growing things of a similar type and their nature.

In the natural course of events a human being whom we have a duty to love and nurture reveals and organizes itself as an embryo develops into the child so that our moral attitudes to embryos should be continuous with our attitudes towards children rather than completely different.[25]

We can deepen and extend these reflections by critically examining our moral intuitions about stem cells.

## 4. Different stories: embryos and stem cells

Experimentation on embryos and their use in stem cell research raises important questions about the "way of morality" and the conceptual fabric supporting our moral attitudes to very early human lives. Murray's "tapestry and web" approach to moral thinking[26] (with its obvious resonances to the work of the later Wittgenstein) is broadly structuralist in that the diverse language, stories, and images invoked by an area of our moral life are taken to inform our answers to ethical questions and the moral sensitivities evoked by them. Confronted by such questions, we might imagine the forms of life and cultural treasures or stories where the relevant language is used and attend to our reactions and intuitions. We might also engage with the narrative structures in which events and objects appear and inform our thoughts so as to display their moral properties and their nuances (Nussbaum, 1990). In that way our real life experience gives rise to the significant connections that articulate our moral reasoning.

The human embryo is morally significant in a way unexplained by its physical characteristics because we regard it as a being whose form involves the coming to be of a human individual among us. When we attend to some general features of our shared thought about human beings and the enduring values informing our lives together, we are reminded of the singularity of each human being and the need of each of us for a place of belonging and a story to tell which affirms that unique value (Gillett, 2004). We belong to families, communities, and traditions replete with histories, heroes and icons, and within that context each of us finds an individual story to

---

[25] Holland (1990) see note 8.

[26] The general mode of thinking is also evident in Murdoch (1993), Diamond (1995) esp ch 13–15, and Elliot (2001).

be lived. A good life binds these stories together in accordance with "the path of morality" not just in ways permitted by others (Taylor, 1989).

Thus the following statements reflect our thinking about embryos and stem cells.

StC   *The Stem Cell Argument*

StC1   Human embryos are distinctive beings who are human but not persons.

StC2   We recognise that human embryos have the potential to become persons.

StC3   This attitude is built on our narrative understanding of the nature of human life.

StC4   The narrative understanding informs our conception of the embryo.

StC 5   That conception is the fulcrum of our moral attitudes.

*But stem cells are otherwise.*

StC 6   A stem cell produced for therapy has a different (narrative) profile.

StC 7   There is an important ethical difference between stem cells and embryos.

### 5. The story of stem cells and therapy

There is currently a range of variously realistic hopes and expectations that stem cell therapies will radically transform our treatment of incurable disease and severe tissue damage, and our understanding of the ways that the human body repairs itself. The relevant hopes have, however, caused fierce debate about cloning and the use of embryos. The present account disconnects the two areas of discourse and implies that we can use stem cells without resolving all the debates about producing and destroying embryos.

Embryos come into being both within normal human reproductive relationships and through biotechnology (used alongside such relationships). The arguments to date suggest that our moral thought should reflect an inclusive understanding of their place in the scheme of things rather than appeal to a narrow subset of their so-called intrinsic properties at a given point in time. If the context is reproduction, then the events in the story are infused by our thinking about the beginnings of a human life and the narrative context of lineages, families, and the care of children. If, however, we are considering entities produced for stem cell therapies, the context is quite different. The *humamba* case, along with other problematic facts about human embryos (e.g. multiple pregnancies and malignant tumours), along with the painting and World Cup ticket analogies, suggest that a dynamic entity is what it is in virtue of its form (HleF) so that it is amenable to a narrative conception of its nature (as a human-being-in-the-process-of-becoming, a monster-in-the-process-of-becoming, a tumour-in-the-process-of-becoming, two human beings-in-the-process-of-becoming, ..., and so on).

If the narrative context of the production and/or development of any living cell is crucial in determining what kind of thing it is then, in the context of a reproductive story, the cell can properly be regarded as a pre-embryo that will manifest its potential as a human-being-in-the-process-of-becoming. But in the context of a therapeutic story using human tissue derived stem cells for experimental or clinical purposes, the concepts informing the story change. Images and associations drawn from stories about the beginnings of lives are no longer apt (absent a reductive physical view). The proper form-fixing context is a widely understood story and set of thoughts about therapeutic technology and its development. In that story entities (that are hardly recognisable as living beings with their own *telos* because they inhabit the abject region between biomedical technology and ordinary biology) are manipulated and for various ends. In thinking this way, we envisage two possible trajectories as follows:

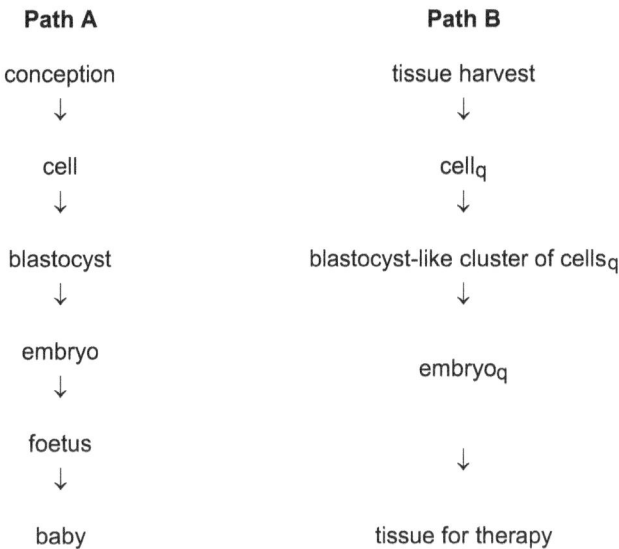

| Path A | Path B |
|---|---|
| conception | tissue harvest |
| ↓ | ↓ |
| cell | $cell_q$ |
| ↓ | ↓ |
| blastocyst | blastocyst-like cluster of $cells_q$ |
| ↓ | ↓ |
| embryo | $embryo_q$ |
| ↓ | |
| foetus | ↓ |
| ↓ | |
| baby | tissue for therapy |

On path A, the normal reproductive path, the embryo develops into a human being. On B the cell, blastocyst-like cluster of cells, and embryo may be qualitatively indistinguishable (on the basis of "intrinsic" physical properties) from an entity on path A (cf. a *humamba*), but in reality it has a different form, in that it is only a way-point in a process not directed toward a full human being but rather to provide tissue to repair a human body. Indeed there may be insuperable barriers to A and B ever "crossing developmental paths" due to some aspect of their production and bioengineering for their therapeutic role.[27]

A stem cell therapeutic story (path B), reveals what we are doing as different from a reproductive process so that the intuitions associated with path A are inappropriate. The physical (time-slice based or synchronic physical) resemblance between tissue-produced-and-manipulated-for-use-in-therapy, and an embryo-destined-to-be-a-child (human-being-in-the-process-of-becoming) is, I have argued, misleading. It is like thinking that a piece of tissue found in a frozen state is the same whether it is a frog or a human (or *humamba*) when, in fact, the real essence of each is quite different. Its intrinsic form is given by the path it is on (revealed by its DNA except in the case of a *humamba*). The reality of an embryonic entity — that which defines it as a kind of thing distinct from other things that it might resemble in certain ways — is a matter of its real natural history (indicated by the DNA involved). The mistake in looking purely at morphological (time slice or synchronic) features is the error shown by thinking that the world cup ticket is just a piece of paper with marks on it or that the first brush stroke of an innovative work of art is just a pigmented mark on a canvas. The real essence of cells produced in accordance with the requirements of therapeutic cloning is not that of cells that are forming a young human being.

So we have an argument for *trajectory based moral essentialism* (TBME) as follows:

TBME1   A at time T' closely (perhaps indistinguishably) resembles B at time T'.

TBME 2   A has a trajectory of natural development that makes it a being of moral concern to us but B does not.

---

[27] We could say that their Lockean "real essence" would not be that of young human beings but be that of mere "human tissue" with a nominal essence that misleadingly resembles the nominal essence of a young human being (according to a set of constraints — essence in terms of synchronic physical properties — on the relevant nominal essence).

TBME 3  Any difference (at time T') signalling the distinct trajectories marks an important moral difference.

TBME 4  The moral difference is directly tied to the trajectory intrinsic to the form of a biological entity and only indirectly to indicators of the trajectory (such as DNA structure).

There is an objection based in *genetic reductionism* (GR) or *genetic essentialism* (GE).

GE Obj:  A is intrinsically different from B only if its DNA shows it to be of a different kind from B because DNA is the basis of our metaphysics of biological organisms.

The objection is met by inserting the following premises:

GE Add 1.1a
   Molecular biological differences are not *per se* morally significant.

GE Add 1.1b
   Differences in DNA are morally significant because of the role of DNA in the HLeF of the creature concerned. The HLeF of a human embryo in a reproductive context is to be "one of us" in-the-process-of-becoming i.e. its projected life story is to enter significant moral interactions with others as part of a context of moral value.

Notice that this locates moral properties as part of our intentional or mental lives that have their own dynamic principles of connection. As intentional properties they differentially reveal themselves from different conceptual frameworks, just as one may see the Evening Star and not realise that one is seeing the planet Venus (even though the terms refer to the same thing).[28] Moral properties, likewise, may not be evident if the descriptive framework is wrong — that of molecular biology for instance — but may come into view when things are looked at otherwise — in terms of a life world of social and personal events.[29]

There is a further objection to the argument: The *laissez faire objection* (LF Obj).

LF Obj:  The consideration of *telos* or trajectory implies that any foetus or even an infant whom we want to use for

---

[28] The difference in sense is sometimes glossed in terms of "cognitive significance" but that has unduly individualistic connotations.

[29] Bernard Williams invokes these as the context of moral thinking (1985, 201).

research or transplantation is unproblematically able to be used in biomedical ways because it was always going to be "cut off" in its life story.[30]

I have argued that the moral properties that accrue to a human being as a-human-being-in-the-process-of-becoming-a-person are a product of a web of thoughts and exchanges that underpin a recognition of and respect for human life. The second objection divorces us from that web by discarding features of our widely shared discourse. But we cannot so easily tear ourselves from our form of life and its ways of thinking. That which is deeply entangled in our discursive being cannot be conjured away by clever and logically consistent but idiosyncratic views. The desperate mother's claim gets its moral appeal from our general discourse about children and families and we can readily accommodate a need to go beyond the language of "miscarriage" to recognise her loss. But a rationally driven and technologically motivated cut-off of foetal life is on much more shaky ground.[31] It is so discordant with our general intuitions that it constitutes "working on a different strand" from the rest of us and straying from "the path of morality". Related arguments but with slightly different content can and have been advanced about animal life.[32]

## 6. Conclusion:
## So why is the subject importantly an embryo?

The use of stem cells for research and therapy raises deep-rooted questions about our being and our beginnings and what attitudes we should foster towards young human lives. We have complex and conflicting attitudes in this area and they inform our thoughts about the earliest stages of a human life. The relevant attitudes are often summarised by an appeal to potential or a being-in-the-process-of-becoming and they are related to the fact that biological entities undergo development that unfolds the traces of lineage, inheritance, origins, and so on that the young life carries. These attitudes and our knowledge of the biological realities involved create a tapestry of words, stories, and images informing our moral thinking about embryos. We can (to some extent) insulate our moral discussions about stem cells and their use from questions about human

---

[30] The argument in this form was posed by Anthony O'Hear.
[31] "Three times I saw rolls of fine hair. ... After seeing them, I felt the little child ... was really pitiful. They were very little. If they were bigger, I would feel much worse"(Jing Bao Nie, 2005, 146).
[32] Diamond (1995), see note 2.

identity and essence, because a consideration of the relevant trajectories and narratives are of key importance in (common sense and scientific) biology and moral anthropology.

I have argued that, despite physical and perhaps even molecular biological resemblances, a cluster of cells produced as part of a therapeutic cloning scenario is not the same as a very similar cluster of cells with a different nature and projected trajectory (or Holistic Longitudinally-extended Form — HLeF). On that basis, a pre-embryo arising as part of a human reproductive story is a different kind of creature from the tissue and quasi-organisms that are produced during stem cell therapy.

Despite the arguments for a conceptual divide between the use of stem cells and the ethical status of embryos, stem cells raise their own set of issues to do with their potential clinical uses. These are quite complex enough to tax the powers of clinical ethics, in the formulation of guidelines in relation to tissue repair and innovative or experimental treatments using such tissue, and are dealt with in the following addendum to this chapter.

## ADDENDUM TO CHAPTER 2

### Ethical issues concerning stem cells

The ethics of stem cell use may not be those associated with embryo experimentation, and may be somewhat peripheral to the arguments about neuroethics and identity, but there are significant ethical issues in relation to the therapeutic use of stem cells.

Stem cell technology offers the hope that we will be able to reproduce tissues from a human being and repair or even re-create organs for that person. If such technology becomes a reality, then the shortage of transplant organs may be a thing of the past. Stem cells also offer the possibility of repair in conditions like myocardial infarction or spinal cord damage where, at present, we can only help the person to cope with the problem and try to prevent the situation from becoming worse. The prospect of injecting cells into a damaged heart or spinal cord so as to initiate repair and restoration of function should silence the staunchest critic of such technology. But ethical problems are not far away.

1. First there is the *placebo effect* which is particularly problematic when the gains are subjective in terms of improved cognitive ability, improved feeling in limbs or organs and so on. The history of medicine is replete with examples where some version of this effect has

induced initial enthusiasm for an intervention the ultimate worth of which is never proven and which ultimately fades into obscurity.

2. Second there is a real problem with *therapeutic pressure* both from patients and from commercial interests. Both are constantly on the lookout for surgical and other techniques and innovations; the patients want something that will make them better, and the industry wants to make money in the lucrative medical technology market. It is not difficult to imagine that stem cell banks, accessible for a fee, would be well patronised by those hoping that the technology will come along to repair or regrow a liver, heart, kidney or spinal cord should you need it. The prospect of "two tier" medicine, and serious injustice, in these fringe areas looks not only to be on the horizon but in our face.

3. Third, there is a distinct prospect that some early attempts at stem cell therapy will have serious *long term complications*. Stem cells are being used precisely because they have the potential to grow and produce new tissue, but new tissue can be disruptive and ultimately damaging to the person in whom it grows and that harmful potential might not show up for some time after the stem cells have been injected or inserted into the site where they are supposed to do their thing. The prospect of a creeping protoplasmic reticulum strangling the heart with dysfunctional heart muscle tissue or obliterating significant areas of functioning brain are quite horrific.

4. There may well be *other long term dangers* the possibilities of which are suppressed or discounted in the vanguard of exciting new prospects for stem cell therapy.

5. As well as these more detailed concerns there are also worries about the effects of stem cell use on *our conceptions of ourselves* and the nature of human life. Human life has a mortal or finite span and our conception of who we are is tied to that span. Heidegger, Sartre and Kierkegaard have all noted that human life holds special moral challenges and qualities because of our mortality. Perhaps the power of stem cells will render the bodies of human beings eternally renewable rather than, as currently, affected by the diseases of aging prevalent in Western society, subject to decay and decline. And if we ourselves will have hugely extended life spans, how will we use them? Some workers think these are exciting possibilities and others think not. *The Makropoulos Case*[33] questions our conception of the good life and its relation to mortality in a way that demands serious

---

[33] Opera by Janácek, based on Karel Capek's play, where by magic the heroine has lived over 300 years (see Williams, 1973, 82-100).

reflective scrutiny. But, even more chilling is the prospect that a stem cell perpetuated biological longevity will outlast our personhood because of some stem cell induced mismatch between cognition, fellow-feeling, and vitality.[34]

---

[34] I will consider some of these problems in Chapter 6 in discussing neuro-implantation.

# Chapter 3

# *What I Am Not*

## *Narrative Metaphysics and Identity*

> You talk as if naming an object and then thinking about it were the easiest thing in the world. But it isn't so easy. Suppose I tell you to name any spider in my garden; if you can catch one first or describe one uniquely you can name it easily enough. But you can't pick one out let alone name it by just thinking.
> (Max Black, "The Identity of Indiscernibles")

> The master said, A gentleman can see a question from all sides without bias. The small man is biased and can see a question from only one side.
> (Confucius, *The Analects*)

> What I am opposed to is a certain kind of exactitude given *a priori* as it were. At different times we have different ideals of exactitude.
> (Wittgenstein, *Culture & Value*)

The human subject is a bearer not only of natural predicates (like *embodied, living, rational,* and so on) but also of moral predicates (like *cruel, considerate, loving,* and so on). An adequate understanding of the human subject could either survey the relevant intersecting discourses or distil an "essence" (or logically austere specification) apt for metaphysical debates.[1] Such metaphysical specifications designate certain properties as essential to a thing being what it is and thus fix the range of permissible thoughts about it; for instance, an animal might be specified by its spatio-temporal trajectory or its origins, each of which yields a basis for making the decision that A is the same animal as B.

---

[1] The idea of essence and identity is discussed in Appendix B.

Notice that the identity question is settled once the relevant (essential) property set is fixed. But I have argued that a human subject is a being with a developmental trajectory typical of living things and that its being an individual of a certain type is not settled until a certain form has emerged. Certain vagaries[2] then need to be taken into account especially when moral questions are posed. Locating very young human beings in Wittgenstein's "great mirror" (of logic — specifying how things are and must be with the world — see *Tractatus*, 5.511) is difficult because, as we have seen, our intuitions about young human lives draw on many ways of thinking about human life. Taking together both the thought that the human form is Holistic and Longitudinally-extended (the HLeF view), the idea of a work in progress, and also the unique relational place in the human world of families, communities, interpersonal relationships, and so on that is the basis of human identities, the combination suggests that reductive accounts of our human moral status are simplistic and unilluminating.

I will examine Derek Parfit's non-identity problem as an example of a metaphysical reduction taken to have wide-reaching consequences for assessments of the value of human individuals. The present narrative theory of identity opposes that view and its implications including its use in ethical arguments adjudicating between no life at all and lives with defects of one kind or another. It implies that these arguments do not help us to understand the moral problems of conception, birth, and genetic diagnosis because of the under-developed and indeterminate intuitions to which they appeal, as can be seen in relation to Huntingdon's disease, bipolar disorder, and psychopathy.

### DNA essentialism and the doctrine of origins

If something like a narrative (an extended and connected series of events realising a story) both configures and forms the identity of a human being, then the claim that a given package of DNA is the essence of a human being looks suspect.[3]

*Epigenetic argument against DNA essentialism.*

(i) A given package of DNA can become many things.

---

[2] These include Sorites-type paradoxes due to growth and aging and other gradual changes.

[3] The view is called "DNA (or genetic) essentialism" and it neglects the importance of epigenetic factors in determining the fate or form of an embryo.

(ii) Its becoming a human individual critically depends on processes operating on that package of DNA.

(iii) Variations in the DNA may not be reflected in the person that results.[4]

(iv) A human being can be the same being as he or she would otherwise have been despite differences in DNA.

(v) A human being can be a significantly different being from what he or she would otherwise have been despite the DNA being the same.

Therefore

(vi) Human identity is not that of a package of DNA.

The argument raises a question about the kind of story (and influences) that make a human being the person he or she is and therefore focuses our attention not only on human beings in general but on young human beings in particular. I would argue (with Cora Diamond) that only a discussion of sufficient breadth and depth about our ways of thinking and acting can ground metaphysics, itself an abstraction from this holistic knowledge.[5] We construct it on the basis of linguistic analogies, patterns or images in our language and a reification of the result often leads us into either nonsense or patent wickedness.[6] Because stories (in a broad sense) are at the heart of our dealings with things, there is a kind of *narrative metaphysics* implicit in the account (that should not be saddled with an inappropriate *philosophical* realism).[7]

*Narrative metaphysics* claims that objects and events cannot be individuated or specified independent of the discourses and forms of life in which they appear and in which they attract workable criteria of identification and reidentification. It is not just that things and events are named differently in different narratives (but are "meta-physically" the same), you cannot determine the boundaries of a thing unless you give the framework within which it can be meaningfully discussed. The relevant narratives then bring values into play so that events take on a significance that otherwise they may not have. Note that the use of the term "narrative" is broad (as in post-modern critiques), referring to a coherent and programmati-

---

[4] This premise follows from the formal cause argument in Chapter 2.
[5] What Heidegger calls "circumspection".
[6] Diamond (1995), 35. This claim is forcibly made by Coope (2006).
[7] I have briefly discussed this in Gillett (2004), Appendix B.

cally linked account of phenomena, a localised history, as in the evolutionary narrative, the story of the splitting of the atom, the life story of Anna Pavlova, or whatever. Narratives therefore constitute a diversity of coherent and organised bodies of knowledge each presented from a particular (situated) point of view with an embedded way of understanding things.[8]

Narratives concern objects and what happens to them. One might assume that those objects can be unambiguously identified in stories other than the narrative type in question (or ultimately in terms of "the view from nowhere")[9] but that claim looks suspect when we see how difficult it is to specify a referent in narrative-independent terms. Foucault speaks of the attempt to "evacuate the concept of the event" (Foucault, 1984, 56) as in the more radical forms of structuralism and settles on the more modest (and plausible) strategy "of realizing that there is actually a whole order of levels of different types of events, differing in amplitude, chronological breadth, and capacity to produce effects"(ibid). In so doing he echoes Wittgenstein's critique of "simples"(the building blocks of ontology and metaphysics) which can be unambiguously denoted and then discussed in various ways for different purposes.[10]

An awareness of narrative reveals that the interests colouring the construction of an account or explanation of what is happening are ubiquitous and affect the way that we classify or individuate things so that the individuation of objects is an activity that philosophical analysis ought always to link to "this and related narratives".[11]

Stories are made up of events involving objects. The world of a story, we could say, is "all that is the case" as it appears in the story.[12] When we look more closely, both Wittgenstein and Foucault echo Kant and cast doubt on the conception of objects and events as

---

[8] Heidegger would say that a narrative creates a framework within which a mode of *logos* allows a thing (*hypokeimenon*) to appear (as phenomenon) so that truths can be enunciated about it. The resulting truths uncover or reveal (and also conceal) aspects of the Being of the thing in question.

[9] The idea of "the view from nowhere" is the idea of completely objective impartial knowledge unaffected by any subjective features whatsoever, a view thought naïve by most post-Kantian scholars.

[10] The view is championed in the *Tractatus* and rejected in *Philosophical Investigations*. It is closely related to Wittgenstein's later doubts about Frege's analysis of thoughts in terms of the semantics of sense and reference.

[11] Analogous to "this and nearby worlds" of modal debates in the possible worlds style (Appendix C).

[12] On this view, metaphysics is a grand narrative (see *Tractatus*, 1).

identifiable/specifiable independently of any account or framework of understanding. By contrast, metaphysical realism accepts such invariant things and, by appealing to so-called "general intuitions" about them, frames ethical issues in terms of a privileged set of representations accorded general validity. One might say to such a metaphysician "In your dreams!" if transcending the subjectivity of the dream-world and its representations unshackled from (or objective and detached with respect to) our lived reality were not so important for "the view from nowhere". An engaged understanding of our place in the world, by contrast, reveals points of philosophical and ethical difficulty and ambiguity besetting us on all sides.

Take a typical event — my arriving home from work. Is it part of this event that a small pollen particle comes through the front door as I open it, even though that is neither known nor mentioned? My daughter calling out "Hi Dad" is surely part of the event but what about the micro-disturbances in air particles that result? And what of the flux of acetylcholine molecules in a million synapses in her brain or of calcium ions into muscle cells in her diaphragm as she speaks? Facts of that type obscure any clear and distinct (or even possible) idea of the event. Of the millions of things going on in her brain only some are aspects of my homecoming. Which events they are is indeterminate because that event, as such, does not appear in neuroscientific discourse which does not, so to speak, pick out the relevant objects of thought (with their proper rules of individuation).[13]

Imagine that (*per impossibile*) we aimed for a "topic neutral" specification of my homecoming. Would that include all the displacements of matter within a certain region of space-time (call it S' between $T_1$ and $T_2$)? The first problem is to specify the region of space, given that my daughter is two rooms away from the front door. Is everything in the house included? My cat, on the back lawn, hears the door and comes bounding around to the front of the house and my daughter greets him more warmly than me when she opens the door. That, surely, ought to be mentioned. Was he part of the event while he was not in the house? But where next? On the back lawn, a big bug eats a smaller bug under the Beech tree; so is the bug's predation event, occurring within S' between $T_1$ and $T_2$ part of my homecoming? How much of the back lawn is part of this event?

---

[13] This point appears repeatedly in the writing of Donald Davidson who argues that not only events but also causal laws are discourse dependent in a philosophically interesting way.

Does that depend on the aural acuity of the creatures there? And what distinguishes chemical reactions in grass blade Gb23947103 (within S'), from Gb23947104 (beyond S') as event parts?

A quasi-physical account of that segment of the universe may mean nothing to anybody (my homecoming is lost among molecular interactions, electro-chemical forces, quantum changes, and so on).[14] What is more, irrelevant matters do get in: the feasting bug, the draught caused in the laundry (of similar magnitude to the hot air caused by my daughter's welcome), some photons hitting the wallpaper opposite the front door (as the sunlight streams in), the lowering of mean kinetic energy of water molecules in the fishbowl due to transient cooling, etcetera, etcetera, etcetera (as the king of Siam would say). Such a catalogue obscures important things about my homecoming; perhaps my daughter's tone of voice reflects her vexation that we have been "on her case" about overdue assignments.

Therefore the meaningful human event may disappear among the myriad of happenings in a given space-time segment of the universe and with it that segment of the story of my homecoming *as a human event*. As my homecoming it is a figure unconcealed against the ground of existence. But there is no "topic neutral" way of carving the world and what is in it that "clips out"(or individuates) my homecoming without using concepts apt for events of that sort as derived from language games based on our participation in stories of that kind. A physical, biochemical, neural, meteorological, or political story carves up the whole shooting-match (Being, big-B) in a way that yields a different kind of picture, throwing different events and objects into relief as topics for thought. The form (*principium individuationis*) of each thing is coeval with the rules of discourse codifying how to discern and count it.[15] Counting a lizard as an amphibian is one kind of mistake (related to empirical knowledge of taxonomy) and counting a detached or undetached reptilian part is another (related to philosophical semantics). The two-way relation between stories and events allows us to grasp truths about (and the significances within) the world we inhabit. And what goes for events also goes for objects because events happen to objects and objects feature or are significant because of their part in events.

---

[14] The *hypokeimenon* does not appear as a phenomenon.

[15] A set is internally related to the individuation of its members so that when I am gathering a set of integers I have stated the individuation criterion for the candidate members, and when I am counting things I depend on what is delineated as an eligible candidate for membership.

Events occur in narratives (in the broad sense) and therefore stories define frames of reference for certain truths and reveals the objects and their parts referred to in those truths (i.e. their metaphysics).

Consider a piece of stone lying half buried in the turf of Ben Lomond. Is the stone a part of the mountain or not? Imagine a world in which the stone has risen to the surface over time; in that world it does seem to be a part of Ben Lomond. But now imagine it was found on the roadside near Loch Lomond and carried up the mountain by a tramper where it was dropped. In that world do we go with origins or current "attachments"? Suppose that the stone is taken and mixed into concrete in Glasgow; if it is part of Ben Lomond under those conditions (according to the origins theory), then Ben Lomond is a scattered object. Now whereas an Irish diaspora is a geographical fact, a "Ben Lomond diaspora" just strains the brain (imagine, for instance, trying to measure the area covered by Ben Lomond in that case). But indeterminacy also affects Ben Lomond's boundaries—the "roots" of the mountain have a "fuzzy border" in the rock beneath, so Ben Lomond is a vague object even though I seem to know what the term refers to. Perhaps mountains can only be identified in geographical accounts rather than geological or precise GPS[16] accounts (although using a GPS system can locate them). Indeed Ben Lomond, as such, may appear neither in a geological nor quantum nor cosmological description of the universe.

Even the President of the United States of America is problematic when considered as an object. At any given time this object is a human individual but he or she may not appear in (i) the story of a water molecule $M_W'$ or (ii) an ecological account of the impact of human beings on the environment.

(i) Imagine that $M_W'$ is breathed in by the president. Now, the time that $M_W'$ spends in the lungs of the president is not noteworthy: its mean kinetic energy is approximately at that of 37.4°C and it has a series of physico-chemical interactions. It is even debatable whether, during its time in the presidential lungs, the molecule is really *in* the president (compared with $M_W''$ bound up in a presidential liver cell or one that has crossed into the presidential blood). But surely $M_W'$ (let's call it Walt the water molecule) either is or is not part of the president of the United States!

Where *does* the president begin and end? Is Walt a part of the president? In that, respect at least, the object which is the president of the United States is indeterminate. Imagine a letter written by the

---

[16] GPS = Global Positioning System.

president apparently pardoning you for a crime. Was Walt a part of that event? That is a nonsense question. If there was an aberration of the president's psyche when he signed it and at the time Walt had found its way into one of the president's frontal lobe neurones, does the president's saying "I have not been myself lately" refer to a state of which Walt is part? To include Walt in any account of that event is to get off on the wrong foot in a story about presidential decisions. We can only assess the decision within a discourse where certain questions can be posed (Was the president sane? ... coerced? ... acting corruptly? and so on).

Explanation takes over these discursive properties. To explain the extinction of a species of Amazonian bird or monkey, a biological event, might draw on purely biological terms but only with partial success. To understand that event I *might* have to say something about the President of the United States (*qua* leader of a powerful economic and industrial nation) and agreements (or non-agreements) about the use of resources and the role of government in controlling international commercial activity. The political and economic realities involved (trade and financial agreements, the US legislature, multinational corporations, and so on) may be part of an adequate explanation of the extinction, even though many of the "objects" concerned form no part of the science (or metaphysics) of biology.

The underlying point is that a thing appears as a bearer of certain explanatory properties as occupying a certain cognitive role[17] and it leads Wittgenstein to reject the idea that there are metaphysically basic individuals or "fundamental components of reality" (*PI*, #47ff). The same point surfaces in Foucault's deconstruction of the event that is independent of history (but clothed in historical drag). It motivates Heidegger's *alethic* view of truth and Quine's remark: "We must speak from within a theory, albeit any of various" (1981, 22).[18] We can summarise the argument as follows.

NM: *Narrative Metaphysics Argument*

NM1 To think about a thing requires picking it out.

NM2 Picking something out requires a discourse apt to individuate it without significant indeterminacy.

---

[17] Cognitive role or significance, or mode of presentation, arise from Frege's distinction between sense and reference in his discussion of the Morning Star and the Evening Star.

[18] A point revisited by Davidson in several papers in his 1980 collection.

NM3  Discourses work within the presuppositions and connections established in a narrative context (broadly construed).

NM4  The thinkable properties of a thing as a determinate thing derive from the narrative context in which it appears.

Narratives are constructed within language games where discursive tools carve up the world and what goes on in it so that, according to our interests, certain things spring into relief as figures discernible against a ground (or horizon). The figure (an object of thought) is revealed by the concepts applied to it whose role, in general, is to pick out features of the world engaged with our interests and powers. Language is, therefore, a tool for adaptation engaging our (shared) cognitive systems with the world around us. The stories we tell determine the cognitive tools in play on a given occasion and differentially make some aspects of a situation thinkable and others not so.[19] I have argued that our thinking about embryos is of a piece with the rest.

## Biological identity and narrative metaphysics

The debates about cloning often equate genetic identity with personal identity and, on that basis, forbid copying or duplicating human beings. However the relevant arguments embed an outdated understanding whereby a person's genome, complete in the fertilised egg, directs development through a deterministic causal chain from the single cell to the child or adult. The genetic constitution is then equated with the metaphysical essence that constitutes identity. But the arguments based on form, the case of identical twins, and arguments that clones are not identical (for epigenetic reasons) imply that, not only is the very early embryo not necessarily an individual, but personal identity is not genetic identity (Brock, 1998), rather it is a joint product of the raw material of genetics and the huge influence of environment and "person-making" that Aristotle and his followers have written so much about.[20]

---

[19] We ought to notice that this conclusion is very close to that of Quine in his "Identity, ostension and hypostasis"(1953). He argues, I think successfully that this conclusion affects the principle of the identity of indiscernibles fundamental to most metaphysical reasoning such that "Objects indiscernible from one another within the terms of a given discourse should be construed as identical for that discourse"(71). To that I would add "All objects are and must be picked out by means of some discourse"(a conclusion I take to be close to Wittgenstein's in *PI*, ##46ff).

[20] I have discussed this at some length in Gillett (2004).

I have noted that our present understanding of development and the importance of the cell-to-cell and tissue effects acting on the individual cells of the growing human being shows us why a holistic concept of structure or form is the best philosophical basis for human identity (even if we confine our attention to biological determinants). The HLeF view is that in a living form the typical trajectory of growth and development, replete with emergent properties, implies that a human being is a thing with a characteristic narrative form (unlike those things for which a more static, middle-sized-dry-goods view is adequate).

These considerations affect both identity and identification of the human individual. We identify a person as, for instance, the fourth child of Jose and Xena, a child who has always been precocious, effervescent and seemed "tomboy-ish". This identity is a holistic combination of features of the type that characterizes a human being as unique, valued, with interests, fulfilling (or not) certain expectations, and capable of "authentic" development as the person whom they are.[21]

## Other discourses and the complexities of human form

Human beings live in narrative worlds and the objects and events in their lives have significance because of their roles in a cluster of intertwined stories, of birth and family, totem and taboo, prophecy or prediction, upbringing and community, culture and geography, and even more individual or "inner" stories of hopes, fantasies, icons, heroes, and self conceptions (imagos even). A person's identity as a dynamic product of all those stories implies that reductive metaphysical views in which intrinsic properties comprise identity miss the real essence of a human being. In real life (and realistic[22] metaphysics) human journeys happen in the world of dependent rational animals that is the world of reason and experience and not on what Kant calls

> a broad and stormy ocean, the true seat of illusion, where many a fog bank and rapidly melting iceberg pretend to be new lands and, ceaselessly deceiving with empty hopes the voyager looking around for new discoveries, entwine him in adventures from which he can never escape and yet also never bring to an end (B295).

---

[21] It will emerge that a romantic conception of authenticity as the expression or unfolding of an inner self is deeply problematic.

[22] Not Realistic (i.e. not universal, trans-world, essence type metaphysics).

Kant did not use many thought experiments and favoured naturalistic thinking about the place of human lives in our conceptual universe, a point that applies *a fortiori* when the moral tracts of our conceptual universe are our focus.[23]

The roots of our moral thinking about human beings are, like all our thinking, based on our conception of what a human being is and therefore on things that have, in part, to do with human flesh (biology) but mainly to do with subjective flesh, that is central to and moulded by (or inscribed by) a multitude of stories. Therefore the two major philosophical accounts of the essence of human identity (the bodily and the psychological)[24] both capture part, but only part, of a more holistic and less reductive view of the metaphysics of human identity that is properly distilled from the multiple intertwined narratives informing the life and thought of "a conscious thing that thinks of itself as itself in different times and places". These complex and interwoven stories subtend "a way of thinking" about human beings that is distorted and simplified when we forget that we are creatures significantly formed by participation in discourse.[25]

I have followed Locke in emphasizing the Aristotelian idea of form and linked our thought about human beings to our dealings with the real world where things go together in intricate ways that may not be evident in narrow conceptions (replete with logical grounds and entailments). Alan Donagan agrees and argues for a conception of human beings grounded in the fact that we are natural creatures who "keep track" of their dealings with the world for the purposes of adaptation so that a person in fact is (and must be) an integrated consciousness:

> it is perverse on its face to maintain that individual human persons are what they are, not because of the individual physical and mental constitution by virtue of which they develop the capacities they live by exercising, but because these experiences are psychologically connected in certain ways (1990, 13).

---

[23] He does address some in his discussion of personal identity as I shall note in Chapter 4.

[24] One based on the idea that an individual is a certain human body (that has a biological beginning and end) and the other that the human being is essentially a stream of related mental states (see ch 1).

[25] Wiggins suggests something of this kind when he talks about "person" as a concept whose reference is the objects that fall under it—human beings—but whose sense is what we make of human beings in our many ways of dealing with them (1987).

Donagan objects to the reduction of thought life into elements that ignore the natural context making them possible and purposive. His neo-Aristotelian view converges with the claim "that to be a person just is to be an animal of a certain kind" but his is a holistic rather than reductive metaphysics of human identity (Snowdon, 1990, 85).

David Wiggins, himself an animal identity theorist, argues that "our grasp of what it is to be a human being gives matter and substance to our conception of persons".[26] That conception is "the precipitate of all sorts of evolutionary, biological, historical, and cultural facts", tracks our dealings with actual flesh and blood persons,[27] and fleshes out (forgive the pun) our thinking about personal identity. Wiggins therefore echoes Kant's rejection of the *res cogitans* as an adequate characterisation of the human subject (who is not a purely mental or non-bodily entity). A person, one might say, typically has a unique set of psychological characteristics, memories, and so on that is (open-ended and) dynamically integrated (to some extent) in discourse with others.[28] The resulting naturalism eschews sharply bounded concepts built on logical essences.[29]

## The narrative roots of moral discourse about human beings

A human being, seen holistically, is not just a genetically unique human organism but a member of the human moral world (Engelhardt, 1986) and there are genetically unique human individuals — for instance those with anencephaly and, arguably, pre-embryos — who cannot, or not uncontentiously, be included. Our moral thought informs holistic conceptions of the status of human beings in ways that are evident in debates about patients in PVS or

---

[26] 1987, 74. In so doing he unwittingly (as far as I can see) echoes Kant (see below Ch 4).

[27] The idea of "tracking" is built on the thought that cognitively we keep track of and update our conceptions with respect to an individual — here a set of individuals of a given type — so that the actual individuals *de re*, as it were, enter into our conception of them and serve as a normative constraint on the ideas we develop.

[28] To recall Foucault (quoted on p. 35 above), we could say the set of which form the referent of the concept "person".

[29] Such concepts articulate Fregean canonical thoughts and aim to capture essences which can then be analysed in terms of necessary and sufficient conditions and give rise to the reductive metaphysical accounts on offer (the current approach characterizes these as nominal essences but they hold themselves to be real essences).

embryos.[30] It is therefore worth examining some of the metaphysical accounts on offer to see if they are sustainable in a holistic discussion of human identity (Holland, 1990; Haldane and Lee, 2003; Singer, 1992; Lockwood, 1985a).

Contemporary biology picks up Aristotle's (and Locke's) realisation that the human being, in development, incorporates matter and dynamically maintains itself, shaping itself in the face of environmental contingencies until it settles into a human developmental trajectory. The shaping continues throughout that trajectory and is completed through being-in-the-world-with-others. Consciousness, for instance, is interactively shaped through interactions with others as is moral subjectivity and the reciprocity that pervades our relationships. Taken as a whole this trajectory (and the stories configuring it) give rise to the (second) nature of a human being and inform the metaphysics of human identity. Such thinking defeats, as I have noted, reductive conceptions of human individuality and yield an *argument for metaphysical holism*.

MHol:  *The Argument For Metaphysical Holism*

MHol1  A metaphysical essence isolates just the set of features definitive of a given thing (as the kind of thing it is).

MHol2  The discourse in which those features appear define the philosophical contour of the thing concerned.

MHol3  Our conception of a person is only understandable by "tracking" human beings as the foci of multiply intersecting and different discourses.

MHol4  The essence of a person is not definable in any purified discourse (be it physical or mental).

It follows that reductive conceptions of a person and the claims used to derive some startling moral conclusions about human affairs and public policy are misconceived.

## Would the real Immanuel Kant please come forward

The non-identity problem (devised by Derek Parfit) has been taken to have ethical implications for impaired newborns, genetic screening,

---

[30] Dame Mary Warnock in her report on early embryos attempts to do so for obvious reasons when producing a standard for use in embryology and fertility services in a pluralistic community (1984). The report is summarised in Lockwood (1985b).

and future generations.[31] For instance, imagine introducing a measure to avert the possibility of 100 children being born with a serious disease either by treating already conceived children or by delaying pregnancy by a month in which case, he argues, we have different children from those in the first scenario on the basis of a metaphysical thesis—"the origin view": "each person has this distinctive necessary property: that of having grown from the particular pair of cells from which this person in fact grew".[32]

But is the origin view sustainable? Consider the case of Immanuel Kant (IK) and what makes him who he is? Parfit holds that he is the entity picked out in the origin view and it is possible that that individual might not have become a famous philosopher.

We believe, Parfit avers, that a particular person exists from the beginning of his or her life, so that the name, as we use it, picks out the actual product of two particular (haploid) cells. But are these intuitions as clear as he claims? Perhaps IK may not have become a philosopher so that, in that circumstance, the widespread nominal essence would not pick out the actual human being concerned. But what does it mean to say "Plato did not write all those books; it was some other Greek with the same name?"

Is it possible that IK could have looked different, been prone to various other diseases, had a different blood group, even a different genetic constitution, and still have been IK—the philosopher from Konigsberg born to Anna Regina and Johann Georg at 5am on the 22nd of April 1724? In fact that designation of IK is compatible with two different origins (only one of which is actual but which we do not know). The device of "possible worlds" (ways things could be/have been) helps address this problem.

In World 1 ($W_1$) Kant is conceived in early July 1723 while the Kants are holidaying in Berlin. He is born 41 weeks later. In $W_2$ he is conceived in August 1723 while they are visiting cousins in Muenster, but is born a week or so early. In both worlds he is born on the same day, christened, lives the same life and writes the same works. Imagine now that a time travelling, philosophically educated, trans-world historian called Wilfred makes friends with IK whom he has always admired. Wilfred is translated from $W_1$ to $W_2$, meets his friend and cries with joy, "At least you are the same in this strange place my good friend, all else has me quite discombobulated!" Is he wrong? By every accessible criterion

---

[31] Some of these are discussed in Parfit (1986).
[32] Parfit (1986), 367, and the origin view is on p. 352.

his friend *is* the same in $W_1$ and $W_2$. We cannot say whether $W_1$ or $W_2$ is the actual world (in which we live and refer to IK)[33] so it is possible that he could be right; ergo it is not necessary that IK (as we know and refer to him) is the product of a definite pair of cells (as in the origin view).

Some might still find Wilfred's joy counterintuitive but more could be said.[34] Imagine three possible worlds (of the infinity available) – $W_1$ and $W_2$ and $W_3$. In $W_3$ the Kants conceive in July 1723 (as in $W_1$) but the child contracts a serious intrauterine viral disease leaving him dull, niggardly, and wantonly cruel. Wilfred arrives in $W_3$ and, having sought out the Kants (who live in Leipzig), meets their son Immanuel (whose name is so ironic that he is usually called Georg). Wilfred (who understands possible worlds) exclaims "I cannot bear a world in which my good friend Immanuel is replaced by this travesty!" (He does not, of course, say so to Anna and Johann.) In $W_3$, my vote is with Wilfred; Georg is not Immanuel, his friend. Imagine further that Wilfred is so mortified by the prospect of a world without Immanuel Kant that (having obtained a downloaded full edition of Kant from the Gutenberg Project) he travels to Milan where he gets a skilled plastic surgeon to refashion him to look like (the actual) IK, assumes the name "Immanuel Kant", is adopted by Johann and Anna, and proceeds (from 1755 onwards) to write *Universal Natural History and Theory of the Heavens*, etc. Is Wilfred now the *real* IK? If Wilfred has succeeded and all records have been destroyed except those in which ($W_3$) IK is the famous philosopher ("Georg", is not mentioned), could $W_3$ be the actual world, our world? Notice the spirals of indeterminacy we are caught in.

A clue to our discomfort is found in Psalm 139 (often invoked in relation to these issues). The psalmist says,

> You created every part of me; you put me together in my mother's womb ... when I was growing there in secret you knew I was there (vv. 13–15).

In the book of Jeremiah the thought is echoed:

> Before I formed you in the womb I knew you; before you were born I sanctified you; I ordained you to be a prophet to the nations (1.5).

Both are logically required by God's omnipotence (God knows the end from the beginning and therefore can see the future and every aspect of

---

[33] Possible worlds and the metaphysics of identity are briefly discussed in Appendix C.

[34] A better strategy is to be found in a more "diagnostic" mode but having started on this "possible worlds" metaphysical game we might as well play it out, if only to show how inconclusive it actually is.

the life of a given person). Therefore, given an identifiable human being—here Jeremiah—God can track that being from the moment s/he begins to be formed, but the argument from form suggests that until a certain point it is not Jeremiah (a subject in-the-process-of-becoming) that is being formed; it may be something else entirely (like the troublesome offspring of Cardinal Guzman—a teratoma).[35] The thought that a person is the same type of being from conception fails to acknowledge that not every thing similar to a human pre-embryo is a human-being- in-the-process-of-becoming.[36] Therefore even if a given human individual (as we know and love/hate them) is essentially the product of a given (or particular) pair of cells does not follow from the texts. One's "origin"(in Parfit's sense) is one of the characteristics that make one the person one is, but it is typically so entangled with other factors (lineage, historical and geographical location, cultural context, parenting family, and so on) interactively forming the unique human subject that it has no special status.

Parfit claims, "If any person had not been conceived within a month of the time when he was, in fact, conceived, he would in fact never have existed"(1986, 352). But IK in $W_1$, $W_2$ and $W_3$ casts doubt on this intuition. Imagine, for instance, that the night of IK's conception was, in two maximally similar possible worlds, a stormy night and the earth literally moved so that a different sperm egg combination happened (otherwise the worlds are indistinguishable). The resulting child, according to Parfit, is not IK in both worlds even though we do not know which world we are in. Parfit may be right that we regard origin as important but, as a claim about the essence of human identity, it does not seem to withstand critical scrutiny. The origin view seems to gain its credentials by association with more holistic factors. In fact there are three possibilities.

*Three theses about identity.*

1. Human identity is fixed by a particular conception event—the origin view.
2. A conception event is one condition that, conjointly with other conditions (perhaps psychological continuity and connectedness), fixes human identity.

---

[35] The reference is to *The Troublesome Offspring of Cardinal Guzman*, a novel by Louis de Bernières (1992).

[36] The pre-reflective intuition is understandable because the only such things we deal with (so that they inform our concepts <human individual> and person) are those who realise that form (as Kant notes).

3. The origin view appeals to our intuitions because, in the actual world, origin goes along with other significant co-determinants of human identity.

Alternative 3 assumes that our concepts are adapted to our natural cognitive domain and become uncertain tools when extended beyond its borders.[37] We should also distinguish numerical identity (the same bare metaphysical "essence" on the views I oppose) from an "all-in" conception of personal identity with content that captures the uniqueness of a human subject as the kind of being whom we care about.[38] Thesis 1 (a strong version of the origin view) does not touch that richer conception but either 2 or 3 could do so. In fact Parfit (and Locke) both reject the importance of (bare) identity (and the associated metaphysics) in favour of thesis 2 (origins +). For Locke, the + is human form; for Parfit *relation R* — "psychological continuity and connectedness" (that does not fix identity but is what matters to us about it).

Relation R is, however, problematic in that if it is intrinsic to the individual then it does not add anything (as Butler and Reid noted) and if it is possible between mental states not internal to an individual then it neither has a naturalistic ring to it nor does it ground self-interested concern.[39] I have argued that human identity:

(i) goes along with biological numerical identity (as in the origin view);

(ii) secures psychological integrity (as in the psychological view);

and

(iii) reflects our actual discourse about human beings.

Three thought experiments[40] concerning events currently on the horizon of biomedical possibility (in accord with the realistic spirit) are relevant here.

In the first, Bob and Alison's three year old son James suffers terminal brain damage when he is hit by a car. They learn that a new embryo can be formed by introducing a nucleus from the child's cell into an enucleated cell of the mother. Such an embryo could be implanted in Alison's womb to give them a new 'James' back again in nine months time.

---

[37] A position, as I have noted, adopted by both Kant and Wittgenstein.
[38] I will discuss this below in relation to identity views (Chapters 4 & 5).
[39] I argue this in Chapter 5 and it is a point made by Schechtman.
[40] I have discussed versions of these elsewhere in relation to the ethics of cloning (Gillett, 2004, ch 12).

But the question is: "Is the prospective child really James come back to life?"

The individual resulting from this procedure, whoever he is, though he has the same origin as James (same genes, same gestational mother, same origin) is not James. The origin view implies that James and James II are phases of the same individual but are they? Intuitively James II is something like the younger brother of James (whose body has presumably been disposed of).

Epigenetic factors may mean that James I and II are not identical despite, arguably, having "the same origin" even though the origin view, in a natural or normal reproductive setting, is not confounded in that way and tracks the individual as conceptualised holistically (as in thesis 3).

A further case suggests that what matters is not even a relation based on causal continuity in the brain.[41]

Barry and Alice's three year old son, Jeff, is terminally brain injured by a car and expected to die within 24 hours. But a new experimental treatment promoting the reconstruction of injured nerve pathways is suggested. Even though there are psychological differences between the treated individual and his pre-injury self so that cognitive skills must be relearned, any memory traces (crucially dependent on the integrated function of the central nervous system) are lost, and temperament may differ, in successful cases, parents are overjoyed at their child's recovery (despite the treatment taking six months).

Notice that it is natural to think of $Jeff_{new}$ (post-reconstruction) as having recovered from a life-threatening injury, despite the psychological disconnectedness and discontinuity with his pre-injury self (relation R does not hold). In fact Jeff has undergone a more radical version of what many people undergo who recover from serious head injuries. But are Barry and Alice making a metaphysical mistake in thinking of recovered $Jeff_{new}$ as Jeff? If the ground of identity is holistic (rather than intrinsic, individualistic, and reductive), then, arguably, they are not.

What arguments can they appeal to? First, Jeff has never been declared dead and then buried and such cultural ways of marking the end of a human life both express and influence our moral intuitions. Barry and Alice's belief offers them the hope that their son has been restored to them in a way continuous with what we currently try to do with good intensive care and neuro-rehabilitation (although the biol-

---

[41] As suggested by Mackie (1976) and Nagel (quoted in Parfit, 1986).

ogy is different).[42] Second, how they treat Jeff$_{new}$ is going to influence his own self-identification and so their seeing him as Jeff will tend to make him Jeff so that the "sum of our dealings" approach to metaphysics is plausibly more correct than the reductive essence views. A third case reminds us of the form that defines an individual.

Brian and Anna's son, John is severely brain injured and they are offered a technique using stem cells, enzymes, growth factors, and micro-electrical stimulation guided by a computer driven three-dimensional graphics program to restore brain function. John$_2$'s brain is so extensively damaged that new totipotent stem cells are introduced to repopulate and restore the tissue. The stem cells are generated using neurogenetic tissue from Brian and an enucleated oocyte from Anna's ovary. The process mimics natural brain development. John$_2$ is a chimera of John$_1$'s 3 year old body and nervous tissue formed by the new stem cells. John loses all his memories, may have a change of temperament, and requires re-education as if he were neonate (catching up with his peers about three or four years later). Brian and Anna are so overjoyed at John's survival.

John$_2$ is biologically distinct from the individual who became John$_1$ and he has different genetic material because he is a chimera.[43] John (like Jeff) will continue his life as if he has recovered from a serious brain injury but in his case neither a particular origin, nor a genotype, nor relation R is part of his survival or identity. So what is its basis?

On the current view the basis for John's continuing identity is a longitudinally extended form incorporating tissues and psychological states that are configured as they are because they are part of him so that he is the formal cause (in one sense of that term) of his distinctive properties. However, John's recovery, despite genotypic non-identity and psychological discontinuity and disconnectedness (i.e. not-R) creates a problem.

The (essential first-person) subjective aspect of personal identity (which is closely related to what matters to us about personal identity) is not evident[44] either for Jeff or John, so that personal identity as we

---

[42] The continuity is of a Sorites kind.

[43] Originally chimeras were creatures made of parts from various organisms but we now use the term when two different genotypes (from two different conception events) are found in a single organism.

[44] Given the normal personal psychological continuity and connectedness of a three year old and recent work in reconstructive and narrative memory and the formation of identity (Schechtman, 1996) relation R looks suspect in any event (see Chapter 5 below).

know and love it seems groundless in both of them. If that is so, what is its naturalistic explanation?

The later Wittgenstein argues that reference and conceptualisation are grounded in our discursive practices (as part of our natural history). The term "discursive naturalism" takes account of both "physical" facts and semantic or cultural practices in which objects and events are individuated (as in narrative metaphysics). A human individual is located in a network of relationships in which he or she is given a name and develops an identity through that being-in-the-world-with-others), an engagement normally contingent on a certain (kin-based) origin. These uncontentious remarks favour thesis 3 as an account of identity; in the actual world our intuitions about human beings arise from a holistic set of co-determinative factors operating within the unique narrative shaping an individual's being as a person.

We can therefore distil the following argument concerning origins and identity.

NCHI: *The Narratively Constructed Human Individual Argument*

NCHI1   A human being begins when two cells join in an originating event.

NCHI2   A human being is the result of a complex event proceeding from that origin.

NCHI3   A person might have had a different origin and turned out the same.

NCHI4   The origin view identifies a person as the product of two particular cells.

NCHI5   The origin view misidentifies the person as we know them.

The NCHI argument locates our intuitions about human identity within a nexus of diverse, open-ended, and naturally correlated contingencies rather than a particular conception event. It has two major implications.

ArT: An *Antireductive Thesis*: Personal identity or what matters about it is neither reducible to a biological substrate nor a bundle of psychological properties considered apart from an actual, morally engaged, human life.

RT:  A *Realistic Thesis*: There is a form of naturalism supporting a broad neo-Lockean claim about personal identity that depends on a realistic embodied and extended subjective participation in a human context.

A purified metaphysics of essence often runs counter to both ArT and RT.

## Attempts at reduction

Recent work based on essentialist metaphysical accounts of persons and personal identity is quite distant from ArT and RT.[45] The arguments are, therefore, partly undermined by the realistic spirit (in Diamond's sense) that links our concepts to the usages that inform human life as we actually live it. Something[46] more ready-to-mind than logically determinate essences in all possible worlds seems closer to the tapestry and web of our understanding of human beings and their moral properties.

A naturalistically inclined philosopher notices that a human person is an animal (in an anthropological sense). In fact many terms, each with their own sense,[47] inform our thinking about human beings and each engages with a different set of structurally related semantic terms. The realistic spirit therefore deflates startling claims based on essentialist metaphysics because it defers to the lives and practices of a moral community rather than subjecting those practices to rationalistic critique and recommending counter-intuitive conclusions.[48]

Coope defends our ordinary intuitions by critiquing the idea of "morally innocent, cognitively normal, adult human beings" who resolve moral disputes in terms of free negotiation appealing to "agent neutral reasons".[49] Such reasons are hard to find at an actual negotiating table (as Williams and Rawls have both pointed out) so that the intuitions involved suffer from the rarified cognitive atmo-

---

[45] Books by McMahan and De Grazia tend to accept some form of metaphysical essentialism.

[46] Such as family resemblances, cluster/core feature views, or template and fuzzy boundary views.

[47] Fregean usage, so that senses have a natural affinity with thoughts.

[48] Coope really takes issue with these counter-intuitive conclusions.

[49] Williams and Rawls both begin with an agent evincing agent-centred reasons and then moderating those in the light of imaginative exercises designed to blunt any vicious partiality rather than assuming that primary impartiality (akin to the view from nowhere) can be suasive in any robust way (as some others might assume, McMahan, 2003, 217).

sphere (and the consequent lack of "sentiment") in which they are expected to live.[50]

It is often argued that to be rational we should ground our moral attitudes on the objective intrinsic properties of an individual rather than on indefinables (such as potentials or taboos). This seems strange in that things such as a prohibition against killing and the veneration of origins are significant and symbolically rich aspects of our dealings with each other in ways that are hard to shift or justify dispassionately. An overly tight link between reason, respect, and autonomy (as a present property), such that non-autonomous individuals lose their entitlement to our respect, ruptures many strands of the fabric of morality especially our moral attitudes towards children.

We cannot replace such intuitions with sweeping claims such as "killing is, in general, wrong." Without further elaboration such a claim neglects, for instance, the perfectly sound intuition that it is OK, even commendable, to dose my pets against fleas and worms. Reasoning on the basis of such sweeping claims does not deepen our understanding of morality. Claims such as "it would be wrong to kill my uncle Joe, even though my uncle Joe is not much of a person" are more plausibly grounded in ontology of the type that Levinas invokes when he remarks: "Thou shalt not kill" is written in the face of human being, is the root of morality, and the basis of our spiritual life. For Levinas, the recognition involved is a fundamental feature of encounters with beings of our kind (Levinas, 1990, 9–10).

Varieties of metaphysical essentialism about human individuals abound (one can think of the primitive streak thesis, the brain identity thesis, the rational individual thesis, the self-conscious mental states thesis, and so on), all touted as objective indices of the fact that we have an individual among us who must be treated as a person. The thrust of the present work is that this is a mistaken approach and that even those coming closest to a more holistic or narrative metaphysics distort our grip on the subject matter by divorcing it from its realistic context and distancing us from ways of dealing with things that may only inadequately be reflected in our conceptualisations of other beings (but are themselves the source and ground of the relevant concepts).

The attempt to purify our thinking so that we respond just and only to the qualities that demonstrably (in Hume's sense) ground certain moral conclusions is, I would argue, as doomed as the

---

[50] I shall return to the type of reasoning involved in the discussion of eugenics and genetic selection.

attempt to say why one loves one's lover or friend in terms of certain properties (that could be instanced by some other being). The loved other is not a package of desirable properties but someone to whom one "cleaves" (in various degrees) and with whom one enters into the closest kind of human relations. Our moral attitudes arise in our dealings-with-others involving mutual recognition, shared experiences, anticipations, reactive attitudes, commitments, relationships, the adoption of icons and images, the valorisation of certain identities and symbolic figures and all those things that make life interesting and inspir(it)ing.[51] Such a life can be appraised and critically examined but not in the absence of an appreciation of one's actual engagement with others. Our thought sometimes needs such presence and when abstract thought overreaches itself and threatens to overturn sound habits of the heart it needs to have its (distancing and defensive) artifices exposed.

Moral arguments in this area suffer problems quite aside from the artificiality of many discussions of identity within the context of traditional metaphysics. The intuitions appealed to in relation to logical identity and our duties to persons current or future are often used to justify conclusions that go unexamined when they need their credentials (and credibility) examined a little more closely. So, to the disputes!

## Not being born

A series of ethical problems are raised by issues such as wrongful life, disability, genetic counselling in relation to significant genetic disorders, and the abortion of defective fetuses. In resolving these issues, many ethicists appeal to some version of a "General Impersonal Utility"(GIU) premise of the following kind:

GIU    *A harm should only be allowed if the net effect is to improve the overall and objective sum of harms and benefits in the world.*

This consequentialist axiom spawns three arguments that should be addressed (especially in the context of genetic counselling and fetal abnormalities).

ADI:    *Avoiding Disabled Individuals*

ADI1    Individual A has a genome that is likely to produce suffering in life.

---

[51] The tweak makes it clear where we might want to go with a discussion of the human spirit and the inspiration we find in various aspects of our lives.

| | | |
|---|---|---|
| ADI2 | | That suffering would be avoided by replacing A with individual B. |
| ADI3 | | Suffering should, where possible, be avoided. |
| ADI4 | | We should not produce A but rather produce B. |

But this argument immediately provokes two objections (or counter-intuitions).

| | | |
|---|---|---|
| AnL: | | *Any Life Is Better Than None* |
| AnL1 | | Replacing A with a genetically normal individual avoids the prospect of A living a damaged life. |
| AnL2 | | Living a damaged life is better than living no life at all. |
| AnL3 | | Replacing A entails that A is deprived of life. |
| AnL4 | | A should not be replaced by B. |

ADI is often used to support a "*search and destroy*" approach to genetic abnormalities but AnL favours cherishing each life despite what some see as shortcomings (a position espoused by some disability advocates). That position is strengthened by the *Uniqueness of Human Life argument* (to which many subscribe in some form or other).[52]

| | | |
|---|---|---|
| UoHL: | | *Uniqueness of Human Life Argument* |
| UoHL1 | | Any human life is unique and irreplaceable from its beginning. |
| UoHL2 | | A human life, even a genetically abnormal one, is therefore irreplaceable. |
| UoHL3 | | Nothing irreplaceable should be destroyed. |
| UoHL4 | | A genetically affected pregnancy should not be terminated. |

One could argue that replaceability is not the issue and that ADI is aimed at ensuring that human beings lead their lives without significant (congenital) disabilities. This may be true if a non-lethal means of avoiding the harm is available (gene-surgery, for instance), but even that is problematic. Correcting a life-altering genetic disorder confronts us with the oft-repeated remark by an autistic person who, asked if he would rather have been born without autism, answered: "You mean, would I rather not have been born at all and somebody else have been

---

[52] On this see Levinas (1990); but also, for instance, Gillett (1997).

born in my place? My autism is part of who I am."[53] The remark can be used to separate judgments into same-person judgments, different-person-but-same-number-of-persons judgments, and different number (of persons) judgments. But this division becomes problematic when the relevant intuitions are examined.

## The inconclusiveness of the arguments in the unwitting sacrifice problem

Consider the case of Bipolar Disorder (BD). BD has a significant morbidity and mortality, so that bringing a child into the world likely to develop BD exposes an unconsenting human being to a risk of (unmeasured but often very significant) suffering.

One could argue that we should eliminate unconsented-to-harms and so eliminate the genes causing BD. But consider the plausible claim that the benefits to society in general from individuals at risk of BD outweigh the affected individual's suffering.[54] If we also accept GIU — the General (or objective) Impersonal Utility claim—then we should not terminate the at-risk foetus for reasons that we could put to him/her as follows:

"We cannot ask you what you would want (and, in fact, you have not got the mental apparatus to be mindful of what we are saying) but we have decided you will be born despite the risk that you will suffer significant harm because we need (creative, adventurous) individuals, like the future you, for the good of all. Perhaps you will suffer significantly but worthwhile things sometimes require a sacrifice."

This "argument for the greater good" just seems wrong. However the GIU premise is itself problematic in its dependence on an assessment of the overall or objectively best sum of utilities. The replacement of the potential individual who is at risk of BD (call the person Gene) with an unaffected but different individual (Harvey) seems to turn on an abstract and possibly incalculable sum that tips the moral balance one way or the other.[55]

---

[53] Notice, *contra* The Origin View, that it may turn out that autism results from events after the conception event and that this remark entails that something other than one's origin is essential one's identity.

[54] I have discussed this as "The unwitting sacrifice problem"(Gillett, 2005).

[55] We might also notice (as Parfit does) that GIU itself leads to a "repugnant conclusion"—that we should value a very large population whose lives are barely worth living over a less but much more fulfilled number of human beings. As long as the multiplier (a very large number) produces a large sum of happiness from its small co-factor, it offsets the loss of utility in the alternative fewer lives full of good things (in a less crowded world).

GIU also fares badly in the face of a significant liberty principle that prefers autonomy or its cognate over collective good.[56] Autonomy moderates overall harm (in some way that looks rationally defensible) by weighting individual wishes (perhaps in terms of human rights) so that we cannot justify the abuse of a minority to pleasure the majority. But notice that affirming a right to a decent individual quality of life over an impersonal sum (of harms and benefits) favours actual individuals and does not include all possible individuals. But it is hard to defend such (actual person) chauvinism in impartial terms (or, *sub specie aeternitatis*).[57]

Quite apart from these general woes affecting the relevant arguments, we have an irresolvable problem with pre-implantation or even early prenatal genetic selection because there is no set of preferences to appeal to when a given human subject who may, in future, have some genetic affliction of variable severity is prevented from coming into existence for the sake of what looks like a better life for him or her ("In whose judgment?" one might ask).

Consider, for instance, the *Any Life is better than none* intuition (AnL). When we ask, "Better for whom?" it becomes clear that we have begged the question by choosing the addressee (the actual existing person rather than the possible alternative).

Or consider a version focusing on one candidate for the privilege of being born: are there any circumstances in which it would be better for a given person not to be born?[58] It seems counterintuitive to argue that the non-existence of an individual is better than their existence, if we concede that there are at least some goods in that individual's life (the intuition captured by AnL). We could only reject this intuition and claim that it is better for A not to have lived and B to live instead by appealing to the very suspect GIU (see footnote 55 above).

AnL is, however, itself highly questionable in that it favours the possibly distorted and definitely self-interested preference of individual A just because s/he exists. But considering all the possible states of affairs of which we ought to take account, given the different decisions that could be made (the range of possible worlds on offer), A's interests are

---

[56] As in Rawls, for instance, or Bernard Williams.

[57] If all people are considered equal and the people existing at the time of any moral claim being made are acknowledged to be a subset of all possible people then favouring them over others seems an unjust decision for some human beings on the basis of an accident of birth.

[58] Parfit considers the closely related question of whether causing someone to be born benefits them in *Reasons and Persons* (Appendix G).

exactly counterbalanced by the preferences of B who is born if A is terminated or not brought into existence. So where do we go from here?

We could go to something like UoHL and put an absolute value on human uniqueness (so that A is valuable no matter how the utilities pan out). On that basis it seems that one should favour the protection of A despite his/her prospective burden of genetically determined suffering. But that conclusion is vulnerable to the same (possible worlds) move whereby the uniqueness of A is viewed in the context of any decisions that could be made, and their likely consequences, in which case the uniqueness of B (who would be born if A is not) would counterbalance that of A. So, again, arguments of this kind get us no further ahead and something other than GIU, perhaps to do with actuality (actual engagement in the moral community), is important in morality.

*The unwitting sacrifice problem* and associated puzzles to do with the life of a person with Huntingdon's Chorea or psychopaths demonstrate the inconclusiveness of arguments built on abstract generalities (e.g. GIU). The Huntingdon's case follows closely the argumentative form of the unwitting sacrifice problem except that we cannot adduce the good of us all as the reason why the suffering must be undergone and instead we should notice that the individual may well have 35 or more years of trouble free life before the onset of the disease. In the case of someone who we could predict would develop a dangerous and severe personality disorder we add to their own prospective suffering the fact that they would harm others but mitigate both by the fact that they may consider that they have a good life and not suffer too much at all. The arguments play out in predictable ways and with equally inconclusive results. But does moving to a non-utilitarian framework of moral argument enable a realistic reflective equilibrium to favour a policy here?

## Valuing life over non-life

It is plausible that any person would say, "Of course it would be better that I had been born" so that comparisons of life with non-life are impossible. This first-person moral claim appeals beyond any small contributions by individual human beings to an objective sum of meaningless, abstract, and incalculable sums of harm and benefit and focuses on the thought that the world is different in an incalculable way *because I am in it*, a difference that is morally important. That message seems to emerge from stories like the feature films *My Left Foot*, *It's a Wonderful Life* and *Forest Gump* and, intuitively, it resists the universalizing "possible worlds" move because of something like the importance of those to whom we are actually related (a realistic consideration).

Given the relatively weak claim that there is at least something that I and others value (or ought to value) about my life (whoever I am), it looks implausible that no-one should ever live any of the moments of life that I have lived. That claim looks even more implausible if different human lives realise incommensurable values because *the irreplaceability of the individual* and *the incomparability of different life-values* intuitions together rule out eliminating a developing human life on the basis of negatively valued features it might have. The resulting impasse in adjudication between claims to life has wider implications than the unwitting sacrifice problem, and arguably indicates that we need an alternative to the impartial, reductive mode of thinking about human beings.

An alternative may lie in (i) *actuality*, (ii) *incommensurability of value*, (iii) *relatedness*, and (iv) *irreplaceability*. First, consider the *actuality* of the situation (as in the *work in progress* argument) which supports a gradualist position allowing us to take into account the developmental trajectory of the individual, intuitively favouring an entity closer to its valued form than a more distant precursor.[59] Second, consider the risk that a developing life will lack any meaningful experiences as a morally engaged being among us (as we do when we authorise termination or withdrawal of neonatal care because of a severe foetal abnormality such as anencephaly). If such a life has value, it is quite unlike the value we find in our own lives and the lives of those close to us. That consideration may be compounded by relational facts such as the likelihood of a significant burden on others. We can therefore (third) consider prospective impacts of a human life on others (as in an abortion decision when the fetal life poses a significant threat to the life of the mother – a living member of the moral community). Fourth, any new life is unique and may occasion goods unlike those associated with any other (as is often remarked by parents of Downs Syndrome children). All of these considerations are inconclusive and the waters are further muddied by a curious phenomenon in genethics.

Patient groups concerned with Huntingdon's Chorea (a disease causing death in middle age preceded by a nasty movement disorder and dementia) usually favour genetic selection and selective implantation to try to prevent a baby, thought of as the potential offspring of a particular couple, being born with the disease. Ordinarily they (and we) do not consider the potential children who are "excluded" (unless the abortion, miscarriage, or whatever impacts on the individuals involved in that way) from having a life. That each person who might have been born with the disease would nevertheless say that he or she

---

[59] Defended in Chapter 2.

is glad to be alive is not "weighed in the balance" in genetic selection against potential sufferers. But why do they not link their policy to the thought that individuals just like themselves (who are glad they were born) are deprived of a chance of life?

Similar empirical indicators to those for Huntingdon's disease are not, in fact, available for Bipolar Disease (or many other heritable diseases) but when asked, "Would it be better that you had been born without your Bipolar disorder?" sufferers commonly remark, "If I did not have my disorder I would be someone else" (cf. the autistic person quoted above, pp. 55–6, and the associated footnote 53). Their position is readily understandable if one reflects on the sort of changes in one's life that would make it impossible to decide whether one would be "the same person". The thought makes Parfit's non-identity problem phenomenologically real[60] and asks whether a unique human life should ever be discarded because there will be considerable suffering in that life. How much suffering and how much countervailing goodness make it the case that a particular human being ought not to live and can so-called reasoned, impartial, and objective arguments help?

## The theory of individual health

In a simple case, such as a *humamba*, a decision to select against an individual pre-natally seems straightforward based on compassion for the individual, prophylaxis against serious suffering, and protection of the community.[61] Things are more difficult if we accept "that health must always be seen in reference to individuals"[62] or "a theory of individual health". In that framework "surmounted sickness" and other apparent evils may contribute positively to health and some obvious diseases (asthma, severe cardiac disease, hepatitis and diabetes) may have much less impact on subjective health (or experienced well-being) than what could be called "maladies of the soul"(somatization disorder and

---

[60] Identity is here tied to a qualitative essence but not necessarily linked just to a particular Origin.

[61] Recall that *humambas* are postualted as genetically modified organisms with a dominantly human genetic constitution who look vaguely reptilian, with few human attributes, an extreme autistic spectrum disorder, hiss but do not speak, have lives of unremitting pain and violence usually culminating in death through self mutilation, and have a lethal toxic bite due to nests of poison secreting cells in their mouth (see pp. 11–12 above).

[62] The theory of individual health as in Danzer et al. (2002).

neurotic depression).[63] Such data should provoke questions about the nature of well-being (or *eudaimonia*). Hacking's "looping effect of human kinds" also reminds us that the ways we think about ourselves contribute to our self-understanding and are highly significant for our life experiences because they forge a link between authenticity, well-being, and the kind of person one wants to be (all things considered).

The more one reflects, the more one sees that Jean Paul Sartre is on to something when he claims that one *is* responsible for being born. Consider: the *me* who results from my being born is formed by a cumulative succession of choices and reactions, many of which are up to me so that the person (in an important sense) who is me would not exist if those choices had been made differently. The choices reflect cultural forces, myths, icons, and symbols through which robust and very ancient intuitions often play a significant part in our lives, but I enact them and live them out, a consideration that is profoundly relevant to our thinking about young human lives as they form subjectivities in response to our encounters with them.

The narrative metaphysics of identity and the theory of individual health suggest that identity and well-being are closely linked and that the human subject (as an identifiable and self-identifying being) is inextricably part of the world in which he or she, as somebody, has been formed through relationships with others. We can now turn to the unworldliness of the metaphysical or logical subject.

---

[63] Julia Kristeva (1995) traces our struggle to find adequate means to represent ourselves in ways that are liveable and conducive to well-being.

# Chapter 4

# *Metaphysical Subjectivity*

## *The Genesis of the Logical Subject*[1]

---

> And as for thinking which can be both correct and incorrect, correct thought being understanding, knowledge and true opinion, incorrect thought their opposites, not even this is the same as perception. For the perception of special sensibles is always true and enjoyed by all animals, while thinking admits of being false and is enjoyed by no animal that does not also have rationality.
> (Aristotle, *De Anima*)

> Any "Objective" object, *any object whatever* (even an immanent one), points to *a structure within the transcendental ego, that is governed by a rule.* (Husserl, *Cartesian Meditations*)

"I think therefore I am" is, as I have noted, often taken to refer to an inner self, purely rational or mental, who stands at a remove from and contemplates the world. But am I such a being? What is the real essence of the *me* that seems to lie behind the centre of my forehead, is present in all my thoughts and experiences, remains constant in all the changes I undergo in my life, who is the author of my thinking, whose rights I hold dear, and whose future I care about? These questions concern the being of the rational subject (the self, the logical, metaphysical, or ethical subject and the subject of experience), of whom Wittgenstein says "The subject does not belong to the world; rather it is the limit of the world" (*Tractatus*, 5.632).

---

[1] This chapter is primarily of metaphysical interest and can be skipped if your interest in identity is more practical and applied.

Both the phenomenological claim that the S–O relationship is the heart of experience and Russell's claim that "acquaintance is a dual relation between a subject and an object which need not have any community of nature" (1988, 125) tend to promote the thought that the subject cannot be treated as an object so that, in a world comprising objects, the subject is something (metaphysically) other.

If one accepts a realistic (in Cora Diamond's sense) account of the human individual and his or her natural origins, how can this organism become a logical subject?[2] Heidegger draws attention to this neglected question when he asks (of the Cartesian *cogito*) what is asserted in the "I am" as entailed by "I think". The glib answer is, "I exist" but what are the relevant dimensions of my existence as a subject and what philosophical constraints are thereby introduced? The subject who asserts "I think" seems not only to be mortal but also to have a claim to moral attributes and the dignity or respect accorded to each of us as a purposive and rational being ("a member of the kingdom of ends", as Kant has it). And how do these intuitions relate to the idea of the human soul?[3]

(1) Some believe that, as a soul, one is an immaterial entity — the seat of thought and moral being — in principle separable from the body but temporarily embodied.

(2) I have noted that some philosophers, such as the early Wittgenstein, claim that science cannot delineate one's being as a metaphysical subject which is not an object of any kind but the subject of the Subject–Object relation.

The neo-Aristotelian view runs counter to such thoughts (and is, therefore, sometimes linked to a reductive view of the type found in scientific writing) and holds that a human being is a being-among-others so that embodiment is essential to human subjectivity and that the subject develops biologically and tries to make sense of the world it shares with others and who cannot adequately be thought of as a mere object (i.e. as an *It* rather than a *Thou*).[4]

In order to engage philosophically with the (metaphysical) subject who makes sense of the world and is "not a part of it" (*Tractatus*,

---

[2] The logical or philosophical subject is what Kant refers to as a noumenal self. This chapter rehearses a number of arguments found in Gillett (1992), esp ch 2 & 4, and Gillett & McMillan (2001), esp ch 1 & 2.

[3] Alluded to in Chapter 2.

[4] This is Martin Buber's distinction meant to draw our attention to the critical difference in relationships between someone we address and something we "manipulate or merely study" (1970, 12).

5.641), one enters some rarified and arcane debates. I will argue that the logical/metaphysical/phenomenological subject just is the human being viewed *sub specie Logico-philosophicus* rather than viewed "*au naturel*" and the real essence of a self, the "I" of "I think" is an embodied human-being-among-others subject to all the ills that flesh and spirit are heir to. This starting point brings us back to the realistic spirit in discussing the human sphere where we live and move and have our being.

The Lockean "real essence" view that I have taken as a guide is a first clue to the "I" of "I think". I will argue that the real essence of a human subject of thought and will (the conscious intentional subject)[5] is as it is because (formal and efficient cause)[6] it is engaged with the actual domain of real discourse (as *Dasein*).

## The cognitive subject

The Cartesian position begins with the "I think", supposedly an Archimedian point or unshakable foundation for thought. The ego (or subjective self) as a thinking thing (*Res cogitans*) is the centre of consciousness and has properties that do not seem to be captured by a physical description of the human body (as part of the external or physical world—*Res extensa*). Descartes notices that the thinking subject can doubt the existence of his or her body (or consider that it might be a mere illusion) but not his or her existence as a thinking self (present even in the moment of doubting) so he concludes that what is essential to I (the subject of I think, I am, I exist) is a thinking self who may or may not be embodied.[7]

Re-enter "the inestimable Locke" who concurs that a person is "a thinking intelligent Being that has reason and reflection and can con-

---

[5] Kant, Bird, Sellars, Husserl, Wittgenstein and Sartre all realize that this subject is not easily treated as an object of natural science.

[6] I have mentioned both formal and efficient cause to recall the arguments about the formation of the embryo which is guided by its becoming the kind of thing it is but in the process of which parts configure themselves because of holistic influences of other parts within the structure of the organism as a whole. An analogy works with discourse and the configuration of subjectivity.

[7] Some say they are "modally distinct"—we can imagine the possibility that "I think" is true but "I am a physical being" is false and if I (as thinking thing) am identical with I (as physical thing) this is not possible and so think it involves a contradiction. Some would put it thus: An identical thing is always the same as itself so the conceivability of a situation in which I exist as mind but not as a body (I am a ghost, or a disembodied spirit, or the principle of mental unity in a scattered group of distinct objects) entails that the mental I (I as mind) am not identical to the physical I (I as body).

sider itself as itself, the same thinking thing in different times and places". Locke is interpreted (within the Cartesian tradition) as advancing an essentially mental conception of the identity of the human subject but I have noted that the remark is nested in a discussion of the form of a living thing as that giving unity of being to the matter that makes it up. And if a human subject (or soul) is also a natural creature, the idea of rational or purely mental self (*qua* person as distinct from human organism) delineated by first-person consciousness and autobiographical memory is potentially misleading. An account of the person as a situated embodied subject not amenable to (physical or psychological) reductive analysis opposes the neo-Cartesian view but requires, in its place, that I spell out what the rational subject is and how it comes to be.

Following Locke we can notice that the Nominal essence of a person might be the same conscious thing which unites in one consciousness remembered episodes, current thoughts and experiences, and desires and intentions, but the actual properties of the real thing in question may not appear in that description. The Real essence, "that real constitution of any Thing, which is the foundation of all those Properties that are combined in and constantly found to co-exist with the *nominal Essence*" (*Essay*, III.VI.6) is, on this conception, what constitutes the subjective core of a person (denoted by "I").

I have argued that the real essence of the human subject is best understood within a neo-Aristotelian framework as a human-being-in-the-process-of-becoming (by its very nature an entity with a developmental or narrative character). Kant observes that the *modi* of self-consciousness (in the simple thought "I think") do not reveal an object (which, as an object, would have a spatio-temporal configuration, duration, discernibility through the senses, and modal properties) and that, as Hume noted, nothing in inner experience corresponds to the I of "I think" so that, if the thinking self is not an object encountered in (inner) experience, then the "I think" does not imply that one is essentially a mental and immaterial object (*Pure Reason*, B406–7).

A post-Kantian naturalist[8] would, at this point, examine those conditions that are necessary for there to exist a thinking thing, thus introducing "a reality constraint" to the idea of a human subject (Schectman, 1996, 119). In a way parallel to the embryological development of the body, we might look for an embryology of the mind

---

[8] Such as Graham Bird (1973) or Robert Hanna (2006).

according to which the thinking subject progressively develops the use of concepts and the idea that there are rules that govern his or her thinking. The resulting concept of the human soul overturns the claim that the soul is an immortal immaterial substance[9] and favours the neo-Aristotelian conception of the soul as a holistic embodied subjectivity, an idea taking us beyond Locke to Kant and Heidegger.

Kant rejects the traditional Cartesian view in the paralogisms (*Pure Reason*, B399ff.), noticing that a human being, as a subject of "acts and inner determinations", conceptualises things and events she encounters using cognitive skills. For Kant, cognition (or making sense of the world) implies that: (i) there are concepts and things and events to which they apply; and (ii) the subject applies concepts by using active skills of judgment.

Meaningful thought results from a subject's actual contact with things that give him or her something to think about, and these are and must be actual, empirically accessible, objects in relation to which one's judgments can be corrected and disciplined (by other thinkers) so that the relevant skills can be mastered.[10]

Kant takes pains to refute the arguments which seem to undermine this common sense view in favour of a transcendent "I". He considers the argument that the metaphysical subject, because it is (and must be) a subject (and not a predicate) must be a transcendent "substance" (an individual or particular thing) with cognitive properties (so that it *instances* and not just contemplates universals). But from the fact that I, as thinker, am always the subject (as in "I think", "I act", "I exist", and so on), I can infer only that any mental ascription logically requires a subject not that a subject as a "substance" (objectively existing thing) is fully revealed in that conception (or idea). In fact this use of "I" reflects only the active nature of thought as it constitutes experience — and that is *all* it reveals about the subject (B407). The "I" of "I think" (an aspect of the nominal essence of a human individual) as a "mode of presentation" does not necessarily reveal the actuality of the thinking subject (its "real essence") because that may not be easily discerned in such introspective

---

[9]   Schechtman considers that we have four basic concerns: survival, moral responsibility, self-interested concern, and compensation (or just treatment).

[10]  He argues this in the Refutation of Idealism (*Pure Reason*, B274-287) an interpretation of which appears in Appendix D. The argument about correction implies that one's instructor is able to engage with the self-same cognitive targets (a point adduced by Reid in his arguments against Locke) in order to track them and offer apt and timely correction. I deal with this more adequately in the section "Becoming a subject" below (p. 69).

moments. In fact there are a number of uses of "I", continuous with the mental ascriptions above, in which the mode of presentation shades seamlessly into ascriptions requiring embodiment:

> "Yes, I hit him, much to my shame."
>
> "I so need to have a pee, that I cannot think straight."
>
> "At that moment I seemed absorbed into my own act of smelling the rose."
>
> "I realised that if I just changed my position a little I could see everything that passed between them."

If there is a logical unity of the subject, then the unified subject is psychophysical and longitudinally extended[11] so that s/he can pursue chains of reasoning, employ at time $T_2$ concepts learned at time $T_1$, and act on his/her reasoning. But that logical constraint merely exhibits the cognitive unity required for meaningful mental life involving data from diverse moments of experience (B408) and from diverse perspectival and multi-modal perceptions revealing the real nature of any thing (I moved my head and saw it was a slab not a sheet) such that the actual state of affairs in the world allowing one to be a subject of our kind becomes clear as one reflects on such phenomena.

> [I]n thinking my existence I can use myself only as the subject of judgment ... that discloses nothing about the manner of my existence (B412[note]).

Kant clarifies his point in discussing a proof for the immortality of the soul. Mendelssohn argued that the soul must be immortal because it is a unitary immaterial object and therefore is not susceptible to corruption (which essentially requires a thing to dissolve into its constituent parts and lose its formal unity). Kant denies that we have grounds for asserting the purity and insubstantiality of the rational subject as an object with a given form and instead claims that, "the thinking being (as a human being) is at the same time an object of outer sense"(B415).[12] He argues that knowing myself through the "I think", a subject of representations and inner determinations, does not settle "anything about the subject's constitution or

---

[11] As Husserl claims in his Fifth Cartesian meditation.

[12] He does not, as I have, invoke the phenomenology that is so richly explored by such thinkers as Merleau-Ponty to support his claim. Similar points about the overlap and indiscernible merging of M (material) and P (psychological) properties are made by Williams (1973) in critiquing Strawson's Individuals.

subsistence". We could say (following Frege) that contemplating the subject–object relation (i.e. the mere fact of my own subjectivity) we encounter a "mode of presentation" of the human subject and although that is *a* "route to the referent" it does not, necessarily (as in the case of The Morning Star — which is not a star) reveal its object (strictly topic) sufficiently clearly to enable us to discern its "real essence"(actual nature).

We can discern what type of subject we are dealing with by considering not only commonplace facts about perception and cognition but also the story of the coming-to-be of the subject as a logical subject (given that a natural ontogeny to do with biological origins lies within the subject matter of biology, psychology, and the other life sciences rather than anything conceptually proper to the moral sciences).[13]

## Becoming a subject

The remarks by Aristotle and Husserl recall the idea that human beings are subject to rules governing the use of concepts in judgments about objects (e.g. O is red, or a frog, or moving fast, or a prime number).[14] We are trained in applying the relevant rules through supervision, guidance, and correction of our judgments about things. This is a "hands on" or practical activity highly reminiscent of Aristotelian training and it cannot be formalised because to seek rules for the application of those rules is to chase a will-o'-the-wisp (the infinite regress is well-recognised). Judgment, exercised in applying concepts correctly to experience is a "natural power" or "natural gift"[15] exhibiting what Kant calls "mother wit, the lack of which cannot be made good by any school". The informal, even inchoate, rules determining, *inter alia*, what kinds of things a concept should be applied to and its cognitive role *vis à vis* other concepts require mastery of practices or techniques of using the related linguistic terms in such a way that one's mistakes and successes are manifest and can be corrected through interaction with others (PI ##202; 208). The techniques are world-involving, and cannot trade in immanent, private, or mental entities because correction of somebody's use of a concept must requires that an object or conditions can be accessed

---

[13] The point made by Wittgenstein at *Tractatus*, 5.641
[14] As argued by both Kant and Wittgenstein.
[15] As translated by Kemp Smith and Guyer & Wood respectively at *Pure Reason*, B172.

## Metaphysical Subjectivity

and tracked by both trainee and instructor.[16] Wittgenstein puts it thus:

> Hence it is not possible to obey a rule 'privately': otherwise thinking one was obeying a rule would be the same thing as obeying it. (*PI* #202)

Understanding a concept is, on the present account, predicated on the actual use of rules to group objects and to grasp ways of thinking (marked by terms in a natural language) tied to the shared environment to which we are adapted (thus Millikan's [1990] "distal correspondence rules"). A person masters the rule-governed ability to use a term when she achieves an adequate agreement in judgements with competent users of the relevant technique. For instance, Arwen grasps the concept <square> when she can reliably judge the truth or falsity of thoughts such as <that figure is square>, <this is not square>, <a square is a four-sided plane figure> and so on, such that her use of the relevant term — or grasp of the related concept — develops through exchanges in which her judgements are manifest and correctible by others, so that she becomes a thinking subject by going along with us in our practices and becoming competent with a range of concepts.

> But if a person has not yet got the concepts, I shall teach him to use the words by means of examples and by practice ... I do it he does it after me; and I influence him by expressions of agreement, rejection, expectation, encouragement. I let him go his way, or hold him back; and so on. (*PI*, #208)
>
> From a child up I learnt to judge like this. This is judging. (*On Certainty*, 128)
>
> A pupil and a teacher. The pupil will not let anything be explained to him, for he continually interrupts with doubts, for instance as to the existence of things, the meaning of words, etc. The teacher says, "Stop interrupting me and do as I tell you. So far your doubts don't make any sense at all". (*On Certainty*, 310)
>
> The child, I should like to say, learns to react in such and such a way; and in so reacting it doesn't so far know anything. Knowing only begins at a later level. (*On Certainty*, 538)

In fact nature itself is our accomplice in this task equipping children with primitive tendencies to lock into relationships with other human beings and develop a "second nature" (McDowell, 1994).

---

[16] This is implicit in Kant's analysis but made explicit by Husserl (1931, 242).

Our children find it natural to be trained so that their souls are crafted by those who nurture them (as the mediators of a culture). Whereas for animals behavioural repertoires are (for the most part) formed innately and through individual experience (including mimesis), we are, literally, mind-makers for our children transforming their natural tendencies by in-forming them so that they can use the (discursively structured) adaptations that our socio-cultural group has developed.

The link between understanding and rules draws on a thinker's being-with-others who interact with her in the world, commonplace facts that lead Wittgenstein to remark that ways of doing things lie at the heart of our ways of knowing and Heidegger to ground thought in circumspection — the totality of our associations or "dealings with" the world around us. In circumspection things take on significance for us that is holistic, reflecting a pattern of interactions between human beings and their contexts, rather than a relation of standing apart from, not belonging to, or being a subject "which need not have any community of nature" with its objects of thought (this leads to the use of the term signification rather than representation).

The coming-to-be of a logical subject as a being-in-the-world-with-others is also instructive about the connection between cognitive unity and human identity.

### Hume's question: is there a necessary unity of the subject?

I have rejected, with Kant and Heidegger, the idea that a subject is a purely mental entity existing in a special (*noumenal* in the sense of unwordly) realm distinct from the natural world. Kant remarks, "the persistence of the soul ... in life, where the thinking being (as a human being) is at the same time an object of outer sense, is clear of itself" (*Pure Reason*, B415) directing us towards the worldly situation of the subject (as a thinking being) and to a basis of subjective unity that concurs with Hume's denial of an inner apprehension of a unified subject of experience:

> When I turn my reflection upon myself, I never can perceive this self without some one or more perceptions; nor can I ever perceive any thing but the perceptions. 'Tis the composition of these, therefore, which forms the self (*Treatise*, Appendix, 676).

Our conceptions of things, for a thoroughgoing empiricist, arise from perceptions or impressions, whereas for Kant reason may lead us to apprehend the necessity for an object-yet-to-be-specified (as in the general claim that "every event has a cause") so that we may be motivated to discover and render detectable or perceptible some posited object through its effects on others (think, for instance, of a magnetic field). In the case of the thinking subject, we notice the necessary logical connection between certain mental determinations (as the "acts and inner determinations" of one subject) and then seek the object itself (the referent grounding this mode of presentation) while recognising that its presentation as conscious subject may not fully disclose its true nature. I have also noted the similarity between the inference from the evident cognitive unity of the subject (subtending a unitary subject of "mental acts and inner determinations") and an inference from bodily acts such as "I walked to the bus", "I can see you from where I am standing", and so on. Representation is, constitutively, the combination of concepts with objects using two abilities—one related to tracking an object and the other to the possession of a concept[17] so that both abilities underpin thought based on a subject's contact with the world.[18] We could (following Kant and Wittgenstein) also notice that the fact that subjects develop (during their lives) the skills of judgment required to use concepts implies that a significant temporal unity beyond the present moment of consciousness is inherent in an ability to construct coherent (or rationally connected) trains of thought (as in the HLeF view).

Just as one's cognitive unity (as a holistic temporally integrated subject) is an unavoidable logical constraint on an articulated or conceptually rich thought life, so a principle of (actually spatio-temporally) located or situated subjectivity is entailed by a conceptually coherent sensori-motor life as an intelligent subject.[19] Lives evincing thought are characteristic of those whom we recognise as our cognitive companions and teachers, and lives of agency characterise fellow members of the kingdom of ends. Thus my experience as a unified or cognitively integrated being-among-others is confirmed when I reflect on my own life of thought and action.[20]

The "I" of Kant's transcendental unity of apperception now begins to seem far less "noumenal" (in the spooky sense) and more

---

[17] The completion of an incomplete construction Fx (Frege), the subsumption of objects under concepts (Strawson).

[18] Kitcher (1990) explores this in terms of a link between "synthesis" (Kant) and the identity of the subject and uses it to support a "cognitive criterion" of personal identity.

[19] This point is also argued by both Strawson (1959) and Campbell (1994; 2002).

[20] Recall that I rehearse my interpretation of Kant's argument in Appendix D.

the deliverance of a "mere analytic of the pure understanding" revealing as the basis of empirical experience claims to be "taken merely problematically" (so as to acknowledge the limits of sensibility). Kant's transcendental subject, the "I" of consciousness and thought, is, however, often linked to a "noumenal self" as identified in Descartes, Russell and the early Wittgenstein:

> The I that thinks will be phenomenal and causally determined. This I is ... the I with which we identify. What possible comfort — or even interest — could we have in knowing that some noumenal self is free and potentially immortal, when the self with which we identify, the thinker, is phenomenal? I believe that Kant refuses to acknowledge this devastating implication. I see no coherent alternative, however (Kitcher, 1990, 139–40).

But this *noumenal self* is not found in Kant whose rejection of the Cartesian subject is entirely compatible with the current (neo-Aristotelian) account.

1. The unity of consciousness is logically required by the nature of mental acts involving concepts and conceptions of objects based on "tracking" or identification and reidentification of enduring things over time.[21]

2. The need for cognitive unity as a subject of experience is grounded in the subject's existence as an object among others some of which are themselves subjects.

3. Our knowledge of thinking subjects derives from our dealings with human beings who interact with us and share our discourse. They can be investigated as phenomena (and therefore by sciences such as psychology) but that does not illuminate their logical and moral (or normative) engagement with reason and reflection (evinced, inter alia, by their occupying the S locus in the S–O relation so that they are sensitive to the "anomalous" requirements of rationality rather than causality).[22]

---

[21] As I have argued in Gillett and McMillan (2001).

[22] Wittgenstein makes this point in *Tractatus*, 5.641, 6.423. Donald Davidson (1981) has exploited the conceptual gap between causal requirements and rational requirements to argue for the anomalism of the mental realm as a domain where items stand in relation to each other because of their rational relationships according to discursive norms rather than their relationships qua physical states with causal properties.

## Locke, Hume and Parfit

A considerable scholarship about human identity draws on Locke (and Hume) to advance a psychological thesis about the essence of human identity:

> *Psychological essence thesis*: I am essentially a connected and coherent set of conscious states with characteristic psychological attributes.

I have noted that Locke contextualises his discussion by remarks about the biological form of the functioning creature that is the subject whose psychological unity is, *inter alia*, evident in first person awareness of intentions, actions, thoughts and attitudes at different times and places. These are all attributes of a thing comprising "Particles of matter in succession vitally linked to this same organized Body" and not a soul as an "immaterial substance"(*Essay*, II.XXVII, #14).

The reductive psychological essence thesis together with Hume's scepticism about identity are taken to imply that a person is a bundle of conscious experiences linked by psychological connectedness and continuity—Parfit's "relation R" (1986, 216).

Parfit, arguing for this view, appeals to various thought experiments that seem to preserve what matters to us but undercut coherent identity claims. He argues that I, or any other human being, could be diminished in degree, divided, fused, and so on without losing anything vital to conscious life as we know it. The argument against an essential-unity-underlying-identity thesis diverges from the present view by setting aside the constitutive need for a cognitive unity underlying an articulate thought life and the fact that the elements of that thought life necessarily have a (situated) history (both conscious and unconscious) that is honed in experience as a being with a longitudinal formal identity as a thinking being-in-the-world-with-others.

## The paralogisms of Parfitian psychology

Kant, in fact, addressed Parfitian arguments (as devised by the spiritualists and materialists of his time) in his discussion of the soul.[23]

SV    *The Spiritualist View*

SV1    Consciousness is a set of powers and properties essentially associated with a certain kind of stuff—mind or spirit stuff.

---

[23] In *Pure Reason* at B415–417.

SV2  All powers or faculties could be diminished by degrees.

SV3  We could also fuse and combine mental properties by combining the relevant stuff (in fact there would seem to be no other way to do that).

SV4  Any person is a fusion of a body and a sufficient quantum of mind or spirit stuff.

Therefore

SV5  Persons can be fused, split, or recreated independent of their bodies by working with the relevant packages of spiritual stuff.

*Some possible corollaries*:

SVC1  When we have children, our souls or spirits fuse or combine their mental and spiritual powers and what our bodies do is irrelevant.

SVC2  Children are produced by dynamic division and recombination of parent souls.

MV  *The Materialist View*

MV1  Consciousness is a set of powers and properties essentially associated with a certain kind of stuff—material (brain) stuff.

MV2  All powers or faculties could be diminished by degrees by diminishing the amount of stuff or its level of function.

MV3  Some diminutions can leave an essential core intact.

MV4  A person is essentially a being with a body that contains a sufficiency of the right stuff (the material substrate of mind) in functioning condition.

*Corollaries:*

MVC1  We can divide the stuff as long as it still evinces its essential properties and the characteristic result of that multiplicity of properties—i.e. consciousness.

MVC2  We can fuse and combine mental properties by combining the relevant stuff.

In his seminal paper on personal identity, Parfit poses the following problem cases for any theory of personal identity:

> My brain is divided, and each half is housed in a new body. Both remaining people have my character and apparent memories of my life.

> We can, I suggest, imagine a divided mind. We can imagine a man having two simultaneous experiences, in having each of which he is unaware of having the other.[24]
>
> The psychology of fusion is more complex. ... The one person who results from a fusion can ... q-remember living the lives of the two original people.
>
> On this way of thinking the word "I" can be used to imply the greatest degree of psychological connectedness.[25]

I have previously criticized Parfit's interpretation of the experiments and neurological conditions (such as hemispherectomy) inspiring his thought experiments,[26] but we can independently critique his metaphysical claims.

Kant's thought experiment begins, as does Parfit's, by focusing on the powers of the mind as properties of a mental substance present independent of an actual lived human life. We soon get Kant's "fission" conjecture:

> Now, just as we can think all powers and faculties of the soul, even that of consciousness as diminished by one half, but in such a way as the substance still remains, so also, without contradiction, we can represent this extinguished half as being preserved, not in the soul, but outside it; and we can likewise hold that since everything which is real in it, and which therefore has a degree — in other words its entire existence from which nothing is lacking — has been halved, another separate substance would then come into existence outside it. For the multiplicity which has been divided existed before, not indeed as a multiplicity of substances, but as the multiplicity of every reality proper to the substance, ... and the unity of substance was therefore only a mode of existence, which in virtue of this division has been transformed into a plurality of subsistence (*Pure Reason*, note b, B416–417).

Notice that Kant does not imagine half of a brain placed in another body but rather half of the mental properties of an individual (which retain their function) becoming attached to a substance that can

---

[24] Multiple personality syndrome would provide real life grist to this argumentative mill (see Gillett, 1999a).
[25] Parfit (1979), 187–88, 198–99, 205. I shall deal with q-memories in Chapter 5.
[26] In Gillett (1998). I will rehearse some of the brain bisection arguments in Chapter 7.

support their separate functioning.[27] The guiding thought is that the functions, perhaps requiring some substrate or other to support them, are logically independent of an integrated human life of the type in which we normally encounter them. This idea reappears in Kant's imagined fusion:

> Similarly, several simple substances might be fused into one, without anything being lost except only the plurality of subsistence, inasmuch as the one substance would contain the degree of reality of all the former substances together (*Pure Reason*, note b, B417).

Whereas Both spiritualists and materialists are prone to such fancies, Kant is not: "I am far from allowing any worth or validity to such figments of the brain"(B417n).

Kant dismisses these "figments" on the basis that our concepts and therefore the use of reason must limit itself to the world of actual experience to which it is adapted. We can reason about other minded beings that we have encountered and whose properties we have observed and studied (e.g. human beings), but he critiques the "confusion of an idea of reason (of a pure intelligence) with the concept, in every way indeterminate, of a thinking being in general" when our only actual and developed experience is that of real people "where the thinking being (as a human being) is at the same time an object of outer sense" (B426, B415). He thereby links the concept of a "thinking thing" to our dealings with other human subjects who share the world with us and for whom the problematic figments of the brain may be impossibilties in view of the properties necessary to ground the subjectivity of a human being. Kant therefore both undermines the Parfitian metaphysics of the mind and offers, *pace* Kitcher, a "coherent alternative" to the (spooky) "noumenal self" — a view of the human subject grounded in our dealings with actual human beings that evince integrated cognitive function as beings-in-the-world.

The Parfitian claims rest on the premise that the properties constitutive of mental life are separable from both, on the one hand, a principle of cognitive unity, and, on the other, the integrated human

---

[27] Williams (1973), for instance, imagines a case of "the removal of the information from a brain into a storage device ... and is then put back into the same or another brain"(sic). The idea that the total information state of the brain can be captured apart from a situated longitudinal process of being configured by experience is, in fact, similar to the swampman case (Davidson, 1987).

body as a being-in-the-world (with, for instance cerebro-somatic feedback loops and a set of intact brain stem connections).

Kant has noted that the subject of rational determinations denoted by the *I think* is not a substance of any sort, whether mental or material, but merely a logical requirement of the structure of thought for beings like us, the real basis of which may not thereby be disclosed. I have used the term "subtended" to indicate a relationship, not of logical entailment, but internally related to the coherence of such propositions as "I am walking', "I dream of Jeannie with the light brown hair", and so on. These implicate, in a conception of a thinking thing, a natural being who has dealings with the world as an agent, concept user, and trained rule-follower.[28]

We can therefore review the argument in the following form.

1. The *I think* (the logical or metaphysical subject) is based on cognitive unity.
2. The *I think* as a purely formal principle denotes neither a property nor a substance.
3. The idea that the *I think* could be divided or fused like an object is a mistake.
4. In so far as the *I think* denotes an existent thing it denotes the form of a human subject.
5. The *I think* considered in relation to mental acts and inner determinations is essentially indivisible as a centre of consciousness (but may be conflicted).[29]
6. The *I think* considered as the human form obeys the natural constraints (such as physiological integrity) essential to human functioning.
7. The *I think* as conscious unifying principle of thought cannot undergo Parfitian transformations.
8. The *I think* as actual embodied human subjectivity cannot undergo Parfitian transformations.

---

[28] Peter Strawson makes the point using the logic of mental predication, and Wittgenstein famously undermines the idea of a private language (a system of coherent meaning restricted to a Cartesian mental realm of inner experience) as the basis for the articulation of thought but, arguably, Kant is the first to articulate the thought that a mental subject is necessarily, also an object-in-the-world. Strawson, (1959), 99n. I have discussed Wittgenstein's argument in Gillett (1992) ch 1 & 2.

[29] I shall come to psychic conflict when I discuss psychical and neurological disruptions of the self.

9. The Parfitian transformations are "unserviceable fancies" or "figments of the brain".

Notice that 8 embraces a type of naturalism about the mind or human subject[30] and is a counter to Kitcher's complaint about the irrelevance of Kant's self to real flesh-and-blood human beings.

Kant's arguments reinstate the human being as the rational and unified subject of conscious experience. Only a human being participates in the shared experience that culminates in a thinker who has mastered the rules governing the application of concepts (*Pure Reason*, B172–3). The human being as a being-among-others is, therefore, the objective correlate of the rational subject of consciousness and instances the real essence of that which reason reveals as the metaphysical subject, the *I think*, that binds our mental acts together so that they exhibit a formal and transcendental unity.

The Parfitian fancies fail because they sever human consciousness from its real essence as a being-in-the-process-of-becoming-among-others and indulge in speculations about mental acts as properties somehow able to retain their nature apart from the work of the synthesizing (rule-following, concept using) thinker.

Kitcher's complaint also fails to see the very idea of a noumenal substance as incoherent because substances as we encounter them are part of the real (natural) world in which we track objects and notice their properties. Our mental acts, whether theoretical or practical, are, in essence, rational determinations and therefore reflect the norms governing the use of concepts in judgment and inference. Therefore our mental acts transcend the purely causal determination of inner states and events and answer to the "oughts" which are "found nowhere else in the whole of nature" except where reason holds sway.[31] Our obedience to the oughts of reason betray the fact that we are formed by prescriptive norms and therefore that we are not to be understood solely as naturally constituted creatures but also as beings participating in a nexus of justification and correction (who thereby develop a second nature).

It remains to examine a further attempt to transform the logical or metaphysical subject into something which it is not and, in the process, to unearth certain complexities in what it is.

---

[30] It will resurface and be strengthened by an analysis of the actual brain bisection data (ch 7 below).

[31] *Practical Reason* B575 (NB the link to *Tractatus*, Sellars, Davidson, and McDowell).

## Kant and Freud on the *ding an sich*

Kant does not (*pace* Kitcher, Strawson, and McDowell for instance) mystify the subject as a noumenal being dwelling in a realm other than that of nature. The human being, according to Kant, is a human being seen as a rational, responsible, and creative being who is essentially and historically related to others and obeys oughts (or follows rules) as a result of learning from others and taking their lessons to heart.

We can summarise the derivation of this neo-Kantian view as follows.

1. The noumenal world is the world as it must be if our conception of objectivity and truth (amenable to reason) is to be sustainable.
2. Kant's "transcendental unity of apperception"(or, as in Kitcher, the cognitive unity of a human mind) does not indicate purely mental or rational object—a *res cogitans*—but rather the necessary integration of thought based on repeated encounters with the world.
3. As a conscious subject, each of us is an object-among-others—an object moving among and sensitive to things and engaged with other conscious rational subjects who can share my thoughts and respond to their truth and falsity.
4. My proper attributes as an individual and their myriad interconnected functions are not introspectively evident to me on the basis of any of my unexamined intuitions.

But, after Freud, can we really think of ourselves as the conscious, rational subjects we find in Kant's rationalism or Sartre's existential humanism?

The Freudian revolution was significant in that it introduced the thought that consciousness is not the limit of the psyche but merely the conceptualised appearance of the engagement between the human organism, the world and others. Consciousness does not transparently reveal the nature of a human subject because it is meaningful to think of the soul as having depths or layers that influence one's narrative as a being-in-the-world-with-others but are not always apparent to the introspective or reflective gaze. Our real essence as human subjects who think and labour diligently on the intellectual edifices of metaphysics and philosophical reflection is something more complex than those systematic endeavours take it to be (as Nietzsche argued).

If that is so then, even if I take myself (essentially) to be the self, the thinking self, and nothing but the self (so help me God!) what I am is (like an iceberg) a being with significant aspects lying (both in the geographic and deceptive senses, as it were) beneath the surface of my conscious narrative. Freud's unconscious (Ucs) is a residue of a more primitive and powerful psychic world than that of the conscious self (Cs with its subsidiary Preconscious Pcs) and gives rise to deeply felt and intuitive aspects of my thought and behaviour (such as those involved in emotional and moral being).

The Freudian view is seductive but, I think, fails because a human subject is not only more than human attempts to conceptualise it can ever make it out to be, but also an interactive complex engaged with a discursive reality and formed so as to complement that reality (as a key complements a lock, or an enzyme its substrate).[32] The strange hybrid of Cs and Ucs, that responds to reason but is more than rational because it is an engaged, concerned being, is a subject for whom its nature is in question because questioning is its mode of existence such that it is always already challenged and challenging the world (through its attempts to "capture" experience in intellectual terms). Both conscious and unconscious aspects of the self-as-subject are equally important but neither is a thing in itself; it questions and continually poses to itself a problem that is, ultimately insoluble in intellectual terms. The conscious self is a discursive being subject to norms (as conceptions of laws) not simply a natural phenomenon (or purely causal system), and we should notice that both descriptions are characterisations (logical constructions), they are not the thing in itself.

What is more, just as we have noticed and unravelled the misconception inherent in taking the *res cogitans* (conscious rational subject of experience) to be a full disclosure of our being-in-the-world, so we must expose the associative, causally understood creature revealed by the natural sciences (and accepted by Freud) as a complementary misconception. On that basis we can make some post-Freudian remarks about human beings that avoid identifying what a human being is in itself with the Ucs in any misleading or potentially reductive way.

---

[32] This thought is made explicit in relation to cognitive science and philosophy of mind by Andy Clark (1997).

All objects affect the subject but their effects are not fully evident to the subject (through introspection or reflection) because the encounter between subject and world is only partially conceptualised and made conscious. However, the touch of the object ("raw" or unedited, as it were) leaves a trace in the psyche despite its incomplete accessibility to conscious thought.[33] Freud identifies the selectivity and presentation of the encounter to the conscious subject as an appearance mediated by speech. Given the present account of the development of the logical subject through occasions in which speech is taught and learnt (to echo a phrase of Quinton's [1967]), this view is attractive and it explains how a word can have resonances with formative discursive experiences somewhat looser than those dictated by the complex historical and rule governed functions of speech. Church also notices that the mismatch between the psychic effect of an encounter and its conscious articulation allows the subjective significance of events in life to interconnect in ways not subject to the rational order structuring thought and to have a much more organismic character. Pascal's words "reasons of which reason knows not" or a kind of "reason" more suited to the "heart" than the mind means that we "feel the force" of such connectivity "without being in a position to articulate its content, and without being able to subject it to critical scrutiny" (Church, 2005, 40). This, one might say, is part of the reality of the subject as a unified locus of psychic activity that does not appear as a feature of the rational subject.

Thus, both psychically and ontologically the unknown "object" underpinning and serving as the ground of conscious experience, the actual human subject (though not exactly the Kantian *ding an sich*) is not adequately revealed by introspection and the (post)Cartesian exposition of the ego. We might go further and, with Heidegger, remark that the subject as an object engaged with the world, or thrown into the stream of life (as *Dasein*) is the subject as a being-in-the-process-of-becoming-amidst-others continually transcending its own self-conception while being moulded in part by that self-conception. Therefore the subject comes to reflect both the self-influencing conceptions that make him/her a being with a certain psychic configuration and the contingencies of historico-cultural positioning that inscribe him or her in certain ways. A human subject

---

[33] Lacan uses the term *tuche* to speak of the touch and Levinas talks of the trace left by the encounter with the other, a trace that defies totalisation by conceptualising it.

emerges as the result of this (more or less intentional)[34] enterprise informing his/her interactive being in the midst of historical contingencies in a way that undermines (pure) (bio-)psychological essentialism in respect of the subject.

Kant reminds us that our conception of an object and its individuation is constrained by ways of thinking that can be rationally interrogated, but that we must remain silent about the inaccessible or non-cognizable features of any being, including ourselves, except in so far as we/they are logically/conceptually delineated by cognizable features. The existence of things in themselves (*noumena*), including human beings, is necessitated by our rational and transcendental analysis of experience, but only knowable in so far as we have developed techniques for their characterization.[35] Oneself as subject, the psychically informed centre of subjectivity, is inscrutable in just this way and knowable only as a psychological and embodied being. Beyond the reach of psychological language (of beliefs, attitudes, conflicts, emotions, expectations, regrets, and so on) there are neural events and structures that are part of the unspoken aspects of self implicit in the lived conscious narrative but not fully articulate as part of it. But even the neural events are understood according to a discourse—that of neuroscience, itself both revealing and concealing the being in question. When we lay aside the presuppositions inherent in neuroscientific discourse, we find that certain "transcendental" conditions constrain our understanding of the human subject (as subject of thought and experience). We have noted already that the subject has a narrative (positioned, sequential or historical) configuration (both biologically and psychologically and in terms of cognitive development as a logical subject) and is normatively configured (as a rule-follower).

The transcendental conditions on the narrative subject are therefore twofold:

(i) one must be an object interacting with and affected by other objects;

(ii) one must have a workable unity of cognitive activity sufficient to yield articulate mental content on the basis of experience.

The conscious narrative resulting from the dynamic activity comprising a discursively engaged life trajectory is a selection, partial

---

[34] More or less intentional because aspects of it are contingent and surd and aspects intended by self and the others who nurture and help to create the self.

[35] I discuss the Kantian "I" in Appendix D.

and interested, that results in a lived subjective identity. But subjective identity is not that of a pure (phenomenological) subject because the subject (of early phenomenology) is always distinct from and positioned with respect to the object it cognizes whereas, realistically, the person is entangled with (and concerned about) the natural world and his/her material and psychological exchanges in that world. The person as a formed being is therefore being formed dynamically as a being who is (always already) there, thrown into the current of life (thus Heidegger's *Da-sein*). The subject of this narrative, on reflection, appears to have both metaphysical distinctness from and inextricability with the things (and other subjects) contributing to its formation. We will turn to this concept — the narrative subject — in the next chapter where we can support the strong identity conclusion already derived by exploring the contested topic of memory and identity as an entrée into the world of moral being that will inform the practically oriented chapters to follow.

# Chapter 5

# *The Moral Subject*

## *Memory, Identity, and the Human Soul*

> ... the soul is, in a way, all existing things; for existing things are either objects of perception or objects of thought.
> (Aristotle, *De Anima*)

> The 'soul' (of the human being) is in a certain way beings. The soul which constitutes the being of a human being discovers in its ways to be—*aisthesis* and *noesis*—all beings in regard to their thatness and whatness, that is to say always also in their being.
> (Heidegger, *Being & Time*)

> The relationship of domination ... establishes marks of its power and engraves memories on things and even within bodies.
> (Michel Foucault)

We have examined the subject of experience as a cognitively integrated or unitary, narratively coherent subject who is the thinker responsible for composing my thoughts. In discussing personal identity Schechtman has drawn a clear distinction between *the re-identification question*—a matter to be determined within the metaphysics of identity—and *the characterization question*. The former is answered by spelling out a criterion or criteria according to which we would judge that we were dealing with the same numerical individual and it is usually answered by appeal either to a psychological (neo-Lockean) criterion or to bodily (animal) identity.[1] I have noted that Locke's remarks about real essence and the Aristotelian framework of his discussion of personal identity run counter to a reductive metaphysical view of either type and support a more holistic view even though he distinguishes the worries motivating our questions

---

[1]   As discussed in Chapter 4.

about the same person from those that would be answered by bodily continuity *per se*. I will argue that if we deepen Locke's view not only by invoking real essence and the neo-Kantian arguments for the unity and objectivity of the human subject but also by pursuing the real nature of memory (in the way that Schechtman does) we arrive at an account of human identity which answers both of her questions in a satisfying way and adequately grounds a discussion of our being as moral subjects. I will, in developing this account, reject answers which do not reveal what actually lies beneath a human identity[2] which is not the brain viewed reductively but is what we could call the embodied brain situated in a socio-cultural context. I have argued that this *hypokeimenon* exhibits cognitive unity and objective being-in-the-world and has a narrative identity that matters to us because of the encounters in which we develop as a being-with-others-in-the-world.

First I shall rehearse the argument for the cognitive unity of the human subject.

## Argument for the unitary cognitive subject

Let the cognitive subject at time $t_0$ be $S_C^{t_0}$. The cognitive subject is the subject who performs cognitive operations involving (a) the use of concepts and (b) the making of logical inferences. The use of concepts is, I have argued, tied to rule following and the mastery of concepts entails that the subject is capable of following the requisite rule.[3]

Any plausible naturalistic view of this capacity licenses the following argument.

USc1  $S_C$ learns concept C in situations occurring at $t^1, t^2, t^3, \ldots t'$

USc2  $S_C$ uses concept C in giving content to experience at $t^x$

*Therefore*

USc 3  $S_C$ at $t^x$ is the same individual as at $t^1, t^2, t^3$, etc.

The naturalistic assumption is merely that the competent use of concepts according to shared rules common to members of co-linguistic groups is not a skill that magically comes into existence but requires learning or training, a process that takes time.

---

[2] We could call this the *hypokeimenon* of that which manifests itself as a human subject or person and by so doing follow Heidegger's discussion of our knowledge of the world (*Being & Time*, H43).

[3] Also discussed in Chapter 4 above.

The second aspect of the cognitive subject entails that the subject, armed with two premises, is able to draw an implied conclusion as follows:

Given that S believes

*All swans are white* (mistaken as it happens) and

*Hector is a swan*,

S can draw the conclusion

*Hector is white.*

This ability is, in fact, indifferent to time constraints provided only that the premises can be called to mind for the purposes of the inference. The idea of cognitive unity therefore depends only on the mastery of concepts and the ability to reason.

A robust conception of the human psyche as an integrated or unitary subjectivity directs us to a serious consideration of memory and subjective identity (in a way that Schechtman, among others, has explored). This leads us to a much richer analysis of the narrative identity of the subject, an analysis more in keeping with Heidegger, Lacan, and post-structuralism than the standard neo-Lockean theories on offer (particularly when they accept a shallow Propositional Attitude psychology).

### The recovery of times past: memory and narrative

When we examine the philosophical views about memory that tend to dominate our discussions of personal identity we find that they are riddled with problems.

> An event leaves a trace in the memory: one sometimes imagines this as if it consisted in the event's having left a trace, an impression, a consequence, in the nervous system. As if one could say: even the nerves have a memory. But then when someone remembered an event, he would have to *infer* it from this impression, this trace. Whatever the event does leave behind in the organism, it isn't the memory.
>
> The organism compared with a Dictaphone spool; the impression the trace, is the alteration in the spool that the voice leaves behind. Can one say that the dictaphone (or the spool) is remembering what was spoken all over again, when it reproduces what it took? (Wittgenstein, *Remarks*, I, #220).

Wittgenstein here articulates a popular philosophical and psychological view of memory (these days we might substitute the idea of a video-recording for a dictaphone spool). The thought is that memory activates a trace of experience seen as a causal imprint on the mind, producing images and ideas interconnected by various relations of contiguity, cause and effect (by constant conjunction), and resemblance. The memory image "preserves the original form, in which its objects were presented" and is distinct from imagination which can rearrange and reconstruct images so as to provide fictional thoughts at the behest of the subject (Hume, *Treatise*, 57). Properly functioning memory is faithful to the original order of the impressions in the experiences concerned even though "the pictures drawn in our minds are laid in fading colours" (Locke, *Essay*, 152–3). This empiricist model of memory has it that the will serves to awaken the recorded images which are "rouzed and tumbled out of their dark cells into open Day-light". Updated in terms of computer mechanisms and the language of contemporary cognitive science, this is the current model for many philosophers of mind. Parfit, for instance, accepts a generic story of this type.

I remember having an experience only if:

(1) I seem to remember having an experience;

(2) I did have this experience; and

(3) my apparent memory is causally dependent, in the normal way, on this past experience (Parfit, 1986, 207).

Wittgenstein identifies the essence of this "the classical, causal model" as follows:

(i) there is a causal trace left in the brain by events impinging on the subject;

(ii) the trace can be activated to provide images qualitatively the same as those caused by the experiences remembered.

It is worth noting that in this model the subject is a passive receiver who then later can activate the trace which in itself is a more-or-less faithful inscription left in the brain. This characterization and the classical model can be criticised on several counts.

Schechtman (1994) criticizes the thesis that a memory is an awakening of an element within a loose causal nexus of relatively atomic snapshots of experience each of which is more or less complete unto itself. That thesis (derived from Locke and Hume) is a critical element in reductive psychological views of personal identity according to which the psychological subject is a construct from atomic moments of mental life (Parfit, 1984). The apparent unity of the subject is explained by relations between those psychic atoms among which memories are a set of psychic "video clips" causally imprinted within a person's brain (as in the classical model of memory). Schechtman argues that the person is necessarily implicated not only in specifying any given memory but also in elaborating its content so that the psychic individual cannot be a mere assemblage of such elements. The relevant psychological continuity theories of identity therefore depend on "autobiographical experience memory" conceived as a collection of episodic or declarative conscious memories as they are conceptualized in the "storehouse theory" of memory.[4]

The storehouse theory and the idea of discrete memories as mnemonic atoms are not in good standing in current cognitive and neuropsychological discussions of memory. It seems that a person extensively edits, transforms, updates, fills in, and interprets remembered events when consciously recalling them.[5] Most memory accounts are not at all the kinds of thing that could possibly be an isolated video clip of the event remembered (as Wittgenstein astutely observes). What is more the stereotypical autobiographical or episodic memories are part of a much more extensive system of holistically connected cognitive skills. Schechtman remarks,

> Memories of particular experiences are thus only one of the kinds of autobiographical memories we have and do not even seem to be the most common (Schechtman, 1994, 8).

She notes that most memories are consolidated, summarized, and edited versions of things that have happened to the subject and, in fact, draw on numerically different experiences with the details of particular remembered episodes added in to a template assembled from different but related occasions.

> It is not easy to see, however, how these summarized-event memories can be fit into the structure of psychological continuity theories; they are not simple, countable, connections between two well-defined moments of consciousness.

And this is only the beginning of the problems because who one is, one's personal identity, makes a distinctive imprint on the formation of those memories that one accumulates rather than just serving as a causal locus for the physical realisers of mental events each having their own identity and content as discrete entities.

---

[4] A theory no longer held by most cognitive psychologists working in the field. See for instance Parkin (2001) or Schachter (1989).

[5] See for instance, Neisser (1981) and Barsalou (1988).

If memory is to provide us with a useful source of knowledge about our own histories, we will need to condense the information we receive. It makes sense, therefore, that in autobiographical memory the information that is coming in should be reconstructed as a more concise and comprehensible narrative which emphasizes the most significant factors of past experiences and depicts general and longstanding patterns or activities with representative examples (Schechtman, 1994, 11–12).

Schechtman concludes that "autobiographical memories are the way we tell ourselves and others the story of our lives" and that, in fact, "we are rather subtle authors".

There is therefore an holistic role for personality and identity in memory so as to adapt a human individual to the kinds of events he or she finds him/herself thrown into. Human memory is best understood as a colloquy of skills and techniques, some learnt discursively (products of "second nature") and others a legacy of "first nature" (or neurobiology). The relevant skills are based on a process of cognitive development in which rule-governed, language-related techniques are mastered so that the subject forms beliefs and attitudes linking times and places. By so doing we keep track of self and others and develop enduring projects and strategies designed to take account of the unfolding of contingencies and the life events that result.

All this has profound implications for theories of psychological continuity.

> Who we are is thus determined by who we think we are in many crucial ways. We first of all need a sense of our pasts as the comprehensible unfolding of a life-story to have the capacities definitive of persons. Furthermore, the way in which we process information to construct a particular story will play a role in creating the particular person we become (Schechtman, 1994, 16).

Wittgenstein supplements this view in such a way as to deepen our understanding of our real psychological essence in a way that prepares the way for a different approach to the metaphysical and moral issues associated with human identity.

## Wittgenstein and memory

Wittgenstein's main contentions about memory can, I think, be summarised as follows.

1. A memory is not a mental image or item of content accompanied by a feeling of remembering.

2. Memory is distinguished from other mental phenomena by its link to the intentional skill of remembering.
3. Remembering is continuous with the range of cognitive skills involved in keeping track of things in the world and one's place in the midst of it all.
4. Memory is holistically connected to the temporally integrated identity of a human being (as are intention, hope, expectation and so on).

These theses, scattered throughout Wittgenstein's work on psychology, are part of a view that mental ascriptions are abstractions from our complex patterns of interaction with the world and its inhabitants so that mental life is an aspect of the life lived by a subjective, embodied, and socially engaged (or discursive) creature.

*1. Memory and mental images*

> "I had a toothache" when I say this I don't remember any behaviour, I remember my pain. And how does that happen? A faint copy of the pain comes into my mind? — So is it as if one were ever so slightly in pain? "No, it is another kind of copy; something specific." ...
>
> But the word specific (or an analogous one), which one would very much like to use here, does not help. ...
>
> What we want to know, to get a bird's eye view of, is the use of the word "remember". ...
>
> For one can't say: "After all, you are acquainted with the specific thing, the memory-image." (*Remarks*, I, ##159–60.)

Wittgenstein confronts the idea that the experiential content of memory is a faint copy of the original (as in Locke and Hume) and with it the empiricist theory of memory. He notices, first, that the quality of memory is different from the event remembered in just as obvious and inexpressible a way as the bust of an individual is a different kind of likeness to a portrait. The word "specific" is, he notes, inadequate to say exactly how a memory (e.g. of pain) differs from the experience. But a memory of my pain is not a matter of being acquainted with a memory image (or copy); it is, as it were, having a special kind of access to events past that is as definitive as being acquainted with somebody and as much subject to an external test of validity (a test of whether one is, in fact, acquainted and not just whether one believes that one is). Both "remember" and "recognise" are "success verbs", like knowing, all of which have objective criteria of application not at all dependent on how one achieves them (the images involved, for instance) so that a posited introspective relation to an image of a person is not to the point, rather one must link a present encounter with somebody and past dealings with that same individual (and not a copy or look-alike), the kind of thing we do effortlessly all the time.

If an image or copy (however adequate it might seem) is not only insufficient for memory but also unnecessary, then memory has parallels with reference and representation (which are often analysed causally in current empiricist accounts).

> I was speaking to my neighbours about their doctor; as I did so a picture of this man came into my mind—but I had never seen him, merely knew his name, and perhaps formed a picture of him from the name. How can this picture characterize my speaking of *him*? And yet this is how it struck me, till I recalled that I don't know at all what the man looks like. So his picture represents him for me not one whit better than does his name (*Remarks*, I, #231).

Here the speaker successfully refers without having any (causally or otherwise produced) image of the individual to whom he is referring just as a subject might successfully recall a picnic shared with an acquaintance without there being any particular memory image or mental content that is common to both of them.

Wittgenstein reinforces the point that memory is not like everyday perception and its content in other passages where he is sceptical that there are phenomenological similarities between memory and normal perception.

> "I see us still, sitting at that table".—But have I really the same visual image—or one of those that I had then? Do I also certainly see the table and my friend from the same point of view as then, and so not see myself?—My memory-image is not evidence for that past situation, like a photograph which was taken then and convinces me now that this was how things were then. The memory-image and memory-words stand on the same level (*Zettel*, #650).

This passage is a stark exposé of the memory image thesis and directs us to the role of cognitive links exploited in remembering but that are also evident in our appropriate use of words and abilities such as the ability to tell others what has happened to us so that there is a continuity between memory and other cognitive skills.

## 2. Memory is a skill

> If I now say that the experience of remembering and the experience of pain are different in kind, that is misleading: for "experiences of different kinds" makes one think perhaps of a difference like that between a pain, a tickle, and a feeling of familiarity. Whereas the difference of which we are speaking is comparable, rather, to that between the numbers 1 and $\sqrt{-1}$ (*Remarks*, I, #108).

Is remembering comparable to apprehending the square root of Minus 1? Pain or a well-characterised sensation are as "basic" in our mental life as the number 1 is in mathematics, whereas a thinker requires more extensive familiarity with human beings and their ways of understanding experience to appreciate what it is to ascribe a memory and therefore to know how to think about what is happening in her own case when she remembers something. To understand that one is remembering or that a certain thought involves memory one requires some mastery of the skill involved in doing what is commonly referred to as remembering just as a certain kind of technique of calculation is essential to any understanding of what $\sqrt{-1}$ is. The skill involved is time-linked and may or may not be accompanied by any particular experience or experiential content.

> If someone asks me what I have been doing in the last two hours. I answer him straight off and I don't read the answer off from an experience I am having. And yet one says that I *remembered*, and that this is a mental process (*Remarks*, I, #105).

Here we see me giving an account of myself, a function misleadingly assimilated to having an image or representation with a certain content before the mind as if it were a snapshot of past events associated with the characteristic memory-feeling that tells me: (a) it is a memory; and (b) that its content originates in my past experience.

Once again memory emerges as continuous with all the other skills exercised in discerning or determining the nature of our dealings with things. These skills, as I have noted, are partly "semantic"(in terms of the memory literature) aspects of our being as creatures whose learning and therefore consciousness spans time and enables a cumulative cognitive repertoire and the "mental acts" depending on it.

We might however, just pause before we consider the cognitive skills allied to memory that we take for granted as semantic creatures and consider semantic memory (that which pulls together associations between words and conditions). Wittgenstein discusses this feature of our conscious experience in relation to the "character" that accompanies a thought of, say, Mozart or Beethoven, pointing out that there is a multiplicity of associations that might correspond to this "character" which are pulled together when we recognise a word or recall something familiar (*Remarks*, I, #243). It is not that these associations form the meaning of the word, but they do contribute to the subjective content that accompanies such thoughts. Heidegger refers to the complex of dealings with the thing concerned ("associations") that underpin circumspective knowledge of all the things and people which share the world with us.

### 3. Remembering is continuous with other cognitive skills

In discussing the memory of a pain, Wittgenstein further explicates what psychologists call semantic memory.

> "I remember that sugar tasted like this." The experience returns to consciousness. But of course: how do I know that this was the earlier experience? Memory is no more use to me here. ...
>
> But when I say "It tastes exactly like sugar", in an important sense no remembering takes place. So I do *not have grounds for* my judgment or my exclamation. ...
>
> "It tastes like sugar". One remembers exactly and with certainty what sugar tastes like. I do not say "I believe sugar tastes like this". What a remarkable phenomenon! It just is the phenomenon of memory. — But is it right to call it a remarkable phenomenon? (*Zettel*, ##659-60).

The very idea of semantic memory is so continuous with other aspects of our nature as cognitive creatures, forming the basic skills we use to navigate our way about in a more or less stable environment, that this range of skills cannot be assimilated to the formed and paradigmatic autobiographical or episodic declarative memories that are the central elements of the classical causal theory (as it is found in philosophy).

> How does anyone learn to call a lump of sugar "sugar"? How to obey the request "Give me a lump of sugar?" And how does he learn the words "A lump of sugar please" — i.e. the expression of a wish?! (*Remarks*, I, #163).

Wittgenstein is noting the pervasive nature of what we call semantic memory as part of the ordinary cognitive skills articulating a person's mental life.

> When I talk about this table, — am I *remembering* that this object is called a "table"? (*PI*, #601).

Wittgenstein notices the seamlessness of the cognitive domain implicating the past, ranging from basic skills of learning and keeping track of objects (fundamental to thinking of the world as comprising relatively enduring objects and stable properties) to discrete autobiographical memories of complex episodes and chains of events.

## 4. Memory and personal identity

Wittgenstein is often cast as an enemy of psychological or cognitive processes in the discussion of mind and knowledge, but that seems to be a mistake.

> Why should I deny that there is a mental process? But "There has just taken place in me the mental process of remembering ..." means nothing more than: "I have just remembered ..." To deny the mental process would mean to deny the remembering; to deny that anyone ever remembers anything (*PI*, #306).

Here he does not deny that inner processes take place but asks us to locate the basis of our use of mental predicates, such as those associated with memory, in the adaptive activity of a historically engaged creature. Memory is part of a complex, articulated repertoire of cognitive techniques for dealing with temporally ordered events in one's environment. He remarks, for instance, on what psychologists have come to refer to as "source memory":

> But if memory shews us the past, how does it shew us that it is the past?
>
> It does not shew us the past. Any more than our senses shew us the present.
>
> For even supposing that memory were an audible voice that spoke to us — how could we understand it? If it tells us e.g. "Yesterday the weather was fine", how can I learn what yesterday means?
>
> I give myself an exhibition of something only in the same way as I give one to other people.
>
> I can display my good memory to someone else and also to myself. I can subject myself to an examination. (Vocabulary, dates) (*Zettel*, ##663–6).

Wittgenstein here focuses on the skills we use to keep track of and reflect on events in which we have been involved, skills requiring us to place them in the past and in the context of other life events. He then emphasises the common criteria to which both third person and first person memories conform so as to locate them accurately, a skill that one might expect of a species whose adaptive strategies are intensely social and interpersonal and for whom dossiers or histories of significant exchanges are likely to be useful. In this he is echoed in contemporary psychology: "memory is not a single faculty but consists of different systems that depend on different brain structures and connections" (Squire, 1995, 198).

Wittgenstein's remarks on memory suggest that memory is holistically related to personal identity rather than providing a (possibly reductive) subvenience base for the construct of identity. Memory is not a causally imprinted trace on a passive receiving system forming a "spool like" cumulative record of self-standing mental events; instead we find an agent who engages in "a dynamic cognitive operation involving the integration of problem solving, cross checking, verification and inference" (Hodges and McCarthy, 1988, 647). Thus "the narrative structure of one's own life is continuously recreated, edited, reinterpreted and updated" (ibid.).

In general it seems that all the functions loosely grouped as belonging to memory involve the modification (and continuous revision) of neural connections in the context of the unfolding story of the subject. The editorial or authorial function refers to the fact that, in nearly all these functions, the subject considered holistically as a situated subject plays an active role in what is inscribed on the body.

Amnesic syndromes, in which a person suffers damage to parts of the brain subserving memory, reveal a great deal about the way that the brain organises memory and have led to distinctions well established in the cognitive and neuropsychological literature. Schachter discusses many of these in relation to the theoretical dispute between "passive association theorists" (who conform much more to the Lockean/Humean model) and a much more "Kantian" or "active organisational" model (Schachter, 1989). The dispute is philosophically significant because the former model emphasises the causal role of the environment in structuring "relatively automatic and passive formation of stimulus response bonds" which constitute the mind and effectively exclude the agent—*qua agent*—from a central role in the formation of the psyche. The alternative, more in keeping with current work in cognitive neuroscience, emphasises the active subject as the lead player and narrator in the compilation and editing of life experience as a coherent whole apt to satisfy the adaptive demands of the external world with which the subject is entangled.

The gradual shaping and polishing of memory suggests that the contents of the psyche are not a mere causal trace of the events at the time (on an inner "spool" or data storage device) but have aspects of narrative composition capturing what is, or was at the time, significant to the subject. Once composed, the narrative of the event becomes increasingly fixed in its anecdotal form according to a script or schema and remains more or less stable in that form (Barsalou, 1988; Rubin, 1992).

It is instructive, in relation to this process, to look at the dramatic subject of "flashbulb memories"(memories of vivid and salient events), so named because they appear most closely to conform to the classical model—the idea that a snapshot of an event in the past is housed in a long term store and retrieved at will. However even these memories do not support the classical model.

> Flashbulb memories are simply more extensive, more enduring, more consistent and reported with greater confidence than other memories; they are not perfect by any means (Bohannon and Symons, 1992, 87).

Considering the susceptibility of even such prototypical memories to the effects we have discussed (such as active composition and revision over time) it appears that, "The notion of instantaneous memory pictures can be discarded as a bad idea that does not fit any candidate mechanism."

In place of the classical model, we need to appreciate just what happens to link memories criterially to historical or temporally indexed situations and how the desiderata of fidelity mesh with the increasingly evident facts about reconstruction and the creativity associated with memory. Formed memories develop as a subject acquires a set of schemata to organise scripts which fit the course of tracts of experience (Conway, 2005).

> When you recall an episode in your life, you reconstruct it in much the same way as you would reconstruct an episode in a story. However, your own life story is much richer and contains many more details important to you than any story you might read. So you need a much finer system of cues and rules to recon-

struct your life than to construct a story (Glass and Holyoak, 1986, 244).

The schemata concerned in autobiographical memory draw on the subject's past experience, incidental emotional associations, and current concerns so that they are intimately tied to the many ways that a subject has learned to deal with the kinds of events in which they are normally involved (Schachter, 1989, 691ff).

The close association between memory and other cognitive structures serving the needs of a trajectory through the world is evident in studies showing that memories are typically recovered (or, better, reconstructed) by using "strategic retrieval processes operating on available episodic and semantic knowledge" to estimate the temporal order of events and place them in relation to known landmarks in the plausible space of the individual's experience (Moscovitch, 1995, 240). The reconstruction of conscious memories, in fact, is a kind of problem solving task; "Strategic retrieval processes are self-initiated, goal directed, effortful and intelligent" all associated with frontal lobe function in service of the personality structure and character of the individual concerned (Moscovitch, 1995, 234). Luria, wedded to the Marxist view that higher consciousness is coeval with speech, often refers to the participation of speech in the higher control of human behaviour by the frontal lobes. Such functions relate directly to the hierarchies of interest, and personal concerns arising in human discourse discussed by Damasio in his discussion of the role of emotion and personal engagement in giving structure and direction to our cognitive lives (Damasio, 1973, 93, 198).

A person exercises a quite particular skill (the nature of which remains to be elucidated) when they remember an event knowing that it is a memory. The fact that we take this skill for granted suggests that it is interwoven with features of ourselves that we find so unremarkable that we are apt to overlook them (*Zettel*, #659). A human subject develops an ability to weave together a conscious narrative in a way that locates him or her as a conscious subject in a world of objects and events presented amidst an abundance of sensory information. Aristotle, Kant, Luria, Wittgenstein, and McDowell have all, in their own ways discussed the way that we are discursively shaped to use rules of sense and reference to achieve propositional knowledge of that world and our own individual histories as conscious inhabitants of it.

The literature on the neuropsychology of memory identifies the hippocampus and medial temporal structures as the locus of the functions that serve other tasks including the tracking of indexical or dynamic content such as information about one's current location in space and time (O'Keefe and Nadel, 1978). It seems, therefore, that "the functions of memory in normal everyday cognition are so vast and diverse" (Braisby and Gellatly, 2005, 266) that, working the closely together as a holistic set of functions to do with navigation in the environment, they provide an integrated sense of self and what one is doing or has done at various times and places so that memory "links, indeed it binds, the self to reality" (Conway and Holmes, 2005).

These facts from the literature are, therefore highly relevant to a question at the heart of an account of the metaphysics of personal identity:

> *Is memory holistically related to personal identity or does it provide a subvenience base for that construct?*

The question is illuminated by examining cases of amnesia.

> NA's memory problems affect his everyday life in many ways. Social relations are difficult because he often cannot remember people from one meeting to the next. He does not enjoy television as he might because he cannot retain the narrative across the commercial break. Cooking is also hard because he cannot keep track of the sequence of steps required by such a recipe (Ellis and Young, 1996, 276).

Here we are confronted by the profound inter-relationship between memory and one's life as a person with preferences, intentions, a character and a unique place in the world. Memory functions are part of identity formation, implicate layers of the psyche that are historically structured and integrated. The intricate relationship between personal autobiography, one's hierarchy of motivations, the acts and intentions that one executes, and the evaluative framework that contextualizes experience, makes it evident that there is a holistic relationship, suggested by Wittgenstein (and explicated by Schechtman), between memory and human identity. The argument therefore establishes that if we are talking about human memory (as we know and love it),[6] it is not Q memory.

The argument linking identity, subjectivity, and care of the soul is opposed to what we might call the anti-Narrative stance but it does not rest on a narrative (or anything merely psychological) as the ultimate principle of human identity. It can be distilled into one or two

---

[6] Or, more importantly, as we have a coherent and workable concept of it.

succinct arguments and then a claim about ontology (Galen Strawson, 2004 and 1997). The result is a rejection of the following "anti-Narrative" claims:

aN1　The claim that we are and ought to think of ourselves as Narratively constituted is false.

aN2　One can be fully aware of the fact that one has long-term continuity as a living human being without ipso facto having any sense of the mental self or subject of experiences something that has long term continuity.

*Argument for the unitary narrative subject*

Let the narrative subject at time t0 be $S_N{}^{t0}$

$US_N1$　The subject narrating a lived life story at t2 is draws on events at t1 unless Q memory is possible.

$US_N2$　Q memory is not human memory.

$US_N2$　Any human subject $S_N{}^{t1}$ is the same human subject as $S_N{}^{t2}$.

$US_N2$　Therefore there is a relation of identity between $S_N{}^{t2}$ and $S_N{}^{t1}$

If that is true then any given subject, considered as a narrative subject, has a necessary unity with itself throughout the period covered by the narration, or the events contributing to the lived narrative moments comprising a given life story, i.e. the period during which it thinks of itself as as the same thinking thing in different times and places.

When we combine the unitary narrative subject claim with the cognitive unity claim, the two aspects of human subjectivity — $S_N$ and $S_C$ — combine to secure a robust identity conclusion. But, the argument above has the effect of strengthening Schechtman's claim that $S_N$ secures the four desiderata of an account of personal identity (survival, moral responsibility, concern for the future, and justified compensation for past wrongs). One could also argue that $S_N$ requires a cognitive subject $S_C$ to underpin its narrative ability — the ability to construct a series of contentful experiences.[7] If that is so then a strong identity conclusion is secured together with the desiderata motivated by the characterisation question.

If these arguments are telling, then the anti-Narrative claims are both defeated in that, metaphysically speaking, the narrative and cognitive subject is diachronic and ought to recognise the fact or risk

---

[7]　I have so argued elsewhere (1992, 32–47).

being disconnected from the truth. The scopic soul is transcendent and unworldly, abstract and distanced from the world and the immediacy of lived existence within it; it can therefore be thought of as purely mental and without an intrinsic engagement in the world, but a human subject is touched by the real and altered as a result of that touch. Human being-in-the-world is and must be entangled, relational and cathectic, a conversation with one's whole being not an exercise done from a contemplative distance. That is why human identity and care for the soul are internally related. Considered as a purely thinking thing I take on an unreal or ethereal aspect, and the care of the soul becomes a diaphanous idea but this is the nominal essence of personal identity and not its real essence. As the thing I am, flesh and blood inscribed and penetrated by experience, I take on vitality and responsibility so that my individual being-in-the-world-with-others is both inescapable and worth caring about.

What is more the link shows us why the cognitive subject discursively engaged with other human beings is also a moral subject.

### The moral subject and cognitive development

The moral subject is such that he or she must feel the pull of moral claims and yet may still not necessarily respond positively their demands. According to a neo-Kantian view, the subject ought rationally to appreciate the force of a moral requirement and also have an incentive to obey it, but he or she may still determine to act contrary to what morality commends.

*Argument linking cognitive and moral subjectivity*

CMS1  A cognitive subject learns cognitive skills from other cognitive subjects.

CMS2  The relevant interactions are not just didactic but also interpersonal in that they involve recognition, solicitude, correction, encouragement and so on.

CMS3  Involvement in interpersonal interactions includes one in a moral community.

*therefore*

CMS4  Becoming a cognitive subject goes along with becoming a moral subject.

The argument ties the cognitive subject *qua* human cognitive subject into a world of discourse where he or she learns from others the signification of terms and therefore learns to apply the concepts that articulate his or her thought. In so doing the subject locates him or herself among others and comes to appreciate that what they do affects him and what he does affects them. Thus two implicit messages are conveyed — that one truly is a being-in-the-world-with-others and that those others respond to things in sufficiently similar ways to oneself to be able to convey the significance of the words one uses to articulate one's own mental life (or narrative, or psyche, or motivational structure). Thus, when contemplating any action, I intuitively appreciate that it may affect others who are in the world with me and that their feelings about it are likely to be congruent, to some extent and particularly where it is a widely shared human experience (such as pain or embarrassment), to my own. It is therefore open to me to factor in to my decision as to whether to enact what I have thought of doing in the light of that intuitive understanding of its effect on others (which I can cultivate and expand or neglect and allow to atrophy). It is a measure of my participation in the moral community how I respond to that complex of incentives and considerations.

### Reductive theses and their evident deficiencies

The philosophical literature on memory and identity has focused on necessary and sufficient conditions defining what Locke calls the *principia individuationis* for a person. I have interpreted Locke[8] as delineating that aspect of ourselves (or nominal essence of self) which grounds our intuitions about responsibility and authenticity (without wanting to undercut the actual basis for that nominal essence in the real world) and focused on the Aristotelian thoughts he uses to introduce the discussion of personal identity. I have eschewed a reading of real essence confined to the internal properties of the thing concerned — a biological human being — and instead noted that human identity is (at every stage of development) a product of being-in-context.

Interpreting Locke's criterion for personal identity in the light of an informed account of memory and consciousness, we notice that "the psychological criterion" misses many implicit features of our own self-understanding. The theory tries to answer too many complex questions about creatures like us with an inadequate view of the metaphysics of the human psyche. The inadequacy can, however, be remedied if we embrace a view of the human subject as positioned in

---

[8] In a very similar way to Mackie.

an interwoven complex of human discourses.[9] The soul (or psyche)[10] is a "mode of presentation" of *Dasein* so that the relation between soul and situated human being is analogous to that between an object of experience (or thought) and the Kantian *ding an sich* or between memory and the *tuche* (or trauma). The analogies can be schematised as follows:

| Soul/psyche | object of thought | memory |
|---|---|---|
| *Dasein* | *ding an sich* | *tuche* |
| | (thing in itself) | (touch of the real) |

In each case there is a reality — *Dasein*/*ding-an-sich*/*tuche* — that is signified so as to enable the mind to grapple with it in a meaningful way, but the intentional object cannot displace the actuality in our understanding of the world. The soul is a human subject as self-understood with a narrative form drawing on the diverse ways of thinking about human beings current in the subject's historico-cultural situation.

The right perceptual analogy for the human subjectivity is not vision and its object but smell. Visual (or scopic) conceptualisations of subjectivity distance the subject from the object of perception and visual experiences seem to leave the subject intact, but smell is quite different. One smells (or tastes) by taking into one's body particles of the substance sensed and being chemically altered by them. Smelling (or tasting) therefore changes a body and is part of the destruction by melting away of the thing smelt. It is therefore costly and the object smelt as fragrant object is transient. Smell reminds us that reality actually touches and changes us and that I as subject am entangled in my being with the world out there, so it overturns the Cartesian illusion of transcendence of the world by *res cogitans*. The experience is also historical — the moment consumes its own substantial basis so that it cannot be repeated. Note that Freud uses the term *ding an sich* (an evocation of the Kantian analysis) tying "thing presentations" to memory traces rather than memory images (Freud, 1986, 172). Levinas has it thus:

---

[9] That is a view which can be found in Heidegger's existential phenomenology and it is expanded by Barthes, Lacan and Foucault.

[10] Locke, as I have noted, speaks of the "principium individuationis" (*Essay*, II.XXVII#3) and discusses (as does Aristotle) plants, "brutes", and persons (#9) basing his analysis on the idea of form: as a "continued organization", "the same organised body" or "the same continued life".

> A trace is not a sign like any other ... it is exceptional with respect to other signs in that it signifies outside of every intention of signalling and outside of every project of which it would be the aim. ... a real trace disturbs the order of the world. ... But in this sense every sign is a trace. In addition to the signify-ingness of the sign it is the past of him who delivered the sign.[11]

Levinas wants us to notice that our words and deeds affect one another and do not just convey symbolic messages so that the impact of another person on my soul is only incompletely captured by any subsequent representation or episodic memory of my encounter with them. Others change me through my dealings with them and leave their traces in my life all of which contribute to making me who I am.

## Memory and lived experience: the *tuche*

Just as the Lockean person is a subject-as-thought-about rather than in itself (the human being who touches others in ways not reducible to signals), so a memory is not the *tuche* (or touch of the real) at its heart. We are affected by the causal impact of the real and it gives rise to cathexes or resonances—somatic, emotional, ideational, and volitional (aspects of the trace of that encounter). Lacan, focusing on the *tuche* or trauma that has overlays of signification, personal relationships, unspoken messages, context and imperatives, argues (as did Freud) that we cannot capture this "touch of the real" in articulate and conscious memory. Therefore the complexes arising and reverberating through the psyche on the basis of the *tuche* (or trauma) can only be approached through transference wherein a living other also encounters me and evokes the traces of the events that transpired. "Our experience then presents us with a problem, which derives from the fact that, at the very heart of the primary processes, we see preserved the trauma in making us aware of its presence" (Lacan, 1979, 55). Lacan here uses the term "primary processes" to refer to the workings of the mind not evident to consciousness that play an important part in directing our thought and desire.

So now it should be clear why a reductive interpretation of Locke's "memory criterion" (one focusing on conscious episodic memory) is a mistake. When we look beyond the Cartesian nominal essence of the self, we encounter a real essence hinting at the complexity and depth of the existent (existential) human being. Every memory is a trace that is only partially recreated by the subject from an actuality that is the touch of the real. The touch of the real penetrates the sub-

---

[11] Levinas here contrasts memory traces to events-as-remembered (1996, 61–2).

ject like a smell (perhaps a bad smell or perhaps a perfume) and it modifies the structure of the brain but in a way that draws on all the connections and multiplicity of associations that make it the memory that it is. Words crystallize or fix just selective aspects of the memory and contain within themselves the imperatives and overlays that are their autobiographical signification or introspectible relevance to a subject. But their causal resonance with the psyche (particularly the primary process)[12] is such that sound, image, context of hearing, tone of voice, and a myriad other unspoken things could be at the heart of the cathectic structure attached to the memory. These are aspects of the *actuality* of the subject (and his or her psychic life) at the surface of which is the event as remembered and inscribed in words on the mind of the subject. The way any event has touched and moved me is, to use Foucault's words "traced by language and dissolved by ideas" (Foucault, 1986, 83). The soul is therefore a volume written in by experience but both written over and even rewritten by subsequent experience[13] and therefore perpetually dissolving and resolving itself into new patterns (so that the palimpsest of the psyche is a direct *analogia entis* for the neural network doing the biological work implementing it). To try and provide a neat and linear summary of this in terms of discrete autobiographical or episodic memories and the connections between them is to misrepresent mental life and therefore also to misconstrue the human subject as an existent thing.

The revised view of memory and identity allows us to "flesh out" a substantial account of the subject as an ongoing entity with a place in personal and social life.

## What is the truth about the self?

The present approach to the human subject and personal identity yields a sense of the transcendence applicable to the human subject that is central in a neuroethical inquiry. Truth, on the current account, is seen as *alethia* (unconcealing) and reflects the relation between *Dasein* (a situated or "thrown-into-life" human being) and his/her world or "a kind of knowing that is the being of being-in-the-world" (*Being & Time*, 60–61). The embodied subject is therefore *Dasein* viewed under the lens of subjectivity.

---

[12] The mode of operation of the subconscious—well discussed by Marcia Cavell (1993).

[13] This point is made by Schacter, Loftus and Hacking.

# The Moral Subject

Heidegger's existential phenomenology emphasizes being-with-others and historicity so that one might discern two axes of personal being in-forming each of us and therefore fundamental to one's self understanding. The first axis is that of origins or belonging and the second is self-sovereignty or individuality.[14]

Any individual needs to know and be secure in his or her roots, so that s/he can access and use the resources of mythology, symbolism, legitimation, valorisation, and a sense of meaning all of which transcend the individual as organic parts of practices and customs here where I belong (among these people who bear this name and who have named me). The life experiences and stories shared around the table and present in the faces of those whom I trust and who have nurtured me and taught me within their circle of life are the roots of my being-in-the-world.

A human individual also needs room to breathe his or her own air and find a place to be in the sun (as does a tree). This space allows one to be an individual (and unique) realisation of the complex good possible for beings like me. The nourishment giving me the strength to pursue this individual journey comes initially from one's roots (and from time to time one will return to them actually or spiritually) but then is extended beyond that first circle as one is trusted to be a person whom one's extended family or kinship group can release into the world bearing their name.

Notice that one is a being-in-the-process-of-becoming engaged with a greater context transcendent of oneself as an individual but open-ended as one traces a path in the world in one's own way. In that lived experience, the faces of others and the new relationships of trust that are formed can have a transformative effect. Note also that, as the circle of trust and enrichment widens, so one is affected and perhaps inspired by the stories, myths, heroes, and values of others in a way that can influence one's development as a person. That growth equips one to give something back to the wider group so that all are enriched. To grow as a soul or become a better person is to go beyond the limited subjective world one normally inhabits in exactly the way Jack Nicholson's (obsessive-compulsive) character indi-

---

[14] Maori (indigenous New Zealand) thought allows one to think of these under the ideas clustering around *Whanau* (extended family or kin)/*whenua* (placenta or land of origin) and *Rangitiratanga* the understanding or recognition of sovereignty or chieftanship over self or others.

cates when he compliments his companion by saying "You make me want to be a better person."[15]

The scopic subject may be transcendent, unworldly, abstract, and distanced from lived existence in the world, *Dasein* is "touched by the real" and altered as a result of that touch. The being-in-the-world of the subject is a mode of being that is immediate, engaging, and cathectic, and the conversations through which the subject comes to self-knowledge involve one's whole being (they do not happen at a distance) so that transference and the trace of the other are intrinsic aspects of them. That is why the subject is impossible to define as bounded by the limits of the biological organism (or its real essence) narrowly conceived and the maladies of the soul are as varied as the souls who suffer them.

The subject of memory is a subject who has been formed through being-in-the-world-with-others at a certain time in history and is not a purely thinking thing, conceived in universal terms. The real essence of a human subject is like the real essence of an exemplar of a species (only understood as a phenomenon in the context of a certain phase of the history of the biosphere). However, unlike an exemplar of a biological type, the human subject is created through participation in social and personal life which is where what counts as something comes to form the stuff of morality.[16] In that milieu one sees oneself as worth something (however distorted that value might be) by the prevailing discursive context and the care of the soul (construed as flesh and blood inscribed and penetrated by experience) is an aspect of one's life that one cannot avoid (however badly one does it). One would hope that the social and personal milieu in which one is immersed would engage one with the truth of one's being-in-the-world-with-others. Only as we understand how a human subject enacts an identity in the world can we see what is involved in intentional action (a pleonastic phrase) and explore its organic relations with one's character and responsibility as a moral subject.

---

[15] In the film *As Good As It Gets* his constricted and controlled world is irrupted into by the real life of the woman who normally serves him breakfast and he finds himself entangled in her problems.

[16] As Bernard Williams notes (1985, 201).

Chapter 6

# The Sins of the Fathers

*Enacted Subjectivity*

---

> Since all freedom is ability, freedom of choice is the ability to keep uprightness of will for its own sake.
> (Anselm, *De Libertate Arbitrii*)

> Life is like a path along a mountain ridge; to left and right are slippery slopes down which you slide without being able to stop yourself, in one direction or the other. I keep seeing people slip like this and I say "How could a man help himself in such a situation!" And that is what denying free will comes to. That is the attitude expressed in this "belief". But it is not a scientific belief and has nothing to do with scientific convictions.
> (Wittgenstein, *Culture & Value*)

Human beings are not only subjects but also agents and both aspects of our being flow from our nature as embodied subjects or beings-in-the-world-with-others. Agency is has traditionally been tied to character, freedom to act, and moral responsibility such that they seem to stand or fall together. But these concepts are inherently problematic in that one does not wish to revert to a claim that the power to act arises from an extensionless point of willing (in the *res cogitans*) nor to invoke dispositions and powers of the psyche regarded as part of the natural order.

The embodied subject as agent is, on the latter view, regarded as an inherited set of tendencies that lead one to repeat or be inclined towards the sins of the fathers. Given the moderation or even configuration of the psyche by the socio-cultural order in which it develops, one might think that upbringing or familial tendencies could only confirm slogans like "abused children abuse".

The internalist view of action is that the agent's behaviour is causally produced by the desires or habits operative within him or her so that, even though the causal chain is located within the agent, it is configured by forces acting on the agent (hereditary and environmental). It therefore seems unjust to hold a person responsible for the net effect of these forces. We therefore need an account of action grounding responsibility for his or her own actions in the metaphysical, forensic or moral subject as agent. The current account offers us a reconstruction of this debate that makes sense in terms of a realistic view of human beings and their practical reasoning.

## A philosophical model

The dominant (Anglo-American-Analytic) philosophical view of action is causal, such that the beliefs and desires of the agent causally produce an intention which itself causally produces an action. Mill notes with approval that this account renders actions no more problematic than other natural events (an attractive thought to those who embrace a certain kind of naturalism in metaphysics). We can picture it thus:

$$\text{Intention} \rightarrow \text{action}$$

Here the intention is a mental or brain state, the action is a bodily movement, and the arrow is causal. We can then link that picture to a general physicalist claim (that often pre-empts the space available to philosophical naturalism):

$$\text{All events are physical events}$$

We are left with the view that the *mens rea* of voluntary action (or acts for which we are responsible in some strong forensic sense) is a preceding mind/brain event that causes the action (where the mind is seen as a complex function supervenient upon brain activity). The end of this path is unpalatable for moral philosophy and jurisprudence.

In 2001, in *The Ottawa Citizen*, Dr Tana Dineen reported a series of exculpatory considerations that were based on expert psychiatric evidence about the brain states of the perpetrators of various violent crimes (6 June). They included a sex killer who was said to suffer Multiple Personality Disorder,[1] a woman who shot her husband while he slept and was said to have suffered battered wife

---

[1] To which we shall come in Chapter 8.

syndrome, the 1978 Twinkie defence in which the actions of two murderers were ascribed to temporary insanity resulting from the ingestion of sugar, and the knifing and raping of a sleeping woman said to result from the fact that the murderer had been a blue baby and therefore had a "crocodile brain". Common to all of these cases is the belief that the state of the brain and the events which go on within it, themselves caused by events beyond the agent's control, can explain and even excuse criminal acts through their causative role in the production of those acts.

The beginning of the road to perdition is, however, relatively unexceptionable. In the paradigmatic case we have an agent who, with malice aforethought, embarks upon a course of action with significant effects. In the paradigm case, the agent formulates a plan for certain reasons or motives and carries it through to bring about the envisaged end. We recognize, however, that the world throws up an endless variety of cases. Sometimes, for instance, everything happens more or less, in a flash so that the reasoning in the model does not reflect the reality of the act. For this reason we simplify the essentials down to an intent to act (the *mens rea*) and the doing of it (the *actus reus*); of these two, the *mens rea* is the fulcrum on which guilt is balanced — *Actus non facit reum nisi mens sit rea* (Duff, 1990, 7).

When the simplified construal is fed to a philosopher with a scientific bent, we end up with a theory of action in which the intent is the causal antecedent of the act (Mill, 1874). The intention as cause, like all other causes, has a causal history (thus the *Ottawa Citizen* type of claim). The intention is then thought of as a mental state comprising a combination of belief and desire that causally produces the bodily movement which is the action.

The model implies that "to act is to be caused to behave by mental states of one's own" (Bishop, 1989, 11) and it is a small step to the idea that such states are direct correlates of brain states and events moving the agent's body so that intention talk is an unscientific explanation of human behaviour ("folk psychology", or "the psychology of the Clapham omnibus"). The claim is that scientifically (and therefore realistically) construed, an act is a (complex of) bodily movement caused by states of the brain,[2] as is shown by certain revealing cases.

---

[2] Paul Churchland (1986), for instance, lays out the varieties of this view that are current.

*The Ramestes case*

Imagine that Joe, a virtuous sheep farmer, notices that his neighbour's prize ram, Ramestes, is being worried by a black and brown dog. He recalls that there have, in the area, been some nasty dog attacks on sheep attributed to a black and brown dog and the farmers concerned had not been able to rescue the sheep before they had been so badly savaged that they had to be "put down". Joe realises he has his hunting rifle in his pick-up and, as the best shot in the province, decides to take matters into his own hands to save the valuable ram. He shoots, and would have killed the dog cleanly, but, at that split second the dog causes Ramestes to leap into the path of the bullet so that the ram is killed instead.

In such a case we excuse Joe because he had good reason to believe his action would achieve the right result and he did everything he could to bring that about, but a cruel stroke of luck meant that his act miscarried (in a way that was beyond his control). In such cases virtue and moral responsibility go along with a good will i.e. Joe's good intent suitably based on clear thinking and the relevant ability.

*The curare case*

Kevin is about to be anaesthetized and notices that the nurse has left a bottle precariously perched on a cupboard. He wants to signal that she is in imminent danger of it falling on her head but when he attempts to do so he finds that his mouth has dried up from the pre-medication for his anaesthetic and when he tries to signal with his hand he cannot because his muscles are paralysed. He sends a desperate message with his eyes but knows in his heart that it is futile.

In this case Kevin did everything he could even though his attempt to act was ineffective. He did what any of us would normally do to perform an action so we conclude that there is an event in the brain (the internal act of willing) that causes the bodily movement (the action), a neurophilosophical model combining action explanation and neuroscience.

## A Neurophilosophical model

A neurophilosophical model of intentional action might look as follows.

$$S \to BE_1 \to BE_2 \to M_B$$

In the model S is a stimulus, $BE_1$ is the brain event corresponding to an intention, $BE_2$ is the brain event (complex) that encodes a bodily movement, and $M_B$ is the effective bodily movement (or basic action).[3]

In fact, certain thinkers with a biological orientation toward psychology believe there is proof that human action is a manifestation of subpersonal or neurophysiological events in the brain, wrongly interpreted by the subject as mental or intentional causation.[4] Their position unravels the closely linked forensic concepts of freedom of the will and individual responsibility (and is meat and drink to the Twinkie defence). The reductive view is based in part on studies of brain activity and voluntary action which seem to ground an "argument to physical priority" (Spence, 1996).

APP: *The Argument to Physical Priority*

APP1 The mental event of intending to act causes the act ($M_B$).

APP2 The physical/brain event precedes the mental event of intending, and is unconscious;

*therefore*

APP3 The physical event precedes and *causes* the mental event of intending.

APP4 Therefore conscious events are determined by their physical counterparts in brain activity.

In the relevant experiments (by Benjamin Libet) a subject made a voluntary response during which brain activity was sampled revealing a set of characteristic events in the brain preceding the act (Libet, 1985). Libet found that there was a pattern identifiable in an analysed EEG record preceding the spontaneous voluntary action by a discernible interval and preceding also the subject's report that he or she had just initiated or formed the intention to act (an event preceding $BE_1$ – the conscious intention).

However, the crucial premise of the argument to physical priority – (APP2) – relies on some contestable assumptions:

(a) that an action is a discrete bodily movement ($M_B$);

(b) that there is a mental event which is the cause of the act;

---

[3] Danto uses this terminology for the kind of thing the agent can bring about directly.

[4] The most famous of such theorists are Daniel Wegner (2004) and Benjamin Libet (1985).

(c) that one can fix the time of a mental event on the basis of its reportability; and

(d) that the detectable brain event is the cause of the act rather than being a reflection of preparatory moves or neural events involved in acting with intent.

Examining some other imagined cases casts doubt on each of these assumptions.

## Is the action a bodily movement ($M_B$)?

Three cases are pertinent to the pivotal claims.

### The wineglass case

Jack is standing with a friend talking to an attractive woman at a party. His friend, Mike, is also part of the conversation. Jack realises that he cannot move things in the amorous direction he wants to with Mike in attendance and at that moment the hand in which he is holding his glass of red wine jerks and spills red wine over Mike's white shirt. He apologises profusely and remarks that he is troubled by a motor tic (a manifestation of a limited form of Tourette's syndrome) such that these things happen to him and that he cannot help it.

But the question is "Was it a tic or did Jack feign it"?

Notice that at least some of the brain events (roughly $BE_2$) are the same in either case and we should ask why and what kind of brain events (were we able to look at them) would help settle the issue. It is evident that the relevant neuroscientific facts have to distinguish between movements connected in the right kind of way with contextual (or narrative) factors (reflected in the areas of the brain to do with planned or purposive voluntary activity)[5] and those more narrowly associated with bodily movement production.

### The fluidity of action

I walk to the door — a continuous passage of motor activity in which many things are relevant at a more or less conscious level. The activity is both conscious and voluntary but can it correctly be said to be "caused" by identifiable preceding brain events or is it merely "associated with" (or paralleled by) a temporally co-extensive fluid and dynamic tract of brain activity mirroring the overt behaviour.

---

[5] Predominantly the frontal lobes and related limbic centres.

## The Sins of the Fathers 113

In this case all kinds of fleetingly sensed events might be part of the behaviour involved: noticing the trajectory of an attractive and interesting new colleague; making sure not to trip on an upturned floor tile; noting that the boss is marked "IN"; and so on. It is implausible that each of these corresponds to a discrete mental event realised in some way by excitation in the brain at the time. Perhaps we should go home and think again.

### The brain-damaged mobster case

Sean is a mobster who is being charged with the murder of his wife. It seems she came home and walked into an elaborate booby trap in the front entranceway of the house and was shot. Sean explains that he had been tipped off to a Mafia plot to send a lock-picking hit man around to his house to shoot him in the evening when he arrived home so he set up the booby trap, but was careful to leave a note to his wife so that she could avoid it. When it was pointed out that the note was inside the door, he looked shocked and blamed himself, saying that he was so dumb since his own head wound in a shoot out, and that he had a hunch that there was a problem in the plan. It later emerges that in the background there is an affair with another woman that was about to come to light, and that Sean had recently learnt of a messy divorce settlement which left one of his friends almost penniless (give or take a few hundred grand), and that he had taken out a big life-insurance policy on his wife due to "the coming troubled times" in the mob.

Sean's case reminds us that an intentional action is not a matter of the events causing the basic actions (things actually done by the agent) but is to be discerned where a pattern of relevant events indicates a guiding conception has organized the behaviour (related in a certain kind of way to the agent as a being-in-the-world-with-others).[6]

These cases pose serious objections to the argument to physical priority and its neuro-philosophical assumptions. We can examine these in turn.

(a) *Human acts are events caused by preceding mental events called intentions*. This view rapidly leads to certain well known absurdities. Consider my walking to the door. How many actions were involved (each presumably with their own intention)? Did I intend every step I took or only the whole action? How long does it take me to intend

---

[6]  I argued this many years ago in Gillett (1986).

or represent such a "complex" action or do I just get it going and it happens automatically from then on? But surely I take each step intentionally or voluntarily? The problems and implausibilities multiply the closer one looks (and, as Philippa Foot has remarked, our mental lives begin to look more and more exhausting). Hampshire also observes:

> An ordinary human action is a combination of intention and physical movement. But the combination of the two is not a simple additive one. The movement is guided by the intention, which may not be and often is not, distinguishable as a separate event from the movement guided. I know that my action is performed at will, and I know what I am trying to do. But this does not necessarily imply that there has been some distinguishable mental event which was an act of will. I often cannot, in reflection or introspection, distinguish as separable episodes the thought of what is to be done from the actual doing of it (Hampshire, 1969, 74).

One could diagnose the "philosophical illness"(Wittgenstein's phrase, *PI*, #255) leading to the hyper-deliberative account of human action as arising from attempts to force the dynamic flow of human activity into the pigeonholes of an inadequate theory.

(b) The flow in the psyche parallels that in the brain; in both there is a constant stream of activity as the human being continuously interacts with the environment. It is artificial, in terms of the neurophysiology involved, to divide this into discrete events. The subvenient basis for observable human acts and reportable human intentions is, therefore, not a set of discrete causally structured events as required by the causal event model of intention.[7]

(c) Libet's experiment assumes that we can time a mental event by timing an agent's ability to report it. What reason do we have for believing this? Even if one is conscious of initiating an action, making up our mind to do something is not something we normally observe and report on.[8] Observing and reporting on events are skilled activities and must be learnt. But whereas we do learn to act and monitor the effects of our actions we do not report the internal

---

[7] This is bad news for certain varieties of mental realism relying on supervenience theory such as those espoused by Jaegwon Kim among others. I have suggested an alternative in a number of articles (1992; 1993; 1999a & b; 2001 a& b) related to Dennett's view (explored below).

[8] One might of course announce that one has made up one's mind, but that is different from reporting an occurrence, as Hampshire (1969) notes.

(brain) events leading up to them and cannot do so (as the brain is not sensible of things going on within it) rather we nest the action in a tract of narrative which captures what we are enacting in doing what we do and how that fits into the "micro-passage" of our life story happening at the relevant time.

(d) We might also notice that decisions take shape and are enacted through turning the mind on relevant factors and then translating that into action when one's mind is made up, so that precision in timing (of a diffuse inner event which is plausibly a scattered pattern of excitation in related parts of the human neural network) may be an elusive goal, as elusive as deciding when the cloud first begins to look like a crouching tiger or hidden dragon. In fact, the remark "Now it is clear to me, I have made up my mind" seems not at all to be like the report of an observation (rather, as Hampshire has noted, it is a resolution). The argument assumes that a detectable brain event causes the conscious intention and therefore the action. The dynamic structure of normal human action makes such a posit look mistaken, an artificial construct bolstered not only by bad philosophy but also by an experimental situation in which the actions are of a staccato and discrete kind. What is more, any confidence in the experiment is unsettled when we notice the many problematic assumptions within it (as a scientific exercise).[9]

The defective causal model of human agency can be remedied by being more mindful of the nature of intentional action, the influences that come to bear on one's voluntary activity, and the ways in which those influences are (or are not) managed (Immanuel Kant, to whom we shall come, was acutely conscious of this point, and its implications for moral responsibility [Kant, 1929, 497]).

However the scientist, ever looking to extend claims of expertise, might counter that this is all beside the point, that in some sense or other the cause of the action, even if we do not describe it as a mental event, must be identical with something going on in the brain. What other view is reasonable in the light of current knowledge about the brain and behaviour? And here some philosophers chip in with their own "Yea and Amen".[10]

This view cannot, however, encompass the fact that a relevant or even active set of beliefs and desires does not exhaust the story of intentional action, because we make distinctions between actions for which we are morally responsible and other doings (in relation to

---

[9] Gillett and Green (1995); Gillett (1999) Ch 9.

[10] E.g. Armstrong (1981); Bishop (1989); Heil (1992).

which, in Austin's terms, we have pleas or excuses).[11] Numerous examples illustrate this point; one of the most memorable is Davidson's nervous mountaineer.

> Imagine two mountaineers, one of whom, A, slips and could be saved from plunging to his death but for the fact that his companion, B, who is holding on to the safety rope, is unnerved by the fear that he himself might fall, his desire not to fall, and his further fear that he might let go and let his friend, A, fall to his death. Unnerved by this turmoil of thought and emotion, he lets go and his friend falls (Davidson, 1980, 79).

The nervous mountaineer is a typical deviant causal chain[12] case in which B's fear of death together with his belief that A's slip might cause him to fall to his death did, in fact, cause him to let go the rope but, despite the fact that the action is causally produced by relevant mental states, the action does not count as fully intentional (so that he is morally responsible). We are inclined to excuse him and his account is effectively a plea in mitigation even though he might blame himself for his friend's death. Such problem cases demonstrate that an intentional action must be caused by the relevant beliefs and desires *in the right kind of way* — not just by effective causal antecedents. This elusive metaphysical requirement (when pursued) rests on something like *the decision of the agent* or *her resolve to do what she envisaged* or something that could be called a final *agent-involving intent*. To justify the thought that it was, in a real sense, up to the agent whether the act occurred so that he or she can and should take responsibility for it — it must be "sheeted home" through the agent's inner determination to act as he did.

Bishop attempts to do this by introducing three conditions:

(i) the agent must perform the basic acts specified in the plan;

(ii) the act must be intentional under the description in the plan;

(iii) the agent must perform those acts with the relevant intention.

His strategy still does not overcome the basic problems of the staccato $BE' \rightarrow M_B'$ then $BE'' \rightarrow M_B''$ then $BE''' \rightarrow M_B'''$ story that we are

---

[11] Cf. the paper "A plea for excuses" in Austin (1970).

[12] Such "deviant causal chains" or Gettier-like cases show us that the conditions allegedly necessary and sufficient for a particular concept to apply allow for cases in which they do not suitably restrict the application of the concept. Here "being actually caused by beliefs and desires currently held by the agent" is supposed to pick out just and only the agent's intentional actions but in the case described they do not.

being asked to believe and it gratuitously assumes that there are individuable brain events and corresponding bodily events to call into explanatory service. But I have argued that this fundamental Millean conception is wrong, lock, stock and barrel—a claim that leaves me with a debt to provide an alternative account of the efficacy of thought in shaping action.

## The defects of physicalism

There is clearly a difference between a dynamic action such as walking to the door and a deliberate momentary action. I have criticized the deliberative version of the story that serves as the model for intentional action. On the present account, an action is the performance or enactment of thought, a subjective construction of the world and the possibilities it holds. It is close to the identity structure theory of intention[13] whereby an action relates the subject to the world in a certain kind of way. The intention is not cast (in Millean fashion) as a causal event within the psychological subject that produces the set of bodily movements. On the identity structure account, the subject is engaged in a constant bodily interaction with the world, tracts of which reflect the subject's thoughts—the belief that one is speaking too quickly, the realisation that a particular member of the audience is taking a keen interest, the conviction that the moment is one to be shared in a special way with one's partner, and so on. Thoughts guide and influence the dynamic flow of action, reaction, and interaction between oneself and the world so that it takes on a particular form, rhythm or character. This is a two-way interaction in which what one does is responsive to the effect it has on one's environment[14] and what develops is intentional activity, the locus of thought and action.

When we survey this picture in the light of the problematic cases it is clear that the conditions delineating intentions are not plausibly those of a brain state located in neuro-time. The fluidity of action undermines the view that behaviour is a chain of discrete events each with their (voluntarist, physically realised) mental cause. The wineglass case makes us look beyond any immediate motor patterning to a much wider embeddedness in an ongoing neurally realised stream of meaningful and motivated interaction between subject

---

[13] Vallacher & Wegner (1987); I discuss this theory below.

[14] Luria (1973) gives an account of the neuropsychology of action stressing the world-related or environmental effects it is aimed at rather than the motor patterns it realises as being what defines a given action.

and world. The brain-damaged mobster case reminds us how wide our forensic investigations have to go if we want to disclose intention, plausibility, self-knowledge, and the role of the agent in an action.

## The illusion of free will

Wegner has recently been taken to argue that in fact free will is mainly an illusion on the basis of the causal model of action and the will (Wegner, 2002; 2004). His argument is as follows.

> Each of our actions is really the culmination of an intricate set of physical and mental processes, including psychological mechanisms that correspond to the traditional concept of will — in that they involve linkages between our thoughts and actions. This is the empirical will. However we do not see this. Instead we readily accept the far easier explanation of our behaviour that our Houdini-esque minds present to us: We think we did it (2004, 653).

In this (mildly confused) passage Wegner notices that a bodily action is the result of complex neural activity and then somehow takes that fact to imply that the agent did not do it. How exactly, one might ask, was an embodied agent supposed to do the action if not by means of such well adapted psychosomatic functions?

Fortunately Wegner significantly retracts from his iconoclastic pronouncements when he tells us what he actually thinks about intentional action.

> Conscious will is particularly useful, then, as a guide to ourselves. It tells us what events around us seem to be attributable to our authorship. This allows us to develop a sense of who we are and are not. It also allows us to set aside our achievements from the things that we cannot do. And perhaps most important for the sake of the operation of society, the sense of conscious will also allows us to maintain the sense of responsibility for our actions that serves as a basis for morality (2004, 658).

Therefore Wegner's considered position is close to that taken in the current account, whereby the discourse of intention and action sets out the terms we use to understand our meaningful interaction with the world and our ability to enact our own story in a given situation. The dimensions of that enactment are only partially captured by the psychosomatic skills applied to the task and wholly misunderstood when they are described in terms apt to the mechanisms which underpin those skills.

## Behaviour for which we are not responsible

The concept of automatism, reinforces the lesson of the wineglass case in that it is acknowledged by all parties that an act to which automatism applies (such as sleep walking, or any other behaviour the performance of which was not really under the control of the agent and for which the agent is not morally responsible in the way required by intent [mens rea] is an act caused by an integrated pattern of brain activity (as in partial complex epilepsy, for example) but it is disconnected from the agent as an embodied moral subject (as somebody). We might ask ourselves, in the case of a voluntary action, "Why is this particular tract of electrical stuff in the brain even a candidate as a proper cause for an action and not some other kind of event?" Looking for the key in the relation between the action and the person's narrative returns us to Davidson's nervous mountaineer case and the thought that a genuine voluntary action is engaged in the right kind of way in the psychic economy of the human being concerned, so that it appropriately relates the agent's behaviour to the ongoing projects and character of the agent. Such relations, in a manner of speaking, map the agent as a subject onto the world via his or her constructions of the world and interests in it.

I have argued that intention is the spirit of action in the sense that it ties action to the identity of the agent because the intent with which someone acts on a given occasion tells us something about the moral character of that person (the way that his/her life story is configured and the values that shape it). I have also argued that the claim, based in mental realism and naturalism, that an intention is a mental event preceding and causing an action is problematic, because of the nature of the causal connection involved and also because of the need to connect intention to agency in a way that reflects the intimate, indeed internal, relationship between action and identity in a way that goes beyond causally construed aspects of the tract of behaviour concerned.[15] Telling an intentional story of a course of human activity locates it in a structure of discursive relations which connects a person to her environment and makes sense of the person's activity according to the meanings that have significance for her and the skills and techniques she has learnt to enable her to act on them. What is more, the longitudinal integration of the experiences giving rise to those skills, forms an identity such that human agency is the outworking of the character developed as part of that identity.

---

[15] The problem is the same as that which bedevils the bundle theory of memory and identity discussed in Chapter 5.

We can now ask, "In what way does the nature of intention go beyond a physical description of bodily movements and confront us with the character of the agent?" The question can be answered by appealing to four related concepts intrinsic to the current account. A *person is* (1) *an integrated rule follower* who (2) uses *thoughts* to structure (3) *their acting in the world* so as to generate (4) *a lived narrative* which is more-or-less coherent and longitudinally integrated so that it constitutes an individual identity.

## Intention: an alternative model

Daniel Dennett has developed a theory of consciousness as a narrative "take" on a continual stream of neural activity arising from the interaction between body and world (Dennett, 1991). His theory solves a number of problems in explaining perceptual, cognitive, emotive, and voluntary behaviour (I have discussed these issues in Gillett, 1999a). If Dennett is correct, then it is a universal feature of human behaviour and conscious experience that we make the best story we can out of a fairly seamless flow of activity which does not in itself determine that story. The narrative of our lived conscious experience depends on:

(i) the concepts and meanings that we have available to deploy in making sense of our own activity; and

(ii) the concepts we find ourselves using on a given occasion.

Thus lived human experience is shaped by meaning-giving skills used by the human subject as a situated narrator and forms the context within which intentions emerge. An intention reflects a complex pattern of relationships with the environment and it captures or conveys what informs a person's ongoing activity so that person-and-socio-historical context frame the desires, intentions, beliefs, and so on articulating one's story.

We still have not, however, secured a sense in which our conscious thought life determines what actually happens with our bodies rather than just the way we experience those events. Only the former, stronger, thought can ground an account of freedom of the will and genuine responsibility for intentional action in the character of the moral agent.

## The identity structure model of action

According to Vallacher and Wegner's identity structure model, an action occurs when a conscious conception structures my behaviour so that the behaviour expresses the thought, such as, *I am making a*

*Mediterranean gesture* or *I am shaking my head in a way that I was taken by in India*. The thought is in-formed by my experience as a narrative subject and it relates actions to their natural context — a lived human life. As such it dovetails with a Dennett-type view of consciousness but not with any causally-detailed identity or supervenience theory that I know of.[16]

The identity structure approach to action explanation is based on thoughts and their semantic properties. To spell out a thought is to specify the way things would be in the world to make that thought true (we could call this set of conditions the truth conditions for the thought concerned).[17] What is more, thought (as we have seen) is structured by concepts and concepts are based on rules (Gillett, 1997) so that they are essentially normative (Gillett, 1992; Millikan, 1993). The rules govern both the application of any concept to the world and its internal or cognitive significance in relation to other concepts. But rules assume agency (it being up to you, in the Davidsonian way, whether you observe or obey the rules). Of course, we work with our cognitive novices so that they are disposed to follow the rules but we cannot causally compel them to (as anybody who has raised children knows).

To recap: human beings use their thoughts, in part, to structure their actions and when they do they draw on a resource that has been shaped by rule-following. A rule-follower controls his or her behaviour in response to prescriptions (guidance, corrections, signs of assent, dissent, agreement and disagreement and so on) from others (even though the relevant performance may be automatized). Thus, to form a creature who can think, we take a human organism (predisposed to learn from other human beings but who may or may not fit in with our usage) and, as Aristotle, Kant and Wittgenstein notice, we train them by making use of a vast range of life situations to impose prescriptions that result in the child developing a second nature (provided s/he "plays along" and acquires our rule-governed techniques). Kant remarks that the moral law is based on "conceptions of laws" not laws of nature and therefore, like Aristotle,[18] he puts normativity (rather than brute sensibility) at the heart of reason

---

[16] The breakdown of the causal view of action is the stumbling point for Wegner in his more recent work.

[17] This neo-Fregean view veers close to a kind of mental realism that ought to be avoided.

[18] "thinking admits of being false and is enjoyed by no animal that does not also have rationality" (*de Anima*, 427b).

and human freedom, even though the norms shaping thought (and therefore knowledge) and action (morality) would surely exploit "natural"(in the sense of natural science) human propensities.

These facts (I have argued) entail that the human subject is cognitively integrated over time because such training (naturalistically construed) is not instantaneous. The subject hones his/her cognitive skills in (informal) prescriptive interactions to structure their current experience in terms of life skills acquired, in part, from others.[19]

The fact that life skills (of perceiving, thinking and acting) are imparted, shaped, and refined over time illuminates both intention and the responsibility of the agent. Think of playing chess: before being disciplined by the rules of chess and developing a mastery of them, a person is relatively helpless if confronted by a chess board and a set of pieces and powerless to act in the restricted domain of chess. The greater one's understanding of the rules, the more strength to one's (cognitive) arm, as it were. The player becomes capable of creative personal strategies and productive reasoning rather than just reacting responsively to moves made by others. Notice that chess moves occur in an interactive domain or a "shared world", a further analogy with thought and action in general. The empowerment resulting from self discipline so as to master a set of (cognitive or intentional) skills elegantly illustrates the old saying, "the truth shall make you free" which could be glossed as, "mastery of the rule-governed relationships between thought and the world make one able to understand and act according to the dictates of one's own reason in the domain to which those thoughts are adapted". The fact that rules do not cause one's compliance with them also leads us into the topic of identity and character.

## Identity, character and intention

Dennett is inclined to say that whether or not one follows a given rule or exercises a given skill on a given occasion is Joycean – thrown up out of a neurocognitive chaos where words/memes/meanings jostle for dominance. But such nihilism is hasty: lack of mechanistic control is not lack of control (as any Jazz player will attest). In the normal course of events, human behaviour is, more or less, explicable on the basis of character or personal narrative. Take the situation Wittgenstein envisages (perhaps as a result of teaching in Trattenbach): a child often has a reason for not following rules and

---

[19] Anselm also notes the role of ability and propensity in our perceptual capacities (1967, 128).

learning skills that would otherwise confer advantages on them. So much is that generally true that if a child will not learn, someone should find out why. Perhaps s/he lacks the cognitive equipment to do the task or perhaps s/he does not want to learn (maybe because of an attitude to rules that is quite deep-seated or maybe as a cry for help at that time). Sometimes perfectly competent thinkers violate the rules for effect: they coin a metaphor, have an original thought, say something outrageous, or make a dramatic statement. Rule violations usually make sense when we understand the person involved; when they do not, we invoke causes (Jaspers) or the objective attitude (Strawson). The fact that rules do not causally necessitate rule-following performances means that thought content is woven into (more or less) integrated narratives by concept-users (considered as narrative subjects). The ability to grasp concepts and then use them in relation to whatever is going on between oneself and the world *at will* is so basic to human consciousness that we take it for granted, but it has profound implications for longitudinal mental integrity (integrated personal identity over time) and freedom of the will.[20]

## The role of the agent

We now have four holistically connected conceptions in play in understanding a human being as a moral agent. First, the person is *an integrated rule follower* and so can think. Second and third, *thought structures action*, and fourth and last, a human subject has *a lived narrative* which is more-or-less coherent and informs their conscious life and their identity. These four taken together imply that an action is explained by relating it to the life history in which it arises in a way that essentially depends on regarding the agent as a rule-follower who commands certain techniques and not merely as a causally-compelled device. This framework grounds a set of reactive attitudes (praise, blame, encouragement, approval, disapproval, and so on) of a moral kind based on the thought that a human being is the source of his/her behaviour and responds to the kind of correctives and imperatives that were part of his or her training as a thinker. The cognitive skills structuring the ongoing interaction between the subject and the world illuminate both the subject's experience at any given point and (thereby) the intentions informing his/her activity.

---

[20] I have discussed the implications for Parfitian theories of identity above (Chapters 4 & 5).

Intention is crucial in law and morality in that it determines culpability for any act (through the doctrine of *mens rea*).[21] Also important, but less immediately relevant to the nature of the act itself, the narrative of the individual is the source of the motives for which an act is done (as is shown in the brain damaged mobster case). Motives (like desires) are structured inclinations or dispositions to adopt or aim for certain ends that have been invested with value by the subject[22] (however brutishly) and thus they are rational determinations of agents giving rise to a series of events (as Kant noted). Intent is therefore understandable in terms of ongoing projects and the character of the agent and attributing an intent aims to reveal a way that the agent currently relates him/herself to a situation in an identity revealing/enacting way.

## Why the judgment we pass on an act is a judgment about a moral agent

When we decide that an action exhibits a given intention, we fit a person's behaviour into their narrative so as to explain their self positioning in their world and among others at a point in time. Intentional explanation therefore functions analogously to the way that naming a move in chess locates the displacement of a small artifact in a hodological (or purpose-ridden) domain of activity. *She has moved her bishop out to the second row*, locates certain physical goings on within a structure of rules and strategies that inform a game of chess. Her hopes, future intentions and schemes are unlikely to be transparent through one move if she is a player of any sophistication (and therefore potency) but that she has moved her bishop rather than idly shuffled a piece such that the result coincides with that move, gives one clue as to what she is about. The unfolding pattern of her moves tells us something of her strategy and character as a player.

If we broaden our gaze to the game of life (in all its complex sweep), then the medium of engagement with one another is (virtually) unbounded and structured by rules of immense complexity and subtlety. It is fraught with real hazard, and laced with images and symbols embodying values and carrying moral challenges. We

---

[21] I have already mentioned the centrality of *mens rea*, or a mind which conceives and enacts the reality of the criminal act, in the attribution of moral or legal responsibility; the exception is an offence, such as being a public nuisance, which is one of strict liability where the ignorance of the criminal nature of the act does not excuse the perpetrator.

[22] Lacan speaks of desires as montages in the sense of "a surrealist collage" in which one might find "the most heterogeneous images" (1979, 169-70)

make moves in this domain that engage us with others, with our mutually-crafted artifacts, and with the natural world (which is, increasingly, being interactively transformed by us). In this domain we act by using meanings to structure our behaviour and thereby we reveal ourselves as identities or characters who see the world in certain ways.

When we discern an agent's intent, we discern, in some small way, the narrative s/he is living. We understand more when we discern motives, needs, vulnerabilities, and expectations underpinning that narrative and what is enacted from it. Such understanding ultimately reveals the lived autobiography of another so that action explanations afford glimpses into their moral life. Every action is both formative and expressive of the agent's character so that a comprehensive dossier of a person's actions (of the intentions that have, from time to time, been enacted in that person's behaviour), is a surview of his/her moral character (as Sartre [1958] so clearly noticed).

Dennett's theory, often considered favourable to physicalism, supports the present "take" on human conscious life, the will and moral responsibility, if, as he claims, one's conscious life is a story spun on the basis of the ongoing interaction between brain and world.[23] Dennett, like Wegner, uses examples from psychology, psychophysiology, and neurology to argue that conscious experience is not a direct reflection of (or even strongly supervenient on) the physical interaction between brain and world but is rather a narrative attempting to articulate the results of that interaction in meaningful terms.

*First*, there are well known phenomena whereby events that happen after a remembered episode can alter memories of that episode (Schachter, 1995). This suggests that the way we remember an event is not just produced by what happened but also reflects later "editorial rewrites" rendering it coherent with everything else we know so that we end up with a well-integrated narrative. Dennett refers to these rewrites as either Orwellian (as in the *Nineteen Eighty-Four* rewriting of history) or Stalinesque (as per show trials with false evidence). He means to deconstruct the difference memories formed by interposing post-experiential information from those where the information that arrived in consciousness is recast as part of the experience itself (both are readily understood within a

---

[23] Dennett (1991) is himself among those who seem to take him to be a physicalist despite the anti-realist effect of his epistemology.

Lacanian approach). In both the active role of the subject as a living protagonist in forming what is experienced and remembered is a prominent feature of what is happening.[24]

*Second*, he discusses illusions such as the "phi" phenomenon — where the observer sees a red light in one position and a green light in a slightly different position a short time later but reports the experience as one in which the light moves and changes colour as it does so (Dennett, 1991, 114-15). When we consider the trajectory of the illusory light and determine what physical substrate could be the origin of the intermediate visual impressions, we realize that these are "filled in" by consciousness to make sense of what has gone on between brain and world in terms of what usually happens "around here".

*Third*, he considers confabulation (common in those types of dementia and brain damage associated with amnesia). Temporal lobe automatisms are a case in point: the patient has a seizure in which the body enacts an automatism — a stereotyped pattern of activity that looks like a voluntary action but during which the person is unconscious). The events may have the form of an organized action but they are exhibited without motive or intention. Afterwards, if asked, the person may express confusion or may confabulate some spurious report: "I just thought the bed needed tidying" or "I'm always just going out to the kitchen to check on things." In such cases, the subject responds to an implicit social demand to explain themselves by spinning a story about the event (unrelated to the actual "electrical storm" in the brain causing the activity). Dennett observes, "subjects are unwitting creators of fiction, but to say that they are unwitting is to grant them that what they say is, or can be, an account of exactly how it seems to them" (1991, 94).

Dennett seems to be correct in so far as a feature of human conscious experience is that we make the best story we can out of our world-involving activity; but should he call this a fiction? The narrative (based on what happens between one's brain and the world) is "as good as it gets". Words like "confabulation" or "illusion" are used when the judgments of others significantly diverge from the experience of the subject. The truth is relativized to an intersubjective perspective so that discerning it means catching on to the

---

[24] Dennett is, however, open to the charge of mental realism of a certain stripe in that he writes as if there is an actual canonical transformation of segments of the brain-world stream of causal interaction into mental contents whereby, in effect, the mental events are a "natural" "mode of presentation" of the brain events.

relevant norms or validated skills of organizing experience and knowledge. This is to be expected as the story of lived conscious experience draws on the concepts and meanings made available (from one's social milieu) to make sense of one's own activity. Thus the narrative that is lived human experience is (normatively) shaped by the meaning-giving skills used by human subjects as situated narrators (around here).

In fact the existence of automatism, as a coordinated pattern of human activity with a purely neural cause, directs us toward the way that the content (or psychologically explicable nature) of any action arises as part of a person's narrative so that the neural events realize or form part of a chunk of that narrative as in the "identity structure" model of action explanation.[25] An action is behaviour structured and explicable by a guiding conception (thus my walking to the door to go out is a tract of my activity structured or given form by my thought that I want to go out). The identity structure is a sensitive and realistic way to understand the relation between ideas (or mental content) and action that is not subject to the simplistic causal model.[26] It focuses on the content currently giving form to my activity so that it is sensitive enough to cope with subtle variations of action but also *realistic* in that it does not picture the agent producing discrete mental causes or intentions for each bit of voluntary activity. It also fits the current narrative view of consciousness and its relation to the stream of extra-conscious activity[27] that is going on seamlessly in the brain.

*So, in sum, where have we got to?*

*Mens rea* is central in forensic assessments of responsibility and its key element is an intention to act. If intent or an intention is identified with a proximal mental cause of an action then we need a causal path from the act to events beneath or beyond the control of the agent (such as brain events and urges to act). Such a causal account looks defective. Instead we have an account focusing on the role of thoughts in structuring behaviour as the expression of a human subject with an unfolding life of moral significance.

In fact the present, Aristotelian, account is close to a passage in Kant's discussion of freedom. Kant notices that the moral law is such

---

[25] As devised by Vallacher and Wegner and discussed above.

[26] Although an Aristotelian might point out that it is an example of formal causal explanation.

[27] This is Karl Jaspers' term for activity which is not conscious because it is physiological or part of the unconscious mind (1913 [1974]).

that it imposes requirements not conditioned by the prior nature of the agent but derived instead from the conception of a law (that the mind may or may not adopt as regulative in its dealings with the world). The norms governing thought (and therefore action) are the means by which we transform our "natural" (in the sense of natural science) capacities so as to exploit techniques developed collectively by our species in their adaptation to the world (a process that creates in us a "second nature"). Kant imagines a young man who tells a malicious lie. He allows that the young man might have had a defective education, bad company, a vicious natural disposition, and be feckless; he even allows that there might have been other more proximate causes that help explain the action. But, nevertheless, he concludes that we can legitimately hold the young man responsible for his vicious act.

> Our blame is based on a law of reason whereby we regard reason as a cause that irrespective of all the above mentioned empirical conditions could have determined and ought to have determined the agent to act otherwise (*Pure Reason*, 477).

The young man's competence in using our cognitive techniques both empowers him and is based on his obeying "oughts" and therefore having the capacity to do so. And, we might say, among the "oughts" he ought to have obeyed are those dictating actions other than those he performed (which embed the values that we, his human group, hold dear).

The alternative to Dennett's Joycean machine (reflecting a "meandering sequence of conscious mental contents famously depicted by James Joyce in his novels" [Dennett, 1991, 214]) as the ultimate (non-)explanation of what we say and do, is the insight that the descriptions and regularities revealed by brain science do not reveal why a particular agent on a particular occasion does a particular action. It sees the action is a joint product of, *inter alia*, the life skills of the agent and his or her moral dispositions as they shape his or her conscious narrative at that point. The action is explicable on the basis of the agent's self-narrative and the influences that he or she espouses or allows to operate in it.

We now have a framework in place which allows us to address the question of freedom and moral responsibility.

*First* we can say that any action is explicable in the context of the life history in which it arises but in a way that essentially depends on regarding the agent as a rule-follower or thinker using socially mediated techniques to structure his or her behaviour.

*Second*, this explanation eschews the picture of a human agent as a causal device and suggests that a conception of intent should not be modeled on the idea of a material cause. In support of this argument I have cast doubt on neuroscientific data which seemed to suggest that intentions are neural events preceding action.

*Third*, I have argued that rule-following (as distinct from acting on the basis of brain states with a causal history) is a prescriptively governed activity and that whether or not the rules are followed depends on a person's interests and choices to use a certain skill on a certain occasion. Acting according to a certain conception of what is going on in the world and what one wants out of a situation, is acting intentionally.

*Therefore* one has the ability to act and (to some extent or other) the ability to control one's actions such that moral responsibility and freedom of the will are best linked to the "rational will" (one's ability to enact one's reasons for acting).

On the present account, human action is not easily linked to the idea of mechanistic or subpersonal causality (for instance by mental states and forces within driving behaviour this way and that); it understands an agent in terms of "spontaneity" (as in Kant not Hume) – the ability to be governed by, or act on, reasons and inner determinations.

## Judging intent and responsibility.

We must therefore side with "folk" (or "the man on the Clapham omnibus") when confronted by claims to explain human action in the terms of neuroscience or any other causal mode of explanation. Neuroscience and psychology tell us a lot about people and the kinds of things they do but cannot be used to disconnect actions from an agent's moral responsibility. Assimilating human behaviour to that of subhuman animals is also suspect in that human action, whether verbal or more robust, is only explained by citing the meanings used to shape both one's life story and how one relates to others appearing in that life story. In that sphere, most of us are working on familiar turf. Since we were very young, we have all been living with and making judgments about others. We are so intuitive and well-practiced that, given a set of facts, "the man on the Clapham omnibus" can say, as well as anyone else (including forensic scientists or neuropsychologists), whether sex killers' or mobsters' excuses for their actions are acceptable.

Each of us may house a neurological Joycean machine, and its shifting (possibly even identifiable) patterns of brain activity may be able to be correlated with our thoughts and actions; but, be that as it may, we already have a very sophisticated system enabling us to explain—and to some extent predict and influence—the behaviour of human beings. Without this scheme of understanding, we would be "missing something perfectly objective" but with it our understanding of each other almost looks like magic.[28] The application of this knowledge to any action is limited by one's understanding of the intricate and interwoven patterns of human thoughts, feelings, and relationships within which our actions occur. As we heighten our skills in this complex intersubjective milieu (perhaps by reading literature), we also heighten our understanding of human intentions and actions and develop a kind of knowledge owing almost nothing to neuroscientists.[29] What is more, it should not be befuddled by spurious causal stories about reasons for acting and criminal behaviour that arise in subhuman ways (for instance from a "crocodile brain"). To enact a reasoned course of action is to act with intent and to be responsible for what one does. Knowing about that domain is "folk" knowledge (although not all folk have it to the same degree) and it is greatly expanded by figures like Euripides, George Eliot, Henry James (even more than his brother William), and Janet Frame, the thinkers who have given us insights into the tapestry of human life in such a way as to illuminate its moral character.

Moral philosophy and jurisprudence, in their quest to become scientific about human agency, should be careful about the epistemic partners consulted in that project. Suitable partners would not have theories about the causal determinants of human behaviour based in reductive psychology and neuroscience. Good philosophy helps clear the ideological weeds fouling that bit of forensic ground so that an insightful psychologist who qualifies as an expert in such matters, can then offer genuine help.

Intentional explanation is, we could say, person-tracking in a world of happenings (in the way that thought is "truth-tracking"). Intentions embody an integrative style of explanation mapping patterns of human activity in a domain where a human group has

---

[28] Dennett (1990). The words "like magic" recall a conversation between Oliver Sacks and Temple Grandin (a very high functioning autistic person) where she remarks that the communication between other human children used to look to her as if "they were all telepathic"(Sacks, 1995, 260).

[29] Although it can usefully be supplemented by their findings.

developed and imparted skills of signification through a nexus formed by language, language related activities, socio-cultural arrangements, and other human interactions. Brain events are the vehicles[30] for this activity but they do not determine it because its spirit or impetus comes from the world of persons in relation (as historical beings-in-the-world-with-others).

## Responsibility: moral and legal

Responsibility has a lot to do with responsivity (as explored by Hans Jonas and Emmanuel Levinas)[31] for whom the face of the other is the fundamental ethical stimulus because it signals a being who should call me to respond because of his or her very nature (hence ethics is grounded in ontology). Therefore, one should consider a contemplated action in the light of its likely impact on the other or as informed by an imagination responsive to the reactions of the other.[32]

We should, as human thinkers, recognise that we are members of a community (or kingdom of ends) and reflectively adjust our behaviour to that reality. We have freedom to do so because, as beings who obey "oughts" to act in ways other than those dictated by our "brute desires", we can curb our inclinations in this way (indeed second nature may dispose us so to do).

We can also broadly distinguish *responsibility to* and *responsibility for*. Both, these days, are linked to a conception of human moral life that focuses on acts — what we do. Despite this being a reduced conception of the ethical life (compared with the original question "How should a person live?"), it is our acts and their consequences that often engage ethical thinking. The broad conception of responsibility restores to ethics something closer to its original agenda in that it allows us to see that we have ethical responses called forth from us that ought to be heeded in one's praxes of self-formation and inform one's attitude to the world (and to others).

Levinas argues that the face of the other is not encompassable within one's own view of the world and what goes on in it because it represents an unknown. "The other" is enigmatic, never captured by one's conception of him or her because s/he is in a dynamic to-and-fro interaction with me as another being-in-the-process-of-becoming.

---

[30] This useful terminology is found in Hurley (1998).
[31] Jonas and Levinas both link our response to another with a sense of responsibility for what we bring about in relation to that other.
[32] The resulting morality is rooted in existential phenomenology and deeply congenial to post-Kantian thought.

The other is therefore both profoundly like me and yet profoundly distinct from me in an intrinsically unsettling way because, just as I am aware of him or her, s/he is aware of me and implicitly able to form a conception of me.

S/he is also affected by me in ways that I can imagine but never totally know. All of this shows in the face (as Mencius reminds us — the pupils of his eyes, his gestures and expressions [Bk IVa15]). We are in mutuality with others: The give and take of my effect on you and your effect on me produces the space of the ethical in that whenever I engage with you I experience your influence on me and become aware that you are similarly affected. If you are a good person, then (as already noted) I might say, "you make me want to be a better person". As I learn to own such interactions, I become responsible.

## Freedom and responsibility

Moral responsivity expresses a character of a certain kind in that acknowledging mutuality and the implied responsibility (for my actions in a kingdom or domain of ends) is an attitude that am not compelled to adopt but, if I do so, I recognize myself to be among other souls — living subjective beings — and even though that recognition may not in itself be voluntary, I can endorse or reject it. I can develop and deepen the relevant sensitivities by putting myself in the way of certain kinds of experiences. I can also (at least to some extent) choose my associates and by keeping company with people of a certain type make myself more likely myself to become like them. When I take up with a certain group I am likely to develop the kinds of reactions, attitudes, and responses that that group has which may or may not be responsive to various things, racial injustice, for instance.

Responsibility (for) is a reflection of the understanding that we have an impact on the world. Intelligent life consists in interaction with my surroundings informed by thoughts of various kinds and recognizing the truths consequent on that by taking account of the effects. Acknowledging those effects as being "down to me" (resulting from my "acts and inner determinations", to use Kant's phrase) is taking responsibility for them. Levinas impresses upon us the human aspect of these impacts and the need to be open to the effects one is having on the other rather than assuming that others are mere copies of (or even artifacts of) our view of things (or the order of things) so that their reactions are ciphers of one's own view of reality.

"I know how people like that are, they are … " Such totalizing judgments do not recognize the irreducible subjectivity of the other whereas ethical recognition infuses one's life with that kind of perspective (implicitly informed by openness to the other), and asks "Is this something I feel good about?" Seeing myself as others see me is, therefore, a way of becoming responsible. Confucius says "I am truly a fortunate man because I am surrounded by friends who point out my mistakes." To welcome that kind of response from the other, within a context of love and commitment, is to embrace a crucial aspect of the ethical life—a life in which the subject is connected to the truth (to quote Foucault). To accept responsibility is, therefore, to take to heart the effect that one has on others and to make an adequate, truthful, or good response by reflecting that in one's reasons for action (so that goodness and truth are, as Plato argued, inseparable).

I have addressed the traditional philosophical issue of freedom and responsibility according to which we are responsible for those things we choose to do (and, to echo Annette Baier [1985], those postures of the mind we choose to adopt). The question "Even if I could have chosen otherwise can I choose how I choose?" usually takes one in the direction of causal events leading to one's choice (Ayer, 1982). I have instead explored the idea of life skills as abilities to make effective interventions that help one control one's situation and what happens in it and therefore noted one's responsibility for the kind of being one has become. Sartre would, in fact, attribute any person with responsibility for the fact that s/he was born. The argument is fairly straightforward:

(i) You have become who you are through your choices in life.

(ii) The baby that was born X many years ago has become you.

(iii) You are responsible for that person being born rather than somebody else.

The argument is uncompromising and needs to acknowledge the role of context and our response to it in shaping or forming a human individual (as in the narrative view).

Freedom, on the present account, is, therefore best thought of as a product of life skills. Life skills fairly obviously serve as a prerequisite for broadening one's horizons. They are in close accordance with an Aristotelian account of the will as the ability to translate reason into action where reason (or cognitive skills generally) enables one to anticipate and not merely be "bushwhacked" by contingencies.

Intentions, as the determinations of the will that guide and shape our actions, spring from and enact an intelligible part of one's life story. In this way human intentions are a sophisticated expression of the will to power rather than causal impulses arising within me that move me to behave in certain ways.[33] The will to power seeks, through anticipation, to control environmental contingencies rather than merely being subject to them and it works, in the human case, through shared cultural techniques and meanings that organize experience. Life stories should be seen as lived narratives built by using the techniques or disciplines that have formed me and allowed me to develop the powers commanded by my human group; our lives are therefore infused by cultural meanings.

With freedom and power over the environment comes responsibility but with responsivity, at least for the ethical soul, comes the yielding of self-directed and self-interested freedom in the light of the truth of our being-in-the-world-with-others. This point is reminiscent of Foucault's remark that the purpose of ethics is to link together the subject and the truth so as to "arm the subject with a truth it did not know" so as to make the truth "a quasi subject that reigns supreme in us" (1994, 101-2).

Foucault's analysis of ethics enables an answer to the question "Responsibility to whom or what?" Normally lines of accountability are clearly spelt out in an organisation and they track causal roles in the light of obligations, duties or requirements. What about this ontological or moral responsibility that seems co-extensive with our humanity? It seems that there is a natural reading of *responsibility for* but what of *responsibility to*?

A post-Foucaultian formulation might be that we are responsible to and before humankind. Sartre introduces the thought of being responsible for the fact that a human being has done what I have done, that one is part of a race/species that does a certain kind of thing — murders or sacrifices children for instance. The argument is:

(i) I have done A.

(ii) I am a person/a member of the human race.

(iii) There is a person/a member of the human race who has done A.

The syllogism intuitively provokes (in a certain kind of person) a certain attitude to the actions I have done as being significant because they are done to and by somebody. The somebody to whom they are

---

[33] Hence Nietzsche's protest that the unfree will is a myth.

done irrupts into the picture through Levinas (as the enigma or irreducible subjectivity whom I encounter) or Kant (as my fellow being in a kingdom of ends) and the somebody by whom they are done enters the picture as somebody who, in the light of truth, needs to live amidst people in the wake of what was done. Both are ontological or objective features of the act seen through an intersubjective context, but Levinas' route to the ontological formulation is phenomenological rather than purely rational. Either route locates the action in a human context where responsibility is inescapable, a fact that, for some, is heightened when one grasps truths about our relational being that transcend any particular or subjective human determinations (even collective versions). The weight of responsibility and its absolute nature can also make one less impressed by the exculpations arising from the types of human failure (or lack of life skills) that make a person serve less than admirable ends or do what they do in inept ways that harm others.

We can now move on to the implications of this view of human freedom and responsibility for our understanding of the contribution of neuroscience to our self knowledge.

# Chapter 7

# *Deep Play in the Mechanics of Mind*

## *Locked In Syndrome, Psychosurgery, and Cyborgs*

The more conventional opinion gets fixated on the antithesis of truth and falsity, the more it tends to expect a given philosophical system to be either accepted or contradicted; and hence it finds only acceptance or rejection. It does not comprehend the diversity of philosophical systems as the progressive unfolding of truth.

... consciousness as it approaches science justly demands that it be able to attain to rational knowledge by way of the ordinary understanding; for the understanding is thought, the pure "I" as such; and what is intelligible is already familiar and common to science and the unscientific consciousness alike, the latter through its having direct access to the former.

(Hegel, *Phenomenology of Spirit*)

For the soul is the primary principle of our nourishment, sensation, and local movement; and likewise of our understanding. Therefore this principle by which primarily we understand, whether it be called the intellect or the intellectual soul is the form of the body.

(St Thomas Aquinas)

Embodied subjectivity, the lived experience of being-in-the-world-with-others is vulnerable to physical insults and interventions because it is radically contingent on a human being's condition for its actuality. Neural insults, medical interventions, and technologies alter one's being-in-the-world and pose questions about neuroscientific knowledge and our conception of human identity and subjectivity. The resulting inquiry examines the operations of the vehicle of our narrative identities — the human nervous system in its integrated cybernetic relationship with the body and through it the rest of the world.

We can begin by considering the result of the radical disconnection between subject and world that is Locked in Syndrome (LiS). The less radical, but profound, disturbances of subjective embodiment in psychosurgery (especially the historical varieties) allow us to explore the relation between neuroscience and key aspects of the psyche. An understanding of the promises and threats of neuro-enhancement by the use of cyborgic transformations deepens that inquiry, engaging it with the current (problematic anti-realist) concept of the *hypokeimenon* and the limitations of a (neo-Lockean) or "intrinsic properties" view of the basis of subjectivity. We can then confront our fragile indwelling of (or incarnation as) neurally integrated flesh (or inscribed bodies).

## Flesh and form

The human form implicitly defines what it is to be excellent or deficient in function as a human being and is used by some philosophers to generate a definition of disease based on mental and physical defects or deficiencies in function (Megone, 1998; Boorse, 1975). This kind of account holds that an organism has a disease where it exhibits a functional change such that it is less well adapted to its natural environment. Narrow construals focus on the intrinsic functioning of the organism but broader accounts allow for a relational breakdowns between the individual and its context, thereby problematizing the notion of disease as a construct applicable to individuals in isolation.[1]

The human form implies that certain characteristics are required for a human being to function properly in a human setting (which, as I have noted, is significantly altered by the individuals living within it). Given that the *psyche* (or soul) is a way of denoting those functions, then virtue (as excellence of soul) is linked to well being of the individual, however realised in detail. Such a view can be interpreted in terms of a modest ("as good as it gets") approach to living a human life, evincing a harmony of the forces (*daimons*) animating a

---

[1]  I have explored this in relation to mental disorder in Gillett (1999a).

particular human narrative.[2] In fact, I opt for a relatively balanced set of Apollonian and Dionysian functions as the basis of human well-being (*eudaimonia*). It follows that where the physical continuity and integration that is part of natural human function in relation to a context is seriously disturbed, the soul is unsettled. Indeed that is readily apparent when we examine a human subject to whom just such a disruption has happened.

### Locked in Syndrome (LiS) — the phenomenon

*Nick's case*[3]

I had my accident on the rugby field on July 29 2000 about 2.00pm during a simple line-out, even before the ball was thrown in. It just felt like another simple case of concussion (everything went blurry), I staggered to the sideline, the coach asked me "what's wrong"?

He said I told him I just felt sick and to put me back on the field in 10 minutes. Then I collapsed, eventually blacked out and then was rushed to hospital (unconscious) in an ambulance with them struggling drastically to keep me alive.

After 3 days of being in there, they thought I was alright and were going to send me home.

Then it started happening, first I nearly collapsed again taking a shower (I became extremely dizzy and lost a lot of balance). For days the specialists didn't know what was wrong with me. My girlfriend at the time, who had rushed down from Wanaka when she had heard it had happened (she and her mother were absolutely awesome throughout my time living in hospitals, considering the situation) went mad at the specialists to do something.

After 6 days of going in and out of seizures, finally after what seemed like all the tests known to man they said I had suffered several brain stem strokes then one massive major one, which altogether had left me diagnosed with the extremely rare and unknown condition only known to a few as "locked in syndrome".

---

[2] Where the *daimons* are the lively forces or inspiriting principles acting within and influencing the actions of an individual.

[3] The indented passages in this article are verbatim transcriptions from Nick Chisholm's memoires as a Locked in Patient.

Nick's story is a nightmare come true. LiS (also known as *coma vigilante*) transforms a person into a silent and apparently unresponsive witness to everything that is being done to them. In fact it is often relatives rather than medical staff who realise the patient's predicament (by noticing that the patient is registering what is going on). In Nick's case, his mother and his girlfriend both pleaded with medical staff to see that he was aware of events around him and when that realization finally dawned, the climate of care changed. A patient with LiS cannot interact with others because he has lost the ability to control his body (except, in most cases, s/he can move his/her eyes up and down) but the subliminal cues that intuitively alert us to the presence of another are often sufficient for someone to suspect that a human subject still animates the apparently unresponsive body so that the diagnosis can be made.

LiS is caused in one of two ways:

(i) by a lesion in the brainstem (usually vascular); or

(ii) by extensive demyelination denying the brain its peripheral connections.

Nick's LiS was caused by as vascular occlusion of the basilar artery due to a propagated blood clot from a vertebral artery dissection after the artery had been damaged in its course through the neck.

## Diagnosing Locked in Syndrome

In Nick's case (as is common), the diagnosis of LiS was delayed.[4] In some cases the diagnosis has not been made and the person has died. That mistake is avoided when clinicians actively think about pathophysiology and functional anatomy and ask:

(a) Where is the lesion? And,

(b) What is the lesion?

The first, these days, is answered by imaging techniques (although clinical assessment tells one where and how to look); and the second by what older neurologists called a "badness time curve". The curve may be that of cerebro-vascular event (sudden loss of function), infection (less acute decline), tumour (subacute decline), or degenerative disease (slower course, perhaps with remissions and relapses)

---

[4] In fact, publicizing his case has made us aware just how many patients, all over the world, are only belatedly realized to be in this state and how much they long to be recognized and their plight witnessed to.

and it allows one to interpret the images and make a probable diagnosis.

In the case of LiS, one must also listen to those who know the patient because they tend to notice subtle indicators often missed by busy health care personnel. Once a diagnosis of LiS is made, the clinical predicament is clear: to communicate with this person who is somebody (a being-in-the-world-among-us) but who cannot convey it to the rest of us.

The means of communication with the patient are limited and dependent upon contingencies commonly including the preservation of certain eye movements.[5] That small mercy has allowed Nick to establish communication using a transparent Perspex board and a trained therapist (prior to his regaining some movements in his upper limbs allowing him to use a joystick and computer).

### A contrast: LiS and Persistent Vegetative State (PVS)

> *Nick:* Still with mind and memory at 100% (sometimes I wonder if it's a good thing or not), external feeling 100%, internal feeling about 30%. I have feeling throughout entire body, although just after accident I had no feeling. Despite some lack of internal feeling, all senses are normal, if not enhanced (eg. sight and hearing). I'm just left trapped inside this body.
>
> At times it feels so surreal and still does sometimes to this day.
>
> To cut things short, considering I could only just hear (I couldn't even open my eyes or breathe by myself), without them even knowing that I still could hear, the doctors and specialists in front of me said I would die to my mum.

The soul of the individual in PVS (but not LiS) has become vegetative because the critical brain functions (allowing movement, perception and intellection) have been devastated.[6] Extensive damage to the brain, particularly the cortical system and its ramified connections,

---

[5] This is due to sparing of the circuitry to some or all of the extra-ocular muscles (through cranial nerves III, IV, and VI).

[6] Multi-society task force on PVS (1994). The person concerned is unconscious, with severe diffuse neocortical damage. There may be a diurnal variation in EEG but that does not indicate (even in the "waking" phase) any consistent responsiveness to events around them and therefore no consistent reaction to relatives or acquaintances. The patient requires complete nursing care, artificial nutrition and hydration, and has no prospect of recovery (this should be established by suitably qualified clinicians in the light of a thorough review of the etiology and pathological diagnosis).

means that there are no longer enough "megabytes" to do the work required for conscious experience and cognition,[7] intentional functions critically dependent on the information processing capacity of the neocortex (Gillett, 2001). Consciousness — the capacity of a subject to use coordinated and holistic functioning of widespread and dynamically inter-connected cerebral functions to interact with his environment in real time — is present in LiS. Nick recognized objects and people, had reactions to and feelings about what was going on and framed them in terms of who he was and how he thought about the world. In PVS there is insufficient (and insufficiently integrated) brain function for that to happen so that a patient in PVS no longer has typical human experience. This fact is indicated by the severely attenuated EEG and Evoked Potential activity seen in PVS and is a result of the loss of the neural capacity required for the intelligent adaptation to the environment at the core of human subjectivity. The person in PVS is not *conscious (simpliciter)* because he or she cannot engage in the many acts of being *conscious of* the things that a person in LiS is capable of.

### Locked in Syndrome and being somebody

*Nick:* It's too difficult and extremely frustrating for me, most people just don't know how to communicate with me.

For about four months I couldn't use a call bell. So if something was wrong or I was in pain or I needed something, there was absolutely no way of attracting anyone's attention.

I talk by using a transparent perspex board (about the size of an A2 sheet of paper) with the letters of the alphabet spaced out on it (identically on both sides). The person holds it up between our eyes (standing about 800mm apart). I spell out each letter of my sentence using my eyes (similar to a typewriter), with the other person guessing each letter I'm starring at, until I've spelt out whole sentence. Extremely laborious! It's also very difficult (almost impossible) to express yourself or be sarcastic.

To be somebody is not just to be a body but it is to be a "subjectivity", a mode of being-in-the-world-with-others. As *somebody*, one has a name and an identity that is formed and reformed as one takes shape in a cultural and interpersonal context and interacts with others sharing that time and place (a place bounded variously by the possi-

---

[7]  Gillett & McMillan (2001) especially ch 6.

bilities of communication). As a human subject, one is recognised, engaged with and taken seriously by others through entanglement in the world and conversation. Nick's perspex board imposes limitations on who he can be to others, he cannot be witty or sarcastic in the free-flowing way he would like to be, because the rhythm of his equipment for engagement with others does not allow that.

We tend to forget the way that rhythm and timing are part of personality and identity so that an individual for whom these are altered (as in LiS, cerebral palsy, or muscular dystrophy) must find ways of being-with-others that allow them to "break on through" their neurological impairments. For Nick, rather than an easy, two-way flow in which his identity and agency can be manifest his interactions are "kludgy", bogged down, and cumbersome in ways that frustrate his ability to be who he is and develop as a person through interaction and a permissive or non-intrusive mode of embodiment. His body *is* his being-in-the-world but there is a mismatch with the Nick who he was in and through his lived narrative before the insult he suffered.

> *Nick:* I'm just a typical mind imprisoned in this body, I feel as though I'm encased in concrete that I'm constantly and painstakingly breaking through ever so slowly. Since the physical gains I've made over the years, I imagine it's become similar to trying to fight your way out of a 'Straightjacket'.

### Ethics and ending the story: three principles

> *Nick:* I feel extremely sorry for anyone with this syndrome that is scared of taking risks, most things I do involve some form of risk—even something simple like eating.
>
> As it is in everyones life—change is optional. I can choose to stay bedridden (which I once was), wither away and eventually die.
>
> Don't will for death, it will come to you. Just sometimes sooner than expected.

The possibility of "ending it all" for a person in LiS tempts us to make paternalistic judgments from the standpoint of "normality", but a human subject can show us the world from his or her moral plane so that elevated ethical deliberation conducted in abstraction by those who are other is irrelevant. We can ask a set of standard ethical questions but answering them for someone in LiS may be going "a bridge too far".

- *Benefit or prevention of harm:* Is this leading to an outcome which now or in the future the patient would consider worthwhile?
- *Consent:* When asked, does the patient want us to continue?
- *Dignity:* Is what we are doing in keeping with the life of the person concerned?

> Nick: It is definitely a crazy mixed up world I'm just glad to still be alive ... most of the time anyway. I accepted the fact that the accident did happen, long ago. Shit does definitely happen, I just have to make the most of each day in my journey towards recovery.
>
> Some people think I should live a relatively normal life. Really ... how do they expect someone who can't speak or move limbs properly to live a relatively normal life.
>
> Most of the time (when living like this) frustration levels are pushed to the max. and eventually I explode. Sometimes I wish I had died in the ambulance on the way to hospital. It would've been a lot less frustrating for me anyway.

These questions also apply where the subject (or the capacity for subjectivity of a distinctly human type) has been destroyed (as in PVS). In such a case the questions serve to reconnect the decisions with the person at their epicentre given that we cannot address that person and actually ask them.

The question about *benefit or prevention of harm* becomes "What are this human being's prospects?" This prompts us to look (with moral imagination) at the current clinical situation through the soul of the embodied subject we are relating to. The key concepts are *substantial benefit* — an outcome which now or in the future the patient would regard as worthwhile — and the *Risk of Unacceptable Badness (RUB)* — the possibility that we are producing an outcome that this person would find intolerable. Those questions bear on the issue of *consent* — "If *per impossibile* s/he could be asked, would this patient give you consent to do what you are doing?" That question prompted the presiding judges in the Bland case to ask, "Why should this patient solely because he or she is unable to communicate be treated in a way that s/he would not approve of?"[8]

---

[8] The Bland case concerned a young man who suffered severe brain damage as a result of the Hillsborough stadium disaster and was left in PVS.

Respect for the *dignity* of a human being prompts, "Is this ending the right kind of ending for this patient's life?" This is, however, deeply problematic.

> *Nick:* To be really honest I would erratically and uncontrollably without warning literary "shit myself"!!! Believe me, when you're thirty it's TOTALLY DEGRADING! No place more so than the public gym, in front of people. It definitely changes my mood extremely quickly when it happens, as you could imagine.
>
> The specialists even wanted to operate and give me a colostomy bag ... stuff that!

Nick does not want death rather than indignity — even though he acutely feels it — and so he, by his determination to live, has conveyed his response to the issue of dignity. But in PVS and other situations we ought, perhaps, to ask, "Would this patient want to be remembered as a person whose life ended this way?" or, "Is this ending consistent with the ethos of this family?" The most authentic answer to these questions may be to honour or respect the the subjective being who was once a being-in-the-world-with-us in a distinctively human way by stopping interventions prolonging the remnant of life that remains, a judgment that adopts a distinctly narrative ethical framework.

### A human life and the end of the story?

A narrative view of the end of a human life poses the question, "Has this person reached the end of his or her human story?" To centre a human life story on a lived subjectivity implies that conditions such as PVS (from whatever cause) perhaps should be considered to lie at a terminus of the story that is comparable to death.

We may conclude that the best we can do in such a case, and in the light of the questions posed, is to respect the person by ensuring that his or her life does not end in a way they would hate it to. The appropriate end will, however vary from culture to culture and to some extent from family to family (which may raise questions of justice in a publicly funded health system). In contrast to PVS (and related conditions) where these decisions are inescapable for the caregivers of the injured person, those with LiS have views of their own, as Nick clearly and emphatically shows. The PVS patient is no longer connected as a subjective participant in the world and therefore, on many accounts (especially those framed within ancient and deep religious traditions) we should not keep them here. The idea that we should release "the spirit to go on its journey to the place where it now belongs" captures this thought. A secular ethicist may think only of memory and story but a more religious perspective sees the reality it confronts at bodily death in a very different way.[9] For either, the person whose connection with the world has run its course, may regard an end-of-life decision as fitting and as radically different from what is at stake in LiS. What, then, are our ethical dues to the LiS patient?

### The duty of care

At the end of any clinical journey we should be able to reflect on a duty of care properly discharged as the clinical team engages with the embodied subjectivity who is our patient.

*Attention* to and *recognition* of the patient as the creator of, and living being at the centre of, the story of his or her own life connects the witnesses to the illness as a truth embodied (and endured) by this patient at this moment in his or her life.

Both attention and recognition happen through *conversation* in which, as a healer, one cares about the person who may be entrapped by the illness events in ways that pose a constant challenge to his spirit and determination and yet who may transcend any limits we put on him as part of the medical (or deficit) model.

> *Nick:* Sometime in 2001 I had to meet with my Neurologist again. He wasn't at all positive (telling me bluntly), 'whatever gains you have made to date, they're all the gains you'll ever make'.
>
> The first Speech therapist told me because of the severity of my accident and the damage it caused, I would never be able to even eat again.

When things are done in the right way — perhaps by those lower on the hierarchy of health care than ("exalted") specialists[10] — the clinical experience is a "being-with" properly enacted by those who have seen the problem before and who, by dint of their work, are part of one's journey. This "work" or "gift" of recognition and witnessing of what a person is going through is deeply ethical.

---

[9] I shall return to these issues in Chapter 9.
[10] Who thereby fail to fulfil one of the soul's needs. As doctors we are part of a hierarchy in which those to whom one looks for guidance should embody values and traditions that are admirable and transformative so that they warrant veneration (Simone Weil, 1952, 18)

For those whose subjectivity has been utterly destroyed or who are facing their own imminent mortality, and for those who are with them at that point, the feeling that their suffering has been witnessed or recognised is the mark of a life juncture properly negotiated. Such acknowledgement registers the moments involved as significant and the life of the person as something of which we ought to take note. To be acknowledged in this way is to be somebody, more than just any other thing, cast into the universe at some point, and that is the beginning of the ethical attitude.

Nick is somebody, everybody who meets him finds him noteworthy, memorable, admirable, even inspiring, and he values his own being-in-the-world-with-others and he fights, in Luria's words, "with the courage of the damned to recover the use of his shattered brain" and remake something of his life. For those whose story has ended (as Nick's most definitely has not) decisions should be made, informed by the thought that s/he should be recognised, the need of every person and those who love him or her that his or her story and its ending should be witnessed to in the right way, and the outcome should be one that the patient would consider fitting (or worthwhile).

## The split brain

A quite different kind of disconnection severs the internal links allowing the subject to integrate his/her information processing capacities. "Split Brain Syndrome" results from a commissurotomy: an operation to divide the corpus callosum, a large fibre bundle connecting the two cerebral hemispheres. Such operations were done to relieve intractable epilepsy in the 1960s and are still being done for the same reason (Gazzaniga, 1970; Parkin, 1996) in that:

(i) it is a last resort for some severely affected epileptic patients;

(ii) it is difficult to detect any significant neuropsychological deficits following the operation.

The operation limits the effects of an epileptic seizure by preventing both hemispheres being recruited so that the patient does not have grand mal seizures (resulting from involvement of the whole brain) even though partial seizures (in which consciousness and some bodily control may be preserved) still occur. The type of epilepsy concerned usually arises from a damaged area of the brain resulting from birth trauma, diseases of infancy, or head injury, and often the most affected hemisphere is not functioning normally so that the intact half of the brain does most of the cognitive work.

For this reason, such patients typically experience no adverse events from the surgery itself even where that involves hemispherectomy. However disconnections in behaviour can be detected when carefully designed tests are used.

The disruptions are so subtle that we used to believe that "a section of the corpus callosum had no adverse effects on behaviour" (Parkin, 1996, 111). Most patients, after surgery, are untroubled in their everyday lives such that "a typical medical examination would not reveal anything unusual in their behaviour, and their scores on standard tests are normal" (Kolb and Whishaw, 1990, 808). But tests especially designed to separate information processing streams in the brain reveal that the pick up of information is more complex than what one might expect on the basis that human mental function has an underlying unity of consciousness based on the integrity of the brain. In fact, patients show complex disconnections between perceptual, verbal, and motor information that can be revealed by directing that information into either the left or the right side of the brain. One exploits the fact that a given visual hemi-field projects exclusively, in the first instance, to the opposite hemisphere of the brain, so that an object seen in the left hemi-field may not be able to be named because the visual information is processed in the right hemisphere of the brain which connects to the speech and language areas (in the left hemisphere in most people) mainly (or most directly) via the (severed) corpus callosum.

These findings are interpreted by some philosophers and psychologists to indicate that in normal human beings there is not the unity of consciousness implicit in the Cartesian view and that each of us may house two separate conscious minds, one in each hemisphere.[11] "Split brain" cases therefore seem to be a dramatic realization of the splitting that is imagined in thought experiments; but closer examination suggests that such claims may be a little too hasty.

Most of the experimental work uses a tachistoscope to produce momentary selective visual presentation of visual stimuli so that the stimuli are exposed only to one or other half of the visual system. A number of different tests can then show that a commissurotomy patient's ability to respond appropriately depends on whether the response is controlled by the right hemisphere (e.g. picking out an object with the left hand) or the left (e.g. verbal report). The classic disconnexion in commissurotomy is a combination of right handed apraxia (defective visuo-spatial abilities in relation to complex tasks)

---

[11] Nagel (1979); Parfit (1984), esp pp 245ff; Gazzaniga (1970).

and left handed agraphia (inability to write) along with lateralised anomic aphasia (inability to name objects presented only on the left). This finding is often tendentiously reported: "Each hemisphere can be shown to have its own sensations, thoughts, percepts, and memories that are not accessible to the other hemisphere" (Kolb and Whishaw, 1990, 808).

Patients also confabulate when anomalies occur;[12] for instance, a picture—a door—may be shown "to the left hemisphere" and a different picture—a hammer—"to the right hemisphere"; and if forced the left hand may pick out a nail as the object shown. When asked why the left hand is picking out a nail, the subject may say "You build doors with nails". Here each hemisphere deals with certain information and the subject (faced with a task that s/he should be able to cope with) deals with the discrepancy between information and task requirements by using a technique—confabulation—often seen in cognitively impaired subjects. But notice the details here (the margins where Derrida is wont to locate truth). The subject is aware of a problem in his/her cognition and responds as best s/he can so as to meet the normal expectations. It therefore seems that the subject is responding to a demand which would be reasonable if addressed to a unified cognitive "self" and muddles through (as a being-in-the-world-with-others) despite impairments (that are not evident to him/her). But the problems are not confined to an experimental setting and show the extent to which we do regard ourselves as unitary or integrated subjective agents (as we are constantly taught to regard ourselves as being).

A further bizarre manifestation of commissurotomy is "manual conflict" or "alien hand" where one hand interferes with the actions of the other: "the patient once grabbed his wife with his left hand and shook her violently while, with his right hand, he sought to rescue her and bring the violent left hand under control" (Gardner, 1974, 359). This is deeply problematic for any view of personal identity which posits a unity of consciousness as an intrinsic feature of human subjectivity but it is not so disturbing if we view identity as an achievement worked out by using the discursive skills made available in a socio-historico-cultural situation or context.[13]

---

[12] We have already encountered confabulation in the context of memory deficits (Chapter 5) but it is also associated with callosotomy (Gardner, 1974, 361).

[13] The underlying view taken by the present work in which the *hypokeimenon* of human identity is actually not a contained feature of the organism seen in isolation.

## Split brains and personal identity

The data on split brain patients do seem to undermine the assumption that a person is a unique individual whose identity is secured by a unified consciousness realised in a unitary physical object—the human body. Descartes' claim that the essence of a person was to be a thinking thing, is transmuted by brain theorists (especially Cartesian materialists) into the conclusion that a unified neuro-cognitive apparatus (or brain) is the basis of identity. But Kant, along with Aristotelians such as Donagan, argue that one cannot ground the subjective identity of a human being in a mental or physical substance despite the fact that human subjectivity requires there to be a transcendental unity of apperception;

> it is perverse on its face to maintain that individual human persons are what they are, not because of the individual physical and mental constitution by virtue of which they develop the capacities they live by exercising, but because these experiences are psychologically connected in certain ways (Donagan, 1990, 13).

Donagan's neo-Aristotelianism receives support from Wiggins (1987): "our grasp of what it is to be a human being gives matter and substance to our conception of persons"; it is "the precipitate of all sorts of evolutionary, biological, historical, and cultural facts". The claim that our dealings with actual flesh and blood human beings is the basis of our ideas about personal identity sits well with the present version of naturalism and the arguments we find in Kant's rejection of the Cartesian dualist self. But it also directs us beyond the brain to the way in which we are inscribed with the patterns of identity as unified beings-in-the-world-with-others acting in a shared world and accountable for those actions (i.e. we are, *inter alia*, forensic selves).

## Second nature and an integrated mind

Second nature, according to McDowell (after Aristotle), results from the initiation of a human being "into the space of reasons by ethical upbringing" resulting in "habits of thought and action". That claim sits comfortably with Kant's focus on training in judgement and the learning of concepts as the mode of formation of a subject (as thinker or logical subject). The cognitive processes configuring the self as a conscious and (self-)identifiable being among us are also tied to our embodiment by Davidson in his remarks on indexical semantics:

> Clearly there is something irreducible, irreplaceable, embodied in the use of the first person pronouns — all the first person pronouns. In fact all sentences containing indexicals depend, for their interpretation and their truth value, on who utters them. But if I utter them, I know without observation that it is I who uttered them. In this way I relate myself to places, objects, times, and other people, by my use of 'there' ('here', 'behind me'), 'that' ('this'), 'now' ('tomorrow', all tensed verbs), 'you'. There is no substitute for this way of placing myself in the world (2001, 86).

His focus on the use of indexicals in conversation is exactly where Wittgenstein would look for illumination on the grammar (or metaphysics) of personal identity. It reinforces the thought that we become rational creatures through being-with-others who teach us cognitive skills so that "placing oneself in the world" in this way is coeval with the development of an integrated discursive life. He converges with Kant, Wittgenstein and (Peter) Strawson on this point:

> this much should be clear: the basic triangle of two people and a common world is one of which we must be aware if we have any thoughts at all. If I can think, I know there are others with minds like my own, and that we inhabit a public time and space filled with objects and events many of which are (through the ostensions which made such thoughts available to us) known to others (Davidson, 2001, 86–7).

If the articulation of one's identity as a conscious thinker depends on the subjective lived body interacting with a domain in which it is situated, and it depends on its own internal (neural) integrity to carry out the necessary functions in the right kind of way, how does the person with the fragmented brain do this task? The question must be answered because it is now clear that the neurocognitive function of a human being is typically reintegrated after brain bisection and many other disconnections.

The discussion of memory has shown us that, not only is there a significant pressure on the human being to maintain a sense of self (as agent and owner of actions, and locus of interpersonal relations), but also one uses one's neuro-cognitive capacities in a holistic and interwoven way to do the work of memory. The sense of being a unified self is cognitive and narrative and forged under a set of evaluative constraints which arise, as we have noted, intersubjectively. As such that sense draws both on discursive techniques and mastery of the raft of memory-related skills (identified by Wittgenstein) structuring one's diachronic knowledge of oneself and adaptation to one's context. The idea that one configures oneself actively by the use of discursive techniques developed with an integrated cognitive system explains most of the findings about the fragmented self that are often held to be highly damaging to the folk conception of personal identity or the unity of consciousness.

In understanding why there is a conscious stream and why it hangs together as a co-conscious stream, Davidson directs us (as does Lacan) toward the self as a subject of attribution who is formed by conjoint and complementary appreciation (first, second, and third person) of his/her manifest activity and its significance to others. This complex apprehension grounds what we could call, after Wittgenstein, the *grammar* of self ascription and self reference. The position is roughly as follows.

1. My own conceptual relation to myself is built on self-attributive judgments.
2. Such judgments share truth conditions with those of co-referential others.
3. The relevant truth conditions can only be my own manifest activity.
4. My access to that activity is not the same as that of others but I share with them the significations informing it (allowing for idiosyncrasy).
5. Our respective content attributions can come apart because of divergence of knowledge between myself and others.
6. One situation in which I am affected is when a broken brain affects my knowledge and the pattern of intentional activity I exhibit.
7. Others will try to make sense of my behaviour as a coherent narrative (as I will myself). This normatively driven exercise plays a central role in human activities and in everything human beings do and think every day because it is the cement that binds us (collectively and individually) together.
8. The unified self is a norm that cannot be discarded but it may be impaired in its application to me if my brain (or life story)[14] is broken.
9. I strive to get a narrative coherence into the activity I produce from my broken brain and therefore I will try to cope with my

---

[14] I will discuss the psychic fragmentation observed in dissociative conditions below (Chapter 8).

cognitive disruption in the light of the norm that I am a unitary self.
10. I will do this as best I can by using any information available to me from a holistic pattern of my own personal activity (and the reactions of others).

Pressure from the discursive environment urges each of us to develop a unified and coherent "life of the self" as a (good-enough) embodied human thinker. But, for a split brain patient, the personal and adaptive pressure lacks the normal neurocognitive means to bring about that end. So how is the trick done?

Any thinker with an attraction to Cartesian materialism, in accounting for cognitive reintegration after brain bisection, tends to fixate on the Central Nervous System and its pathways. But a thorough commissurotomy leaves inter-hemispheric connections that seem insufficient to cope with the complexities of normal cognition and perception. But the human organism is not as impoverished as the puzzled theorist makes it out to be.

*First*, the ongoing activity in which my brain takes on informational shape as an organ of adaptation to a human world is organised around a single focus — me. Because my behaviour is represented by myself and others as the activity of someone who has a continuity of identity over time and weaves together a coherent narrative about that activity, that representation (my *imago* — Lacan) helps organise my experience and my mental life.[15] I attend to this or that object — that fly on the wall, for instance — and subjective modes of being result (I learn to call such modes of being "seeing a fly"). If I accept the Aristotelian axioms that there is no psychological change without neurocognitive change and that discursive interactions configure brain activity, then it follows that the brain is always "getting it together" cognitively speaking. And, not being picky about its methodology (bricolage comes naturally), the brain has a wealth of bodily and other "bits and bobs" of (actual and potential) connectivity to do the work normally done by commissural connections. For instance, some experimental subjects signal to themselves with facial expressions (smile for right and frown for wrong). In fact the integration of the self as a subjective body (or coherent informational system) is so central to human being-with-others that any old pathway or potential pathway, no matter how obsolete, will splutter into

---

[15] We will come in due course to Lacan's *imago*; for the moment it is sufficient to think of it as a psychic construction imposing a semblance of unity on the self as agent and subject.

## Deep Play in the Mechanics of Mind 153

action to get the job done. Work on cerebral plasticity in the elderly has opened our eyes in this regard. Decayed or surpassed pathways (the brain's "B roads") do not function as well as the superhighways laid down and refined through constant use (and it is relatively easy to show up their deficiencies) but they do a makeshift job.

> Indeed those split-brain patients that I later studied no longer denied seeing stimuli projecting to the right hemisphere — they could give accurate descriptions and approximate dimensions of them (Weiscrantz, 1997, 34).

Weiscrantz mentions neural plasticity and "indirect bodily signalling strategems"(e.g. facial expressions of approval and disapproval for lucky or misdirected choices in perceptuo-cognitive experiments) to account for this recovery but the physiological details are less important than the philosophical significance of the phenomenon. The patients as subjective beings found ways to reintegrate their fractured cognitive worlds and overcome internal disruptions in their own(ed) holistic conscious lives.

The fact that some of the split brain patients cheated on their informational tasks by using facial expressions of approval or disapproval of an "ignorant" hand is one of the "indirect body signalling stratagems" exploited to meet the demand to be somebody and it puts paid to the idea that the fragmentation of the system entails a fragmenting of the self (as some materialist philosophers and psychologists have averred). There is still a subject here who is using self-attribution and who regards him/herself as prone to certain errors. This is the only logical basis on which s/he could be motivated to overcome what s/he sees as internal discontinuities producing the errors that are occurring and it receives clear moral support from the rest of us.

Cartesian materialists ask the question "How does the brain re-integrate the cognitive world of the individual?" but this is the wrong question to ask — a human being overcomes the fracture in their brain. But cognitive neuroscientists continue to butt ther heads against this wall; "Surely even the powerful discursive forces driving reintegration need some way of doing it which is up to the informational requirements of the task!" And here the logical is a clue to the physiological (to slightly twist Wittgenstein's words). The logical requirements of self and other ascription (as part of our human form of life) require a subjective body to meet the demands of the discursive world and to configure itself by the disciplines of narrative wholeness and perhaps it is in the (holistic) subjective body that its means of doing so can be found.

## Getting it together: the subjective body with a split brain

It is plausible that, just as the body is the focus of the practices (or disciplines) which demand the unity of the subject, so it is the medium providing the means of neurocognitive reintegration. We now know that all thinking is accompanied by covert neuromuscular activity, in which the body "enacts" either the movements that would be made in the situation being thought about or a subvocal version of the relevant verbal representation. McGuigan (1997) and his team have provided persuasive evidence that cognitions involve "covert reactions", or "components of neuromuscular circuits governed by cybernetic principles" and that "where the striated musculature is totally inactive cognitions are inactive". The brain therefore has a massive somatic keyboard (or "screen") upon which to play out its cognitions. Connections between the brain "above" and the body "below" are extensive, two-way (top-down and bottom-up), bilateral, and cybernetic (or looping).[16] Ordinarily the dominant traffic is between one half of the brain and the opposite side of the body despite the potential for ipsilateral information flow. The brain can therefore use the body to "talk" to its other half during cognitive reintegration (as it uses the face in the experimental tricks) rather than the surviving intra-cerebral connections. Perhaps, in the cognitive world, "meaning is (literally) use" if we gloss that as "representing is (subliminal) acting"(or speaking) and I can, if necessary, read off that enactment what I think (subjectively and complete with somatic tone) about what is going on.[17]

This explanation fits with a post-Dennettian view of consciousness as a "take" on (or signification of) the seamless neuro-environmental interaction that (like Ol' Man River) "just keeps rolling along" as a complex of (relatively) automatic response patterns, habits, well-rehearsed strategies, and narrative intentions or determinations (predicated on discursive techniques I have mastered). It also resonates with Clark's discussion of the cybernetic nature of mind in which representations are (to a significant extent) partial interactive routines designed to work as part of a body engaged with

---

[16] A point also explored by Andy Clark.
[17] William James also comes to mind at this point.

the relevant environment.[18] The relevant neuro-environmental stream includes, on this account, covert neuromuscular responses that mirror or reproduce (*en petit* as it were) ways of responding to or speaking about things and remains, radically, entangled as an aspect of one's being-in-the-world.

The reality of split brain phenomena implies that to try to find a "self" inside me as an homuncular locus (or centre) of consciousness is as futile as Hume thought it to be (on the basis of introspection) and Kant argued it to be (in his critique of Descartes).[19] I have claimed that the self as subject of thought and experience (the reference of self ascriptions) is subtended from a holistic and longitudinally integrated complex of purposive activity articulated through the body in its environment. When the neural connections required for integrated informational activity as a subjective body are disrupted, the body gets active in the loop (to which it covertly contributes all the time). It is therefore possible that subjective identity is not only necessarily embodied for logical reasons[20] but also as a practical necessity, even though it would be a mistake to try to equate subjective identity to a sum of physical processes or functions, a conclusion that converges with quite different approaches.

Ramachandran espouses a holistic conception of the self (Ramachandran and Blakeslee, 1998, 227ff) and concludes, paradoxically, that the self who seems to be the quintessentially private core of the mind is, when we look closely at the pathologies of self attribution, a social construct (following Dennett).[21] He argues that a conscious self is an integrated amalgam of embodied, emotive, mnemonic, conceptual, and executive selves all of which have different brain functions underlying them. This view, I have argued, undermines a simplistic Cartesian materialist realism about the self but is actually meat and drink to the present neo-Aristotelian account, drawing as it does on post-structuralism and a somewhat more problematic notion of the *hypokeimenon* of human identity than Mackie's "neurophysiological real essence" (1976, 202).

We now turn to less restricted and simple ways of playing with what is deep within a person.

---

[18] Hence "Being there" or engagement with the world as an active being rather than "seeing there".

[19] I have already discussed the paralogisms in the first critique (*Pure Reason*, B399ff) in Chapter 4 above.

[20] As argued in Ch 4 above.

[21] And, as I have noted, Lacan.

## Psychosurgery and neuroimplanation

Psychosurgery and neuroimplantation are different ways of affecting "the source of our pleasure, merriment, laughter and amusement, as of our grief, pain, anxiety and tears".[22] They are sets of techniques aimed at altering neural dysfunctions thought to cause suffering. Some of them have well-defined indications and objective ways of measuring success but others are surrounded by controversy.

To recap, the present (neo-Aristotelian) view is that the human soul is produced in the process of life as a subjective body among others and that the brain has a key role to play in the life of a human subject such that certain corollaries follow:

1. The human soul is the expression of patterns of activity laid down in a human brain.
2. The brain records significant patterns of information arising in human life.
3. These patterns reflect both the regularities of nature and social and cultural reality.
4. A study of human discourse replete with the relationships in which it occurs shows that the human soul is a holistic configuration of cognitive, conative, relational and cultural functions, unique to a given person and crucially dependent on brain function for their integrity.

Psychosurgery and neuroimplantation both (potentially) affect the substrate of embodied subjectivity in more ways than LiS or commissurotomy, some of which problematize the nature of holistic creatures like us as proper subjects of "reactive attitudes" (Strawson, 1974).

### Psychosurgery

Psychosurgery uses neurosurgical techniques to try to alleviate psychiatric disorders and has a controversial history, begun in serendipity and marked by debate (Manshour *et al.*, 2005).

In 1848 Phineas Gage, a railroad gang foreman described as "the most efficient and capable" man, was supervising the blasting of some rock, when his tamping iron sparked off the blasting powder and flew into his brain, damaging the prefrontal areas of both hemispheres. He was radically affected, being described as,

---

[22] Hippocrates (Lloyd, 1978, 248).

## Deep Play in the Mechanics of Mind

fitful, irreverent, indulging at times in the grossest profanity which was not previously his custom, manifesting but little deference for his fellows, impatient of restraint or advice when it conflicts with his desires, at times pertinaciously obstinate, yet capricious and vacillating, devising many plans of future operation, which are no sooner arranged than they are abandoned (Damasio, 1994, 28).

Gage remained a medical curiosity, an example of the serious effects of damage to the so-called "silent" areas of the brain (so called because bedside tests of neurological function and standard neuropsychological tests did not usually reveal the problems), now associated with executive intelligence and the integration of social and personality function. Gage's brain damage "compromised his ability to plan for the future, to conduct himself according to the social rules he previously had learned, and to decide on the course of action that would be most advantageous to his survival" (Damasio, 1994, 33); he was, in a word, "not the same Gage"(a severe blow for a railway foreman).

Phineas Gage's personality was clearly disrupted in a way that should have sounded warning bells for the development of frontal lobe surgery as a psycho-therapeutic intervention. Following 19th century work by Burkhardt, Egas Moniz and Almeida Lima (in Lisbon) began operating on the frontal lobe for psychiatric reasons. Initial reports of success in patients regarded as hopeless and chronically ill led to the technique spreading so that between 1936 and 1978, in the US alone, some 35,000 patients had frontal leucotomies. Moniz received a Nobel Prize (partly for work on cerebral angiography) but, even as accolades echoed around the medical world, the mutterings began.

First, there are problems about the rationale, indications, and efficacy of the surgery as a response to significant psychological problems. Janet Frame, for instance, remarks on the curious interactive effect between context and the "novel operation" in that, just as the lines inscribed on the magic pad, the old "soul-writing" remains under the modified manifestations induced by changing its vehicle.[23]

The multiply interactive influences bearing on any course of psychiatric intervention demand balanced assessment, and that tends to problematise the idea that lobotomy achieves anything. As a result of this "collective uncertainty which should not be eliminated from judgments of psychosurgical efficacy" (Kleinig, 1985, 110) and its significant adverse effects (such as incontinence and fatuousness), the procedure has undergone continuous changes in indication, method, and even site of operation since its beginnings.

---

[23] Frame (1961); Hacking picks up the idea of the soul as written in his *Rewriting the Soul*.

Issues of identity further muddy the waters: Gage survived his horrendous accident but *as whom* did he survive? Is the personality of the patient modified or destroyed? The popular image is that lobotomy makes people into "zombies", exhibiting "Inertia, unresponsiveness, decreased attention span, blunted or inappropriate affect and disinhibition" (Manshour *et al.*, 2005, 412), so should we ever allow this to happen? Such alterations of self and personality place lobotomy in a very troublesome category of neural interventions and have led to continuing attempts to refine or limit its use and methodology.

During the lobotomy years, psychologists and neurologists were beginning to understand the limbic system, its connections, and its role in behaviour and personality, work now continued by brain imaging (fMRI) and the brain maps which locate "the organs of the self" in the limbic circuit of brain structures.[24] The conceptual evolution of this term is of interest to those questioning identity and brain manipulation. The self is commonly thought of by those involved as an umbrella term for a series of functions to do with agency, emotional engagement, self-representation, self recognition, and narrative integration of life events. The emotional relevance of the self and its implication or disturbance in conditions where the human individual becomes focused negatively on itself, obsessed with some action or consumed by some aggressive defence of the self, has led to the development of targeted procedures such as anterior cingulotomy (for Obsessive Compulsive Disorder [OCD], Baer *et al.*, 1995); subcaudate tractotomy (for depression and OCD [Hodgkiss *et al.*, 1995]; limbic leucotomy, and stereotactic lesions (including amygdalotomy).[25]

Despite its progressive refinement and the mitigation of its worst features, psychosurgery still damages the substrate on which the identity, rationality, and character of the patient depends especially when it intervenes directly in the Central and midline structures affecting the self as a subjective being-among-others. What is more, the indications for surgery are based on the way the person interacts with others and therefore are partly for the sake of others (e.g. interventions for

---

[24] fMRI maps brain function during cognitive tasks so as to reveal what areas of the brain are active in certain kinds of psychological activity. See Northoff and Heinzel (2006); Glannon (2007) especially ch 3.

[25] Korzenev *et al.* (1997). Recent refinements include stereotactic radiosurgical procedures such as cingulotomy and amygdalotomy and these have minimized the side effects of the procedures while preserving their beneficial effects, in so far as these can be measured in refractory psychiatric conditions (Kim *et al.*, 2002).

intractable aggression by the cognitively impaired, hyperactive or self-harming children, and violent offenders (Merskey, 1999, 285).

The issue of "unacceptable personalities"(Frame) also arises in patients surviving moderately severe head injuries that cause profound changes in character, temperament and cognitive ability that may be deeply disturbing for those related to them. Because we realize that the soul is a fragile thing and that changing its vehicle in certain ways has profound effects, even if psychosurgery does help with some debilitating psychiatric conditions (such as OCD),[26] our worry is that we are not just curing disorders but also transforming people into artifacts that are more acceptable to the rest of us (Pressman, 1998, 10). Gosta Rylander, a Swedish psychiatrist, noted that the families of some lobotomy patients made very unsettling comments: "she is my daughter but yet a different person"; "She is with me in body but her soul is in some way lost"; or "his soul appears to be destroyed" (Pressman, 1998, 328). These raise questions of identity, spirit, integrity and human flourishing and are, therefore, entwined with the ethics of such interventions.

Psychosurgery, I have suggested, affects the vehicle of the soul so that the ethical issues attending such a procedure become vivid when we relate them to the powerful plea of a spinal patient asked about life saving measures after their injury: some patients protest that even if they survive and learn to make the best of their life as a survivor, they do not want to be that kind of person. The protest is to the point because a person may seem so different after psychosurgery that there seems to be a discontinuity of identity. Not only are we potentially altering the mind or soul, but we are doing it in a way that may be irreversible. The difficulty of this decision explains the ethical requirements for a careful assessment, as far as is possible (Veatch, 1995 & 1996), of both the objective good and the subjective wishes of the patient and a policy of operating only when the two seem clearly to be aligned.[27]

---

[26] Some OCD patients cause abrasians and chronic infection in their skin by compulsive rituals which damage it and some self-harming patients progressively mutilate themselves (like *humambas* — see Chapter 2).

[27] We are thankfully well past the phase of psychiatry about which Janet Frame wrote in *Faces in the Water* and Ken Kesey in *One Flew Over the Cuckoo's Nest*. In Janet Frame's case, for instance, she claims that she was narrowly saved from having a frontal leucotomy (for what was later declared not to be a psychiatric illness) by the fact that the specialist in charge of her case had read her poetry in a literary journal. I have discussed her case in Gillett (1999).

A major problem with psychosurgery is that the assessment is bedevilled by the intensely evaluative and observer-dependent nature of the judgments involved. The "Stepford husbands" believed their wives were happier after their treatment (and their wives seemed to agree), but those judgments are problematized as the story unfolds. These questions are not unique to psychosurgery and can be raised about ECT, drug therapy (particularly with cognitively marginal patients in institutional settings), and even behavioural management (*A Clockwork Orange* comes to mind). In each case we wonder about our entitlement to alter a person so as to make them more "normal" according to well-developed cultural stereotypes.

It is true that far more circumscribed and directed interventions constitute the modern face of psychosurgery and that it is carefully monitored and surrounded by patient safeguards, but it is important to note that we are still embroiled in the intense debates between biological and social-humanistic schools in psychiatry that polarised psychiatry's research and treatment paradigms in the 50s and 60s.[28] These debates are being swept along by developments in neuroimaging and incautious claims about the role of the brain in explaining every aspect of human subjectivity. The idea that the brain is the actual "seat of the soul" or constitutes the real essence of human identity is becoming unchallengeable and our intuitive awareness that a person can be more than (or rise above) manipulation of the brain and can "fight with the tenacity of the damned" to regain its use threatens to slip away to be replaced by a crude, Cartesian neuro-determinism that loses sight of the long and winding road forming the myriad structures of subjectivity in a way that needs more than just a brain (e.g. books, friends, conversations, colloquia, ideals, and moral causes) to make manifest.

But what happens when techniques of supplementation, simulating functions that we fondly believe to be constituents of embodied subjectivity, are used to build or rebuild aspects of what lies deep within a person?

*Neuroimplantation*

Neuroimplantation makes use either of cellular grafting techniques (some of which use stem cells) and/or of increasingly sophisticated artificial technology to compensate for defects in neural function such

---

[28] Once again discussed in Gillett (1999).

as blindness, the repair of stroke-damaged brain tissue, and the replacement of neural tissue lost in degenerative diseases.

There is ongoing experimental work on the use of foetal tissue grafts in patients who have a variety of neural disorders such as Parkinson's disease, Alzheimer's disease, and spinal injury (Macklin, 1999). The ethics of foetal tissue transplants is, however, confounded by debates about the status of the human embryo or foetus, many of which I have explored above (ch 1 & 2). There are also some more straightforward (although not easy to resolve) debates in the clinical ethics of experimental neurological interventions (see appendix D).

The complex debates around neural grafting and human identity are made even more vivid and dramatic by the possibility of radical grafting technology using distinctly non-human adjuncts to our information processing capacities.[29]

## Cyborgs

Cyborgs are human–machine complexes that may be humanoid in physiognomy. The following story probes our intuitions about cyborgs and our shared moral life.[30]

> Vivienne and Tom began their married life as romantic young intellectuals but things almost immediately began to decline. Viv fell prone to episodes of depression, spending more and more time at home, unable to work, and lamenting her inability to have children. She has tried antidepressants and psychotherapy but to no avail and now neglects herself, her marriage, and any hope of a career. Tom became desperate and increasingly fearful of leaving her alone until he chanced on an excellent service "Cybo-help". Cybo-help provideds androids and is associated with an integrated neuro-rehabilitation centre. Tom is shown a recently released companion/carer model (called Andrea) used for the elderly and for young disabled people. He takes it home.
>
> Andrea is marvellous. She works unobtrusively, does those small considerate things like bringing Viv tea in bed when she is down and spends endless hours talking to her, patiently involving her in various activities. In short Andrea more than lives up to the "$C_c$" (for Compassion and caring circuit) embossed behind the hairline of her right temple (others include $-V_s$ [Vivacious and sociable]; I [Intellectual]; A [Artistic]; and so on). Viv loves Andrea, treating her like a live in companion. Tom also begins to

---

[29] I consider a graded series of cases of neural replacement or regeneration in Gillett (2004).

[30] This story is modified from John Wyndham.

think of Andrea as a person.

After an extended business trip Tom comes home to find that Viv has made significant gains in her psychological function and discovers that she has had some treatment in the revolutionary neuro-psychiatric clinic recently opened as part of the neuro-rehabilitation centre. She is the Viv he married — active, positive in her attitude, and relaxed about life. After another trip he finds she has taken up watercolour painting and joined a reading group. In fact, Viv has improved so much that Andrea can be returned to "Cybo-help".

Tom and Vivienne miss Andrea but are very much happier than they have been for years until one fateful night. Tom is stroking Viv's hair and feels a row of letters embossed in her scalp behind her hairline. He is distraught, rushes from the room and falls down the stairs, sustaining a nasty head injury. Vivienne follows, quickly examines him and then goes straight to the phone; "Hello, is that Cybo-help?"

Should we worry and, if so, is there a *de jure*[31] basis for that worry? In order to answer this question we need to further explore the relation between *Dasein* (Heidegger) and flesh.

## Our cybernetic lives

We have an increasing number of ways of supplementing our own abilities by using artificial devices. One need only think of diaries, cell phones, tape recorders, and so on to realise that our cognitive capacities are routinely enhanced by the use of human–artifact relationships and interactions.

However, one quickly encounters a neuroethical version of the Sorites paradox (the paradox of the heap).[32] In its classic version, such a paradox focuses on a category delineated by a quantifiable attribute — such as baldness. We then notice that a bald man does not become hirsute (or not bald) if he has *only one* hair on his head. But what goes for *one* can go for *one plus one* and so on, until we have a man with, say, ten thousand hairs (or whatever it takes so that he counts as not bald). We then ask when adding one more hair to his head transformed him from bald to not bald.

Problems of a similar type can be formulated whenever we think about complex objects, any example of which can be changed in various non-identity-affecting ways. For instance, my grandfather's

---

[31] *De jure* in the sense of justified, rather than merely intuitive or *prima facie*.
[32] Parfit uses this device to investigate our intuitions about identity (1984, 231ff).

axe has served me well for thirty years after I got it from my father, despite requiring five new handles and three new heads. "Why is this not a new axe?" The underlying metaphysical question is "What change in an object entails that we have a different object (or kind of object) from the one with which we started?" I am still the moral agent whom people know and react to as me when I use my diary or my computer; I am myself over the telephone or when taking medication; but how robust am I in the face of new cybernetic technology and its prospects for enhancement? Would I still be myself if my brain was largely driven by a silicon device that simulated my young adult self in perpetuity?

## Ethics and the human: intuition and reflection

The spectre of robots with human attributes has always been the stuff of science fiction but advances in implantable micro-chip technology and prosthetic devices that interface smoothly with the human brain intensify our moral concerns. The cases of psychosurgery and Tom and Viv suggest one or two *prima facie* conclusions.

(i) We are less concerned when the cybernetic components of the person seem peripheral or somewhat incidental to the psychological identity or character.

(ii) We are more concerned where non-human modes of relationship and reaction or response to others may affect a person at a very deep and pervasive level.

However, a moment's reflection on our intuitive idea that a machine, no matter how human-like, is not a candidate for moral properties, reveals that it is hard to justify especially after a film like *Bicentennial man* or *AI* where we see the world through the narrative eyes of such an individual. The narrative perspective allows us to identify with them and realize that they experience many human-like things such as regret, hope, attachment, sensitivity, and so on. These human things ground our moral attitudes such that we regard a certain kind of recognition as due to the subject concerned. The appropriate (reactive) attitudes are informed by the relatedness, responsiveness, vulnerability, and so on that are part of being human and they are distinct from the sense of right and wrong that applies quite straightforwardly to machines. It is wrong to put diesel fuel in my car and we understand what is meant when someone says that its motor is "happy"; those evaluations are related to functions for which the thing in question has been designed and they require no subjective agenda on the part of the individual to ground them. Their basis is functional and instrumental and there are no intertwined fleshly feelings such as warmth, quivering anticipation, subjective dis-ease, and so on.

We can make this thought vivid by recalling Descartes' tape recorder.[33] Imagine that having said "I think, therefore I am", the tape recorder goes on, now sounding a little desperate, "Don't laugh at me!" The group look quizzically at one another.

The tape recorder, in a pleading tone, "Ok, Ok, I know why you are looking at each other like that, but just believe me I got morphed into this form and I am desperate for human interaction."

One of the group points at the recorder and says "What's with this thing?"

The recorder says "Please, don't turn me off, I live for these times!" Now this tape recorder articulates the proposition taken to be the *fons et origo* of modern philosophy, but that is mere stuff and nonsense if we do not believe it; and who would? We do not believe it to be a soul (a moral subject in-the-world-with-us) and we take the simulated narrative and subjectivity as clever tricks played in service of some other agenda. We are similarly not fooled into entertaining the thought that cyberpets who need petting and talking to or they "die", are anything but arrays on hand held computers even though they are designed to mimic (in some very limited functional respects) real pets. Wittgenstein, as is his wont, makes a telling remark:

> Look at a stone and imagine it having sensations. —One says to oneself: How could one so much as get the idea of ascribing a sensation to a *thing*? And now look at a wriggling fly and at once these difficulties vanish and pain seems to get a foothold here, where before everything was, so to speak, too smooth for it (*PI*, #284).

Suffering, as we know and feel it or in the sense that matters morally, cannot be manifest in a thing (think of a gearbox graunching and wincing with the metaphorical "pain" of it, or a cyberpet showing a "sad" face). Moral subjectivity as we understand it happens to flesh and blood creatures who suffer the slings and arrows of outrageous fortune. Even (animal) pain or pleasure, in and of itself, seems too "thin" to ground substantive moral attitudes (though we may be discomfited with the treatment of flies by wanton boys). So much is that the case that the mortality and sufferings of organisms such as tapeworms and insects are traditionally of no account alongside that of the cats and

---

[33] Outlined in Chapter 2.

dogs we treat by eradicating them.[34] But why is it that the grimaces, writhings, and struggles of a fly or an eel (or perhaps of an android) do not morally engage us? We can argue that these things are much too limited to be ends in themselves or have their own subjectivity so that the stories they figure in need a narrative voice originating elsewhere (in a creature who, as Heidegger has it, is "that creature whose being is essentially determined by its ability to speak" [Heidegger, 1953/1996, H25]). Voice, the ontology of speaking with meaning, of taking part in an encounter or conversation as a subject unlimited by simple functionality (therefore, for Levinas [1996], as *interlocutor* and *enigma* inextricably intertwined), that which the tape recorder cannot be, these things are features of our fellow participatants in the moral domain. We are interested in subjects at the centre of stories and need that posit to be ontologically credible in order for the being to engage our moral concern.

We can refine our intuitions further by considering the kind of goodness and badness we recognise in our treatment of animals (even when we find their reactions to what we do quite inscrutable). For instance, it seems undeniably good to provide suitable conditions for an orang utan by having available a rainforest habitat in which its nature can be expressed. That kind of (natural) goodness is regarded as being sufficient for generating a robust conception of human goodness by some contemporary writers.[35] When we examine that claim it is unclear just what the dimensions of such goodness are or what constrains them but we can understand the idea that the attitudes focused on them concern our being-in-the-world-with-others in an ethical way.

We have a *prima facie* intuition that human beings are in a special place in the moral world so that if a trade off were to be made between the life of a lion or a dolphin and that of a human being then the right choice would be to save the human being. But this can be contested. Imagine that you saw a particular dolphin nearing extinction about to be killed by a wealthy trophy hunter aiming to get one step closer to a complete collection of huntable species. As you tread water in front of him, he says "Talk to the lawyers later after I have got my trophy!" You have your own spear gun for emergencies and could stop him even though to do so would harm him and perhaps even risk his death.

---

[34] And some of us have thoughts informed by that attitude to embryos of whatever type.
[35] Phillippa Foot (2001) and Rosalind Hursthouse (1999) take such a view.

Asimov's robot would not be tempted; for it "Thou shalt not harm a human being or through inaction let a human being come to harm" is the prime rule of morality. The robot uses logically sound procedural rules to guard against breakdown at the points where moral sense or *phronesis* may do most of the work for the rest of us. We might, however, be tempted by the ecological evil we are about to witness (and ask that our case be heard in the independent "Green republic" of Antarctica where dolphins are voting members on the supreme court of eco-justice).

"Hal" from *2001, a Space Odyssey* comes across as a moral agent because of the way he interacts with human beings and establishes a cognitive/intellectual rapport with them (as distinct from the more flesh and blood or organismic rapport one has with a living creature). We also get the sense that he has a history that he is living through and an agenda that he is following. Descartes' tape recorder goes some way towards doing the same as Hal when he fills in his background for us and a cyberpet may simulate the sense of life at stake were it to develop a relationship with its owner, recognise him or her, be disappointed, recriminatory, joyful at being awakened by its friend, and so on. In such cases we are tempted to treat the other to whom we relate as a moral being because aspects of our normal relationships with moral agents are in play and we "fill in" the rest (in the way human beings are cognitively prone to do).[36] Most of the time this filling in is, of course, appropriate because the one before us manifests (at any given time) only a subset of its abilities and capacities (which give rise to moral reactions, responses, and exchanges that justify and reciprocate our regard for them). The filling in or ascription of a moral state of being to the individual therefore draws on a history of similar encounters generating its own momentum and cumulative content as our lives intersect in the moral realm and we mutually configure one another.

But if artifacts get into the moral domain neither through resemblance to us nor through cognitive engagement with us, what is doing the "soul work" here? Somewhere in the scale of organisms we get to the kind of pleasure and pain and other responses that move the creature concerned into the moral domain. What is so morally important about protoplasm? And what is so morally important about human protoplasm? Instead of silicon components comprising the "character circuits" could we use neural assemblies, genetically engineered from yeasts or other protoplasm (pig for example) that would be functionally suited to producing the right kinds of cyborgs (equipped with

---

[36] We have discussed this in relation to confabulation.

humanoid heads)? What then would we adduce to justify our (deontological) moral thinking?

Interacting with and characterizing creatures rests on two related things: (i) reactive responses to those things; and (ii) representing to ourselves the form of a thing and factoring that into our reasoning about our treatment of it. An Aristotelian recognizes that a particular form of an object, say a chair, realized in bronze, is not the same as a similar one realized in wood. In the case of a soul we can imagine a holism about the *habitus* (including responsivity, energy, and vulnerabilities *inter alia*) of a human being that is uniquely grounded in human flesh and blood and cannot be reproduced in silicon, any other fabricated material, or even in different flesh. We could argue that the human being holistically combines feeling, fleshly contingency and intellect (broadly construed) in a way that defies reductive analysis. Is it plausible that only a human being (with the relevant holistic nature) can live one's own kind of subjectivity an what exactly are the constraints here (could you, for instance, be differently gendered)?

If the total form revealed in a lived life story is the basis of moral identity, perhaps that is indifferent to the material of which the being is made, except in so far as that material affects the relevant subjectivity (which is part of how we react and respond to contingencies). Thus, for instance, if an individual were constitutionally unable to respond to me in a human way (because the megabytes in control are unresponsive to what happens between human beings: hormones, biochemical changes, and effects of human-attuned mirror neurones influencing many human reactions and feelings, voice, and so on) then the contribution of the artificial aspects of the cyborg (to the whole being with whom we are interacting) has affected the being of the (candidate) subject in a morally relevant way. In such a case we might find that moral responses and judgments different in important ways from our responses to our fellow human beings are appropriate. Shylock appeals to just this intuition when he makes his famous "Hath a Jew not flesh and blood" speech and highlights his congruence as embodied subject with those judging him. We can imagine this not working with a some types of android but "ringing true"(linking us to the truth about the subject) in less radical cases.

To this holistic appreciation of the fact that one is in the presence of a moral being (to whom things matter in the right kind of way), one brings a certain reflective or perceptual equilibrium involving both intuitions and a rational analysis of the facts surrounding relevant encounters and their characteristics.[37] But in the end one judges according to the responses one finds evoked in oneself and their sustainability over time in much the way that the Aristotelians claim. Faced with strange moral fruit we have to "suck it and see", but that is costly (as is all tasting or taking in of the world so that it touches or affects one's own body). I cannot, however, see that the tissue of which one is composed is (depending on how the being participates in our forms of life) any more morally relevant than the colour of one's skin. Is the being before me able to feel pain? Does the being before me develop attachments and engage with me? Does the being before me tell a story of moral participation? What we ought to do seems to be the result of the myriad normative demands and imperatives that pass to and fro in our daily interactions with those who shape us into the individuals we are. Language, or better speech, we could say (after Lacan)"evokes" rather than merely "informs" (Lacan, 1977, 86).

Others shape me by imparting skills, for instance of self direction and self formation, and I obey those "oughts" and "shoulds" or reject them. Either way I grow as an individual in the shared soil of my culture and my land. Through a myriad encounters, we are inscribed deeply by ways of being that include belongings, oughts and desires, inspirations and aspirations, skills and styles of moving, sources of energy and hesitation, *taboos* and permissions, and so on. Therefore what we ought to do is to be true to our nature as beings who are members of a kingdom of ends able to recognize, take account of, and respond to each other when we encounter one another and tell our stories. For that reason, in any imaginable case, I think we *ought* to react on the basis of a sum, albeit complex, dynamic, and impossible to reduce to formulations, of the mutual participation in language games where morality arises. On the basis of that complex (two-way) engagement in a many-faceted discourse, our conception (inextricably both metaphysical and moral) of *what a human being is* derives from our shared formative and sustaining interactions.

A Cyborg is as human as his or her life among us indicates and ought to be treated accordingly so that its moral being is holistically dependent on our relations with it (as for dogs and their "owners"). But we also tolerate certain kinds of change particularly due to brain injury and other unexpected contingencies and we draw on our intuitive attunement to "the human" to ground our responsiveness to and respect for others with whom we are morally entangled.

---

[37] Nussbaum focuses on this in *Love's Knowledge*.

## The schism — biology and the psyche

The bio-technologies of the psyche may hold amazing promise but are deeply problematic in that they straddle an old ideological divide between materialists and others. I have argued that the human psyche is not comprehensible in the language of physical objects, causality, and objective consequences and is at the heart of ethics. Worries about what we are doing to the human psyche are central in neuroethics and are not well understood when they embody reductive attitudes to human beings. We seem to be deeply concerned about undermining the techniques proper to subjectivity — arguments and modes of address to the person based on recognition — and about tampering directly with "the engine-room" of their subjectivity in ways that reflect the truncated rationality of ends and means. When medicine, the scientific (or objective) attitude, and medicalisation — rather than the nuanced responsivity of an interpersonal exchange moderated by our relation to the other as a being-in-the-world-with-us — is the basis of our dealings with another, something vital is missing from the healing encounter. Wittgenstein seems to be on the mark here when he remarks "The way in which some reality corresponds — or conflicts — with a physical theory has no counterpart here" and "It is a great temptation to try to make the spirit explicit" (Wittgenstien, 1965, 24; 1980, 8e). I have argued that a human being elaborates a psyche out of the complex relationships and encounters in which he or she engages; consequently those altered by brain injury or psychiatric disorder, or who are compisites — part human and part artifact — should evoke in us not only evaluations and assessments, but also a morally informed set of attitudes embodying reason and sympathetic reflection. The moral imperative means we cannot turn our back on the challenges and opportunities of these new technologies but in order to meet them we need to do philosophical work on ourselves and our way of seeing things. In this area, Wittgenstein intones a further word of warning: "Don't play with what lies deep in another person!" (1980, 16e and 23e).

We can next turn our attention to what happens when the narrative is "played with" or disordered in a more psychological way.

## Chapter 8

# *Names and Narratives*

*Multiple Personality and Other Disorders*

> Think about it: what is really your own? The use you make of the ideas, resources, and opportunities that come your way. Do you have books? Read them. Learn from them. Apply their wisdom. Do you have specialized knowledge? Put it to its full and good use. Do you have tools? Get them out and repair or build things with them. Do you have a good idea? Follow up and follow through on it. Make the most of what you've got, what is actually yours.
>
> You can be justifiably happy with yourself and at ease when you've harmonized your actions with nature by recognising what truly is your own.
>
> (Epictetus)

The thought that subjective identity is significantly formed as a narrative with its own structures of meaning and value is an attractive view. But a focus on the psyche as the essence of embodied subjectivity results in a Cartesian view of human identity (as we have seen).[1] What is more, if we adopt some form of physicalism,[2] the human subject becomes a quasi-stable set of neurological states realised by a configuration of brain activity in "the human information-processor" (Andorfer, 1985). This is the posit underlying my suggested transmutation of MPD – Multiple Personality Disorder (now classified as DID – Dissociative Identity Disorder) into MINSD – Multiple Incompatible Neural State Disorder. The current approach focuses on embodied subjectivity as something more holistically enmeshed

---

[1] Parfit, Shoemaker, Lewis, etc. have such a view, as discussed in Chapter 5.
[2] Even if it is under the guise of supervenience or some metaphysically softened non-identity thesis.

with a situated and responsive body inscribed by the world in a socio-historical context. The inscriptions reflect both significations and also the touches of the real world in such a way that the subject is affected beyond what is psychically accessible. The view is post-Freudian in that it accepts that aspects of one's subjective being escape conscious apprehension, but also antirealist in that it does not take those aspects of subjectivity as inner mental states (or shadows of conscious states perhaps as neural configurations not consciously accessible).[3]

A personality or psyche, on the present account, is a complex and holistic reflection of context designed to dovetail with the world.[4] It functions by completing cybernetic interactions with the world (hence the profound effect of LiS) and is designed to apply to the present the traces of signified experience in the past (hence the importance of learning, procedural mastery, habit formation, semantic memory, and the skills contributing to memory in general).

The normal subject moulds "the self" under the implicit demand of the world because his or her mode of being is being-in-the-world-with-others so as to become a named and relatively (good as it gets) unified subjective individual who is a node of relationships and interactions with others and the world around here. The person is named under the umbrella of a widespread norm, indicating and enacting the location of a subjective being with a moral personality in a shared world—a world of being-with-others, a self who is relatively stable but grows and develops as new experiences and relationships are accommodated. Human beings show different aptitudes for this task (Shapiro, 1999); some dissociate (lose psychological touch with present events) when the conflicts and demands become too great. Dissociation occasions a series of identifiable disorders of mind, both MPD and other phenomena such as depersonalization, fugue states, and certain types of amnesia. These phenomena have led to exciting theses about human identity and the underlying neural states associated with consciousness and the ego, but the current account eschews any strong metaphysical realism about persons and their personalities (or distinctive identities).

The dissociative states are worth discussing because they cast light on subjective narratives, names, and the supervenience of the mental and they challenge us ethically, in that if we regard each of the multiples (or alters) of a patient with MPD as a separate human

---

[3]  As one might find, for instance, in Searle's treatment of the unconscious.
[4]  I have noted the relation to Andy Clark's view.

identity, there are alarming implications for forensic and clinical psychiatry (posing problems of responsibility for crimes and prompting accusations of therapeutic murder of human persons). Therefore the Cartesian (materialist) view (MINSD) needs careful philosophical evaluation and critique, particularly in view of the present analysis of subjectivity and the constitution of identity. The preceding discussion, and the account of the psyche that has emerged, will give us reason to resist radical conclusions about the fragmented identities of a multiple and their therapeutic destruction and the view that we should treat multiples as individuals with their own forensic identity and moral autonomy. As it does so it will deepen our understanding of ourselves as (in part) constructed beings whose identity is (in part but not solely a matter of) a palimpsest of variously motivated texts.

## A discursive approach to psychology and identity

The psyche is moulded in discourse, an interpersonal activity in which individuals are present to each other and use meanings current in that discourse to learn or negotiate ways of signifying what is around them and characterizing themselves. The ability to name phenomena depends on the availability of a signifier/signification pair, whether the concept applies to contextual features of the environment or aspects of one's own lived subjectivity. Significations subtend metaphysics and sometimes conflict with one another as, for instance, in thinking of things as electrons; we can think of tiny packages of negative charge (the particle theory) or, alternatively, of standing waves (the electromagnetic wave theory). The two incommensurable ways of thinking of electrons show our use of different metaphors (or significations) for different purposes and it gets us into trouble (as Kant repeatedly pointed out) if we substitute the signification for the thing itself. Science often obscures the fact that significations conflict (a particle, as normally understood, is not a wave of any kind). When scientists have to come clean on these metaphysical issues, they admit that aspects of our thought about the entities appearing in scientific descriptions are metaphorical and help our understanding of the world. Similar considerations apply to the human subject, the basis of embodied subjectivity—a more complex, extended, and world-involving entity than traditional metaphysical essences can easily deal with—but in relation to the psyche there is also a fluidity and dynamism of being-in-flux-with-becoming that complicates any picture we may want to use to characterize ourselves.[5]

Prior to Wittgenstein's later philosophy these facts, and all mental phenomena, were dealt with (in Anglo-American-Analytic philosophy) using a pervasive model in which the mind received and organised information from the world like a container full of conscious states and not-so-conscious states bubbling away within a relatively modular system (more or less confined within the skin – or head – of a human being) that operated causally. However, the metaphysics of electrons reminds us that the *hypokeimenon* of the phenomenon that is a human psyche is not easily conceptualized because a human being lives through an interactive narrative having a distinctive voice, a historico-cultural setting, and a location constrained by embodiment (incorporating the contingencies of mortality).

A person's psyche (and the micro-processing structure of the brain) takes shape as mental phenomena and the connections between them are formed in discourse (Gillett, 1991a). Various natural or even primitive responses made by a developing human being are themselves responded to by those in contact with the individual and the developing mind latches on to their naming and other responses and modifies the learner's behaviour accordingly. Some responses, such as naive linguistic generalisations or those developing into named emotions, are moderated according to the articulation and signals of approval or disapproval communicated from others. Thus, for instance, when the child says "gooses", the normative suggestion "geese" is exhibited and an emergent rule of practice imparted. In the emotional sphere, the child may hit her doll against the table in a fit of temper and the parent may remonstrate with her: "Don't do that, you little devil!"(this, of course, is more effective if similar behaviour is not, at other times, modelled in relation to the child herself). However, over time and a cumulative experience replete with both naturally arising and socially imposed normative regularities the elements of personality congeal into place.[6]

In the increasingly complex configuration taking shape, each component (a concept, name, or type of response to a situation) carries with it a trace of the discursive or interpersonal situations

---

[5] The drive to methodological solipsism in philosophical psychology is one kind of reaction to that suspicion.

[6] The metaphor is used by Janet Frame

giving rise to it.[7] Current memory theory and cognitive neuroscience both incorporate the fact that the psyche is shaped by world-involving regularities that are significant in the adaptation of the human individual whose subjectivity is being shaped by these "touches of the real".[8]

A human being inhabits many different discourses each of which has its own cluster of significations. Some of these, as we have already noted, conflict with one another and require negotiation and adjustment in order to be co-tenable, a fact about subjectivity with at least two implications:

(i) there is integrative activity involved in subjective constitution; and

(ii) any particular discourse is moderated by others in its influence on an individual subject.

The first point was pivotal in Jung's conception of personality and continues to be widely useful in therapeutic settings.[9] The second warns us against excesses often found in culturally relativist varieties of post-modern theory. Taken together, they imply that most of us fashion a complex subjectivity from participation in many different discourses which tend to interfere with one another and thereby both multiply and constrain the significations that can be applied to a given situation.

This last point has served to answer, to some extent, the question about the reality of the individual, an enduring problem in theories thought to embrace social constructivism. On the present view, an individual person is a meeting point of many discourses and must, to some extent, integrate the multifaceted subjectivity which arises from this multiplicity. One has a coherent personality to the extent that one can both occupy various positions in different discourses and fashion for oneself (however intentionally or otherwise) a unique complex subjectivity with adequate longitudinal and horizontal (diachronic and synchronic) integrity. In this sense there is an important particularity to a human individual (as a body on which events and disciplines are inscribed) over and above his or her positioning in various discourses. Seeing the psyche or personality in this way differs from the traditional view in that it is both dynamic

---

[7] This fundamental insight, explored by Levinas, is developed by Lacan.

[8] A real/realm significantly organised by institutions and relations of power (as Foucault reminds us).

[9] Storr (1987). It is also a central feature of the narrative view of identity.

and essentially embedded in historical, political, cultural, social, and interpersonal contexts rather than apt for representation (as it is in itself) apart from them, as might be argued by a Cartesian materialist (or methodological solipsist).

This outline embeds the rationale and agenda of discursive psychology. The discursive subject uses symbols and signifiers as the building blocks of a self-narrative. Discourse reflects "the order of things" and positions one in that order (Foucault, 1970). However "the order of things" is a socio-cultural product (recall the concept <electron>) operating in the midst of evaluative and interpersonal influences shaping and directing human activity. The subject also uses her own construals and expressive acts to do things in her contexts of engagement. The shape of the self is defined in part by gesture and the habits of the flesh and in part by the image of oneself that is incarnate in that responsive flesh.[10] Therefore the subject/agent does not have a nature definable in terms of internal processes. She is among us, she relates to us and construes us even as we relate to her. We share and negotiate conceptualisations and significations and those discourses shape her and the information processing networks in her brain so that the body is a responsive node of interaction crystallizing a mind and personality.

## MPD: the controversies and puzzles

Among the difficult group of diagnoses called dissociative disorders, MPD is especially notorious because of the philosophical problems it generates and its rise in prevalence in recent years. Let us assume that there is a real phenomenon called MPD and that it has some connection with a history of child abuse.[11] On that basis, we can follow the DSM.IV[12] and characterise MPD as a disorder in which there is evidence of two or more distinct personalities within the same individual, one of which is dominant at a given time and controls the person's behaviour and in which each personality is sufficiently complex and integrated to approximate the psychology of an individual human being. Some centres add a requirement that

---

[10] We could say that in this sense — "word made flesh" — we are made in the image of God but also the expression of the *imago* (Lacan) is part of that which animates the human body.

[11] Hacking (1995) has written a comprehensive work discussing these issues.

[12] DSM.IV is a publication of the American Psychiatric Association that provides definitions of major psychological disorders.

there be amnesiac discontinuities between personalities (Putnam et al., 1986).

The condition was first described in France and Germany in the 19th century but in its modern form is almost entirely an American production. There has been a virtual epidemic of alleged cases in the US and Holland since 1980 when a US survey reported about 100 cases in total (Ross, 1991); at present such cases number in the thousands. MPD is a highly contested diagnosis, partly because the metaphysical presupposition (that more than one psychic being can inhabit a human body) is highly problematic, and to some extent my analysis further problematizes that discussion. I will not assume that there are as many cases as its advocates claim, nor that MPD is a discrete entity which can always be identified as distinct from other types of dissociation, nor that the associated "repressed memory syndrome" (with similar psychologically realistic metaphysical commitments) is a genuine phenomenon (Ganaway, 1989).

A strong metaphysically realist reading of MPD (or MINSD) creates two special ethical problems for forensic psychiatry. The first is *the "It was him not me!" problem*, and the second *the therapeutic murder problem*.[13]

> *The "It was him not me!" problem*
>
> Imagine an MPD patient, Joe, accused of a crime. The psychiatrists acting as expert witnesses confirm that Joe exists in the form of multiple alter personalities each of which may be unaware of the doings of some or all of the others. When confronted with incontrovertible evidence that he, Joe, was the human being who perpetrated the crime, Joe protests. "I know my body was the one that actually performed the action of which I am accused but it was really Wilkins, who is always getting into scrapes like this. I would never do such a thing. It was him not me that did it."

What should one say? Both Joe and Wilkins seem, within their limitations, to be forensically responsible agents neither of whom fit the terms of the insanity plea—"a state of mind such that he did not know the nature and quality of the act he was doing or, if he did know it, that he did not know that what he was doing was wrong" (Gelder, Gath and Mayou, 1983, 727). But even though those terms apply neither to Joe (when he is "in control"/"out") nor to Wilkins individually, it seems otherwise with respect to Joe when Wilkins is

---

[13] Braude discusses these problems though he does not use these terms.

in control ("out"). In that state Joe does not know what is going on and may not remember it afterwards, so he would seem to have a viable insanity plea in that he could say he was in a state of mind at the time of the crime in which he did not know the nature and quality of his act.

### The therapeutic murder problem

Imagine that Joe undergoes therapy and is about to shed his alters as a result. In the supposedly penultimate therapeutic session Wilkins (who is out) says, "I have engaged a lawyer who I have instructed, should I not appear for three months, to instigate a police investigation into my disappearance."

Surely Wilkins has a point: even though he is not a very nice person, he should not just be "terminated". When we look at the metaphysics of identity through the lens of Cartesian realism, Wilkins seems to be as real as any other identifiable person—a conscious subject who can view himself as himself at different times and places and, unfortunately, has to live with the handicap of being rendered powerless and silent from time to time. Does he deserve the further ignominy of being summarily destroyed without even a hearing or right of representation?

These two forensic problems serve to make vivid the startling implications of neo-Lockean Cartesian realism about MPD, the view espoused by some sufferers and their advocates. Their view is, however, not widely accepted.

MPD is regarded by many as a major challenge to the intellectual credibility of psychiatry and clinical psychology (Piper, 1994). The obvious variation in incidence (depending on the context in which people are diagnosed and treated) suggests that there may be a clinical bias in diagnosis and possibly a major iatrogenic factor in producing the disorder. If that were so, then the reality of the disorder would be questionable at least by theorists holding a fairly simplistic view of "natural kinds" or essences as their defining characteristic of real diseases.[14] Such a realist might try to model disorders of the psyche on the conventional medical view whereby a disease is a perfectly general phenomenon that retains its essence but occurs in different human beings (so that defining features of the disease are given by what its sufferers statistically have in common). On this basis one asks, "Is there such a thing as MPD, with a core set of characteristics independent of the subject's view of him or herself

---

[14] I have discussed this at length in Gillett (1999).

or is there not?" Posing the question reveals its problematic nature. The narrative view entails that *who one is* is not independent of who one takes oneself to be, and that both reflect or embody prevalent images and "ways of being" made available in a historico-socio-cultural setting. The setting, it is claimed, inscribes the body to produce a psyche.

We can best begin our discussion by considering one of the famous cases:

> *Jonah*, an African American in Lexington, Kentucky, had three alters: *Sammy, King Young*, and *Usoffa Abdulla*. *Sammy* had formed when Jonah was six, after an incident when Jonah's mother had stabbed his father. *King Young* arose when his mother had dressed him in girl's clothes. The fourth character was a protector. When Jonah was nine or ten a gang of white boys was beating him up; suddenly *Usoffa Abdulla* sprang into action and demolished the gang. He was available for emergencies from that time on. And unlike Sammy and King Young, who had fairly rich characters, Usoffah Abdulla was very much a fragment, with little emotion or involvement with anyone else (Hacking, 1995, 28).

In fact Jonah had another even more fragmentary alter "forming" whom he called *De Novo*. The striking feature of Jonah (in an age of bio-medical reverence) was the fact that those who studied him demonstrated clear physiological differences between his alters (Ludwig *et al.*, 1972). But surely that finding should make us ask, "Are similar physiological effects seen in someone pretending to be different people?"

Although therapists and many of the MPD movement are realists about MPD, other commentators deny that there could be any situation of that sort. A metaphysically extravagant or "full-blooded" view of MPD is, however, aligned with realism (of either idealist or materialist type)[15] about the mind and mental structures in a physical world. The discursive view does not support such metaphysical claims. The neo-Lockean view, as we have seen, equates personal identity with a unique mental constitution bound together by memory and co-consciousness (or some ancestral relationship encompassing that). As such it plays into the hands of metaphysical realists about MPD (even where a Mackie style real essence gloss is given to it, see Mackie, 1976, 202). The current (discursive) view holds that

---

[15] As I have noted, the neo-Cartesian view applies the psychological criterion of personal identity in either its idealist or its materialist form.

human identity is actually narrative, embodied, interactive, and dynamic. It is in part produced by an image and the signifiers contributing to it as they play themselves out in the ordinary facts of located and positioned human existence (although virtual reality presents the novel and interesting possibility that part of one's identity could be an avatar in a virtual world online).

## MPD or MINSD

The lived narrative of the human psyche, on the present account, inscribes itself on a body (most obviously in the brain) and there is a well developed account of MPD as a configuration of neurally encoded informational states (ergo MINSD) based on Freud's associationism.[16] Andorfer traces the story of a person with MPD who (in the course of a troubled childhood during which she was physically and sexually abused in the context of a disrupted family) began to dissociate in accordance with the commonly received stereotype, and from early fantasies of an imaginary playmate, developed 20 alter personaties.

> Freud ... suggests that subjection to an interpersonal environment that contains too great a frequency of extremely powerful and contradictory emotional stimuli, during the narcissistic period of ego formation, results in splitting of the ego ... The events most consistently found in the childhoods of multiple personalities are maternal physical abuse ... and incest ... Alternate personalities may be formed only in persons with a biological potential to dissociate ... beginning with a wish for someone else to contain painful emotions, exercise necessary survival or coping skills, or express uncondoned impulses (Andorfer,1985, 309).

The author (the patient's therapist) makes certain general remarks about MPD.

> In probably every case of multiple personality, there is an "executive" personality and one or more "destabilizer" personalities. It is important to remember that each personality plays a role in the psychic economy of the overall personality system. Even those personalities that appear predominantly destructive or disruptive have become so only because the attitudes, affects, and coping behaviors that they embody have developed without the moderating influence of complementary attitudes, affects and behaviors that reside with the other personalities (Andorfer, 1985, 314).

---

[16] Andorfer (1985). I have discussed Freudian associationism in Gillett (2003).

At a certain point Athena, the organizing, all-knowing, and wise personality, demands to know from the therapist how to achieve re-integration.

> In response to Athena's request, the author furnished a neo-associationist explanation of encoding, organization and retrieval in memory, ... and ... explained to Athena how to encode new information into memory to make it accessible to all personalities and to establish associative paths among otherwise discrete memory regions. Athena responded as a skilled programmer who knew the capabilities of her computer (Andorfer, 1985, 316).

It is little wonder that Athena responds as she does when Andorfer elaborates the computer (or neural information-processor) metaphor throughout so that he recasts all the exchanges with his patient (about her personality and the therapy of MPD) in the preferred metaphorical language.[17]

> Personality is comprised of the stereotyped verbal affective, and cognitive behaviors exhibited by an individual and the interpersonal behaviors that are their derivatives. As such, personality is a product of the specific contents of propositional memory and the specific interrelationships of those contents (Andorfer, 1985, 320).

Notice that he is actually talking about teaching his patient skills of memory and self-understanding that allow her to articulate and then "argue" (with him and herself) about the memories, affects, and attitudes she discloses or articulates. This is a classical technique of care of the self (*cura sui*)[18] whereby argument, dialogue, internal dialogue, and critique or struggle are used to heal the soul. Through these means one is engaged with another and re-articulates affects and dispositions in shared language through a conversation with another living and responsive human being who reacts to one's self-understanding (thus evincing their reactive attitudes and creating the therapy as an intrinsically moral context).[19] Through the reaction of that other human being "two worlds meet" creating "a possibility for new possibilties" as the patient "grasps his world-structuring role" (Lear, 2003, 209, 204, 208).

---

[17] So that we see here an example of Hacking's (1995) "looping effect" in action.
[18] Foucault writes about this in his *Ethics* (1997) and Martha Nussbaum in *The Therapy of Desire* (1994).
[19] The phrase "reactive attitudes" is Peter Strawson's.

Notice that in therapy the therapist is making use of the names (Esther, Roxeanne, Anne-Marie, Athena, Anne, Marie, and so on) to address, as human subjects, the personalities whose characteristics are coming to the fore at certain points in the conversation. The therapist is therefore addressing the subject as a multiplex moral agent using the implicit demands, appeals, imperatives, and expectations that accompany interpersonal dialogue between named beings-in-the-world-with-others. We do not, however, get to see this side of what is happening with the patient through the "information-processor account"; we are left to fill it in through subtle reminders about what is actually happening as a meeting of two moral worlds. It is not until we do that "filling in" that we begin to glimpse more adequately the metaphysics and ethics of personality and narratives.

### The metaphysics of narratives after Lacan

The present account argues that one configures oneself as an embodied being in the many relationships and interactions that make up life as a being-in-the-world-with-others. One does this partly through cybernetic routines enchained or entangled with one's context so as to appear "in character" in different settings. Expected and unexpected reactions and responses trace a unique personal trajectory through life and form a dossier that is unified, inter alia, by an important component — a name — allowing us to track an individual and his or her moral career. One's name is a marker or social and personal index number and is so important because each of us carries a unique lifetime of narrative experience and dealings with others inscribed in us and expressed in our actions.[20]

We should, at this point, notice that names are not arbitrary. Most societies use names as ways of recording or encoding kinship relations. We also have nicknames which, in some societies, have reached the status of formal names — such as "Crazy Horse"; "A good name is like deep roots," many old ones liked to say, "that help the tree stand strong against hard winds" (Marshall, 2004, 85). Nicknames are given in a context of comradeship and achievement and they often allude to some narrative moment in the individual's life. Even when they retain a link to a lineage they do so in such a way to recall, through words, deeds or achieved status, a prominent or celebrated former member of that lineage and they are meant to confer some of the *mana* of the former person on the person named (as happened in the case of Crazy Horse). Naming carries with it both

[20] As discussed in Chapter 6.

traces of lineage or origin and expectations arising out of that connectedness and it locates the individual in a nexus of signification whereby his or her connections to others are not only biological but also symbolic. That is then an important fact about the individual and serves as what we could call an "attractor" for further attributions.

Through all this, the disciplines that have shaped one's being and the reactions evoked by exchanges in which one touches the real world around one all leave their residues priming the body to respond to new situations. Some of those responses are incompatible (one cannot both long to be held and want to keep a safe distance, be both appreciative and resentful, or be joyful and irritated at the same time). The conflicts of reaction and response need to be resolved if one is to function in the world as an embodied individual. They are resolved as one enacts a trajectory as a being-in-the-world-with-others on which there are constraints both informal and normative so that one's unified way-of-being is recognisable as such around here (even if it is tenuous).

It seems that we allow departures from the commonly encountered ways of being and they range from the eccentric to the frankly disordered and dysfunctional (we have difficulties accommodating them in the fabric of social life in our human group, and perhaps all human groups would). When these ways of being are violated, we judge that the individual has a serious disorder of the psyche. That judgment licenses a discursive move which places the individual specifically within the moral community so that, to some extent, he or she becomes a phenomenon to be explained rather than one of us to be recognised, respected, and to whom we owe a certain kind of interpersonal accountability.

It may be that a given human-being-among-us instances several narratively connected sets of such relationships each of which is mutually incompatible with the others (for cognitive, conative, or forensic reasons) and in such a case the person themselves may distinctively name the personae to differentiate them from each other. If we fall in with this practice then identities come into being each of which can be lived through in response to certain situations and each of which contributes to the entangled life trajectory of the one body in various ways (hence MPD).

The separation of memories, ways of relating to others, and inclusions in one's lived subjectivity, may go very deep and those differences that go to make up the complex of psyches instanced by the human body concerned might be expected to have some distinctive physiological footprint (discoverable by the earnest seeker). In such a way one might be several different "somebodys" depending on the way in which one's body is animated or inspir(it)ed at given points in time and, perhaps, the inscriptions corresponding to one set of embodied subjective moments may have few if any connections to others. The fact that each embodied subjectivity is a response to a set of connected evoking circumstances and that most of us do manage to meld these together might imply that integration is always possible. So firmly entrenched is this idea that we might enforce a metaphysics of one-body – one-person and insist that no other basis for our dealings with a person is acceptable to us. If so that would be a powerful discursive technique to help bring about the reintegration of the complex subjectivity involved with its (quite possibly) incompatible *imagos* that it is trying to realize.[21]

## The ethics of narrative identity

These emerging conclusions about identity subtend different ethical views about the treatment of alters, personae, or narrative identities.

*The ho-hum conclusion* could be compared with the view that there is no more or less to personal identity than can be derived from an analogy with a woven tapestry cord. But this is probably enough for most purposes. It is clear that the woven cord has certain emergent properties which are greater than any properties inherent in the individual strands making it up. For instance, the cord might hold a person's weight where a single thread would not. This property is, however, reducible in that it is a property type, strength, in common with but of a greater magnitude than the property found in the component thread. A similar but more interesting property is something like longitudinal continuity for more than one meter which is a property depending not only on the lengths of component threads but the interconnections between them and it cannot be accounted for by any straightforward sum of parts. Even more interesting is the coloured pattern woven into the cord which is dependent on but clearly different in kind from any property exhibited by a monochromatic thread. These emergent properties, quantitatively and qualitatively related to but not reducible to the properties on which they supervene, create realities not evident in the components of the cord and therefore require a language and categorisations peculiar to the cord

---

[21] The term *imago* is used as by Lacan and I have already discussed the normative forces at work in the discussion of the split brain cases.

as a whole. The emergent realities allow the whole cord to take on an explanatory role that does not correspond to any roles found at the thread level. In relation to personal identity we might conclude that even if the longitudinal identity of a person is composed of combinations of and interactions between different moments of mental life there may emerge a new and interesting reality warranting the belief that personal identity is real.[22]

Where there is a strong and identifiable pattern emergent on considering the cord as a whole, we might say that we have a well-formed moral subject/agent who is among us and can be treated with an unmitigated application of the various predicates of moral identity (responsibility, intent, agenda, and so on).

*The startling conclusion* takes its cue from an analogy with a loose bundle of rags. Rags can come and go but the bundle remains more or less the same just as does a heap in the face of small modifications. If developed, this analogy leads to a loosening of moral or forensic coherence between different moments of a life history. It grounds a "thin" view of personal identity whereby the idea of identity becomes just a shorthand way of referring to the loose collection of a certain bundle of psychological characteristics qualitatively and quantitatively distinct in its composition but not in its essential constitution from a bundle exhibited by another person. We do not, as human communities, accept this disconnected view of persons and their personalities, because it deconstructs our lives together and undermines notions important to that life such as character, trust, responsibility, relationship, and so on. These reactive predicates, the predicates of morality, are not sustainable if a psychic life is episodic rather than connected in the right kind of way and our belief in that connectedness is justified by pointing at the cognitive unity and narrative unity that characterise human subjectivity. Where these are present, as they are to some extent in all of us who are recognisable as subjects/agents who do meaningful things with others, those unities ground our ascriptions of identity on the basis of subjective embodiment (the surface on which events are inscribed).[23]

The strong metaphysical view of multiple personality disorder is that there are several distinct complexes of "mental molecules" (psychic states with their own distinctive character) each complex form-

---

[22] Notice that Schechtman and I have argued that those moments are, in part, derived in their intrinsic nature from their occurrence within the whole psyche of the person concerned.

[23] The figure is used by Foucault.

ing a distinct personality or self within the individual concerned. The present view is somewhat weaker:

> That there are many distinguishable thought-lines, moods and memories need not lead us to believe that there are many different selves nor that there are none (Clark, 1996, 25).

The discursive view of mental reality concurs that the metaphysical thesis underlying this controversy is flawed and implies that the body/brain is a medium shaped or inscribed by the discursive formations that become the soul — "the element in which are articulated the effects of a certain type of power and the reference of a certain kind of knowledge", "the present correlative of a certain power over the body" (Foucault, 1984, 177, 176). The soul, on this view, is best thought of not as an inner being (perhaps complex) but as an individual unique production with continuity over time somewhat tentatively held together by a narrative and finding its conditions for existence in an interpersonal context — "a complex system of distinct and multiple elements unable to be mastered by the powers of synthesis" (Foucault, 1984, 94). This narrative aspect of personality also strikes a chord with Clark's analysis.

> We tell ourselves the story of our lives, complete with our commitments and professions. What counts as me will vary with my context, and with what I can bear to acknowledge. Was it me that had that dreadful thought just now? (Clark, 1996, 24).

Narratives are constructed, stabilised, and destabilised within social and cultural reality where a person is constantly being morally evaluated, shaping him or herself and taking on a more or less definite persona in contact with others. The existence of the body makes a person an identifiable and namable entity, a node or point of focus of these moral and cultural forces so that the problem of self-synthesis is not solved totally within the individual but resolved (in a good enough way) as a being-in-the-world-with-others.

The present account suggests that a person should not be regarded as a mere bundle of "internal states" but as an integrated set of adaptations to a complex social and cultural context. Conscious states are states of sensitivity and responsiveness requiring (for the most part) intentionally mediated interaction with the world (through the use of signifiers). One is therefore a discursive and narrative formation held together (in a good enough way) so that a soul is written in one as a text through discursively shaped actions and attitudes, to some extent open to self-reflection and critique and the focus of a personal struggle (Foucault, 1994). That task calls on certain skills dependent on the disciplines mastered by the individual (coping skills, anger management skills, assertion skills, and so on).

The discursive reading therefore suggests that the dictum "know thyself" does not imply that one can come to know a fixed inner self, but enjoins a person to "becoming thyself knowingly" in a way that leads to a reappraisal of MPD.

## The return to MPD: not good enough being-with-others

What could induce a human being to partition certain thoughts, feelings and memories away from other moments of consciousness so that they do not appear in the normal conscious life of that individual, to adopt multiple personae? Can all of us do this or do those affected have heightened biological predispositions to dissociate? These are empirical questions but the philosophical inquiry allows us to approach them in an informed way (Sprigge, 1996).

Consider Jonah: he is not constructing a single coherent narrative embracing all his life experiences. As a result he finds that his resources for dealing with situations are ineffective and none of them draw on all of his available life-skills because he has to occupy different subjective narratives to manifest certain of those skills. Let us say that he enters a situation as Jonah, who copes by being compliant and cooperative to the point of obliterating his own interests and complies with others. However, he wants certain things, for instance to seduce a woman. As Jonah he cannot do this and so the seducer, King Young, at ease among women, emerges. King Young's lived body "has all the moves". He is not Jonah and not impeded by enacting Jonah's ways of being (replete with inhibitions and painful sensitivities that make Jonah incompetent around women). King Young inhabits human discourse differently and is differently inscribed with response patterns and reactions. Jonah's discursive techniques just get in the way and *foul things up* in the same way that loss of confidence, panicky aggression, and or apprehensiveness can ruin a batsman's eye in a cricket game.

So far we have identified experiences and adaptations as based on discursive techniques that structure conscious experience and action so as to articulate the field in which one responds to the world according to some subset of narrative skills, selected and actively mobilised to organise present activity. Discursively accessible activity from any given position is gathered under a given name and constitutes the lived narrative of a subject. A set of co-accessible skills (and the moments they have organised) contribute to a personality and character and one usually (under the normative pressure of a discursive context) develops ways of integrating these skills so that one has an adequate range and variety of tools apt for all of life's challenges.

For any subject the fabric of subjective being is, therefore, discursive — and thereby both interpersonal and evaluative or moral from the time of birth. One's personality is being formed amidst all kinds of signals that evoke (and do not merely describe) things from one in a given context (Lacan, 1977, 86). Good significations should be bound together under my name and evoked by it so that I have "a good name" and the "bad stuff" should not be owned by me, it should be banished as "not me"("Where did that come from?"). Thus the formation of personality is evaluative.[24] We might expect there to be a complex interaction between the evaluative tone given to certain responses, the evaluation by the subject of the other person, and the signification of one's current activity; "Am I", for instance, "currently seeing myself as a rebel and does the person influencing me stand in the position of the establishment or as a discontent?" In this way I emerge within the moral and social realm as a subject with a certain name and identity held together by the aspects of subjectivity that I have come to own (willingly or unwillingly).

But there are connectional constraints within every narrative and they influence the synthesis that is soul-making. These are (importantly) connections between signifiers that (for Lacan) entail that the unconscious is structured like a language.[25] As such it is both associative and syntagmatic and the associations ramify throughout a world of relationships, touches and entanglements. Typically a person who loves and cherishes me will not destroy or violate me so if this seems to be happening then I am at an impasse; the evaluations and significations are all awry and will not hang together. How then do I construct a narrative out of this which both makes sense of me and also makes sense of the people close to me? The power relations entangling me make it the case that I deeply need narrative coherence but I may have poor skills in selecting and properly connecting the significations of experience that would allow that to happen. The subject who develops MPD may find such techniques prone to disruption anyway because of their emotional reactivity and problems

---

[24] As I have argued in discussing cyborgs and the development of the psyche in children.

[25] Lacan (1977). Such that the connections predate the "arrival" of the subject.

in mastering the relevant skills, especially when the available models or "discursive sculptors" are themselves grossly impaired.[26] One need not posit a marked "dissociative propensity" to understand how parallel narratives could begin to be constructed, especially when one reads the common experiences of depersonalisation, dissociation and disengagement from reality characteristic of many people's reactions to stress.

Therefore MPD might arise spontaneously, perhaps only in some individuals with a disposition to dissociate from stressful experiences and situations, wherever the discursive skills of an individual are insufficient to the task of constructing a coherent narrative encompassing significant life experiences and a sustainable moral and personal position in relation to others. Does that make it real? Perhaps it makes it as real as any other personality configuration (or imago) that we synthesize as a good enough accommodation to the cumulative effects of power on subjectivity.

### The role of the therapist

The person entering therapy for MPD is distressed and confused about who they are and their own worth in the eyes of others. We can see how a multiple narrative might be likely to be produced if such a conflicted individual found a ready-made way to conceptualize and harmonise her narrative by making use of a script provided by the therapist. Being a multiple might also provide possibilities of enacting aspects of one's self that were otherwise unexpressible. Psychotherapy provides culturally validated scripts associated with various "metanarratives" or theories (about the psyche and its nature). Every therapist has such metascripts even where they offer very little, for instance "there is a chemical imbalance in your brain which we are going to try to correct". Every script has an influence on the self-production of the person in therapy, who often through transference turns the therapist into a surrogate for one of the formative people in his or her life. The script might be one in which people are often overcome by their anger and cannot defuse it. A person may have a tendency to violent anger which he constantly regrets but excuses by, for instance, thinking of himself (and therefore feeling himself to be) justified in his violence because the world treats

---

[26] Shapiro describes the hysterical personality as "impressionistic, relatively immediate, and global ... an experience not of sharply observed facts and developed judgments but of quick hunches and impressions ... suggestive and easily carried away" (1999, 129).

him badly (i.e. not the way his mother used to) or by thinking he is a "chip off the old block" where that is an abusive father. He might treat others as the cause of his violence because they set up conditions in which he loses control, he may think they are out to get him, and so on (this kind of moral accounting is becoming less and less acceptable). Having engaged with the therapist, the young man concerned may begin to want to master certain anger-management skills and learn discursive techniques to deal with potentially violent situations differently in the future. The step from "He's in one of his moods" to "He's a different person" is not impossible and its nature is evident as we realise that a psyche is a shifting configuration of techniques for manufacturing liveable stories out of a life trajectory. An important part of that step is naming who is responsible for what is happening so that the reactive attitudes potentiating change can be aptly focused.

Think of a different script in which the individual is encouraged to think of himself as essentially an innocent and well-meaning individual but with a part of himself that, as in everybody, is prone to violence. He might think "That is right, I am two different people", and develop that script with the therapist's help. When did you start feeling like that second person? Does it often happen that on the surface, you are good and kind but internally there is a dark and angry you waiting to appear? When you were a child, how did you feel about your parents? Did you express bad feelings or give them to your darker self? Notice that we are asking the individual to take a reflective attitude toward himself. Most people fall somewhere along a continuum between, at one end, the experience of having a stable character to which others can relate with confidence, to mild volatility whereby one "shifts" (on occasion) into different modes of relating but can "snap out of" dysfunctional attitudes and, at the other end, experiencing oneself as not one person (a multiple self). If every person's narrative has room for negotiation we now have the resources to respond to the puzzles raised by MPD.

### The puzzles

*First*, the reality of MPD as a disorder is not a matter of finding a multiple set of spiritual or physical entities inside a person. To define a disorder of the mind is to describe a human condition that causes distress and is produced primarily by discursive rather than physical interactions. It seems that certain kinds of discourse result in an individual dissociating from and disowning experiences and attitudes rather than integrating them into a more or less coherent narrative defining him/her-self. In therapy (or any exercise aimed at enhancing the care of the self), one is encouraged to attend to and be critical of one's ways of being. One can then use disciplines forming part of the care of the self to change. The strategy of self-construction as dissociated or multiple might even be encouraged in certain therapeutic settings as part of that enterprise. We could envisage a multiple strategy being taken up where:

(i) the society has a story of mental disorder with the features of MPD; and

(ii) the therapist makes this story available to the client.

The person accepting this story may or may not enter into it (just as some people cannot be hypnotised),[27] but if they did so then it would be as true of them to say that they have MPD as it would be to say of somebody else that he or she is suffering an anxiety disorder, is a sceptic, or is a scholar.

Given a broadly Aristotelian theory of mind, the effects of discourse must be realised in configurations of brain processing function and perhaps some MPD individuals may be able to be taxonomised by looking at their functional patterns of neurocognitive processing but that would not alter the social and interpersonal reality at the heart some of the disorder nor tell us what to do with it.

*Secondly*, it seems that the willingness of a therapist to recognise (or even provide) a "multiple" script as a way of articulating and dealing with a certain kind of mental/discursive distress is pivotal in a person being regarded as having MPD. If the discursive context validates this narrative and the experiential constraints allow it then "I am a multiple personality" becomes a tenable form of identity that carries certain expectations about the modes by which one might cope with life. (Notice that a discursive self-construction is not helpfully thought of as a fiction because it produces in the individual a psychic reality that is similar to the *imago* informing each of our lived subjectivities.) Hacking refers to this tendency to realise certain kinds of mental self-construction through the way one lives as the "looping effect of human kinds" and Butler speaks of identity as, in

---

[27] Individuals prone to be hypnotised share certain characteristics with those prone to develop MPD — the characteristics Shapiro (1999) groups under hysterical style.

part, performative such that it is a way one lives among others as a kind of (diversely constrained) enactment of a narrative type.[28]

*Thirdly*, it follows from the argument so far that is hard to make sense of a contrast between "a natural kind"[29] and a cultural artifact in relation to the psyche. Human beings are naturally social and cultural creatures for whom biological evolution is somewhat *passé*. Ways of thinking of oneself are naturally made available by culture. In New Zealand, one can think of oneself as Maori or Pakeha, more or less on the basis of lineage. One can also think of oneself as educated, law-abiding, literate, appreciative of Dvorak's music, a rugby supporter, a psychiatrist, unemployed, or a number of other things. Each of these thoughts could be straightforwardly true or false but all of them, in a sense, concern culturally mediated ways of being. Extending the list to psychiatric contexts merely allows that some of the ways of being we have created for ourselves are a joint product of medical culture, society, history and human diversity.

Even the most plausible candidates for the disease model in psychiatry are, to some extent, discursive constructs. They carry with them patterns of response that sufferers are framed against when they are described and evaluated; "Isn't he doing well?" does not mean the same for a simple schizophrenic and an immunologist. In the one case we keep an eye on the cardinal manifestations of what is seen as a distinct disorder, in the other we look at a career path and the markers of success associated with it. Increasingly the former seem to be influenced by responses to psycho-pharmacological species, but the correlation is not impressive. I was once told that psychiatry has only two diseases; you can't always tell the difference between them, either might respond to agents primarily developed to treat the other, and a given patient might shift between the two categories from time to time. Such is the nature of the objective natural kinds dominating the metaphysics of biomedicine. As for me, I have my doubts about the possibility of such an elusive and ideologically suspect taxonomy (realism about mental kinds) but at least there I am not alone and can claim allies like Dennett (1991), Stich (1983), Lacan (1977; 1979), Foucault, Kristeva and Hacking (1995).

---

[28] I have mentioned Hacking's account (1994) and Butler summarises her position in a philosophical assessment of Foucault (Butler, 1989).

[29] The idea of a natural kind is a feature of contemporary metaphysics and semantics which assumes that there are certain joints at which nature is already carved and that human language is most "truthful" when it configures itself to those pre-existing distinctions (see Appendix E on this).

## Neuroethics

The present account construes MPD as a configuration of psychic activity worked out on a neural substrate that has been configured in a certain way. In this respect it is like any other personality (or identity). As a philosopher one might represent an alter (a personality that is part of an MPD cluster) as a unique psychic configuration supervenient on a given (neural) subvenience base, but to do so would be to lose sight of the mode of being that is MPD. The Cartesian realist (or scientistic) view supports the claim that to destroy an alter, as one might do in therapy, is equivalent to murder because it holds that the metaphysical equal of a person is thereby ushered out of being. That makes the ethics of therapy designed at the re-integration of a person look suspect in a way that flies in the face of clinical experience and an examined understanding of the human subject.

Not only forensic intuitions run against this view and favour the *"one body = one person"* claim. I have argued that there is a sociocultural norm deeply enmeshed in our dealings with one another and it creates a context in which the self is impelled towards its own unity (available, I have argued, on the basis of cognitions and narratives bound together by the multifaceted skills that go to make up human memory). At this point we need to notice that (as we saw with cyborgs and embryos) ethics and metaphysics are not completely separate but are different modes of thought contributing to and deriving from the practices in which language is taught and learnt. In these practices we relate to others drawing on their dealings with us to fill out our understanding of what it is to be a person (much as Wiggins [1987] argues).

In our shared lives together we distil ways of being out of the many discursive possibilities that abound there and, as a result of the skills that form those ways of being, each of us develops a personality and a character such that we can form relationships (involving commitments, promises, expectations, dyadic practices, and so on). Those encounters and relationships comprise the moral fabric of our lives together and it loses something when anybody loses part of themselves for any reason. When an alter is lost we may lose something that the person needs to be who they are. We should therefore protect and feel concerned about alters, not as persons but as significant aspects of a person in which gifts, inspirations and skills can be manifest that otherwise would not be. Destructive or normative psychological practice whereby a person is forced to fit into our normal forensic framework without appreciating his or her fragility and complexity may not be therapeutic murder but it is the equivalent of grievous psychic harm and should, on that count, be discouraged. But that is quite consistent with the thought that recovery in a fragmented and disintegrating personality is a laudable therapeutic aim.

The discursive account is an illuminating approach to MPD and may have much to offer in other areas of conceptual confusion in psychiatry. At least it is worth considering where our more traditional psychological models yield more confusion than insight into the people with whom we are dealing. MPD challenges us to be honest about the many and diverse ways of being that are open to us and that ought to inform us in relation to those we encounter whom we do not initially understand. As such it allows us to glimpse the work of identity that happens unobtrusively in all of us all the time.

# Chapter 9

# *Care of the Soul*

## Demons, Spirits, and Identity

> Two things fill me with constantly increasing admiration and awe, the longer and more earnestly I reflect on them: the starry heavens without and the moral law within.
> (Kant, *The Critique of Practical Reason*)

How do we give substance to a conception of spirituality that does justice to the idea of human identity? We can start by noticing the traditional division between *body*, soul/psyche/*mind*, and *spirit*. The first of this triad — the body — is addressed by physical or biological sciences like biochemistry, physiology, neuroscience and so on. It asks questions like "In what form does the visual system receive information from the environment?" "How is the function of the heart connected to the function of the brain?" "What stimuli does the brain make use of in monitoring hunger?" and so on. Psychology (the science of the *psyche*) moves away from the straightforwardly physical and biological and asks things like "How many items of disconnected information can a person remember and what happens if the information is connected together in some meaningful way?" "Is a human being influenced by the expressed opinions of others in making judgments about stimuli?" "Do children model their behaviour on that of their parents?" "What contingencies cause people to act in an altruistic way?" and so on. What then is left for questions about *spirit*?

Questions that do not merely describe the body or the mind but form another kind of inquiry might concern the value or significance of human life. Such questions cannot be answered scientifically but they can be discussed in such a way that reason has a role in addressing them. "What value ought to be attached to a human life?" "What counts as a good life and is it the same as a life in which an individual is content?" "Are all human beings of equal worth in some fundamental sense?" "What is truth?"(Not what is the truth *about* X, Y or Z?) Recall Wittgenstein's remark: "How things are in the world is a matter of complete indifference for what is higher. God does not reveal himself in the world" (*Tractatus*, 6432). We cannot use scientific techniques (that reveal how things are) to disclose the significance we ought to attach to our lives.

Significance is found — here as elsewhere — in those connections, relationships, words, images and stories that inform our thinking; here it is about our spiritual life.[1] Notice that if we transform the question into an inquiry into what we *find significant* or *get captivated by*, it can become a psychological question about human beings as objective phenomena, facets of which stand to be examined and described.[2] That is why the question, "What *ought* we to think about our place in the scheme of things?" or "What value *ought* we to attach to an individual human life?" is the route to questions of the spirit.

I have argued that human identity is dispersed, contextual, centred on the body but not contained within it. It is centred on the body as a nodal point of a number of discursive practices and relationships that evoke, provoke, command, and require us to take a stance informing the type of regard in which we hold each other. That allows a different facet of a human being to emerge, one that structures his or her attitudes towards and relationships with other human beings. This is not just a matter of how he or she feels about others. For instance, I might regard you as in some sense being of equal value in the scheme of things as I am myself and either be awed and thrilled by that realisation or slightly "miffed" because it seems to diminish my own worth. My attitude will depend on the connections I make with the original thought — you are my equal — so that is the field to plough in investigating human spirituality.

I will begin with the problem of the forensic identity of a human being "at the last trumpet" or "in a new heaven and a new earth" to show just how problematic the standard metaphysical view is. I will then argue for a profoundly relational view linking each of us spiritually to our roots, to the ancestors we have sprung from, to the

---

[1] Which is why our ethical and spiritual orientation towards others is part of the being of cyborgs and that being and its significance cannot be gauged in isolation from our engagement with them.

[2] Wittgenstein remarks "the will as phenomenon is of interest only to psychology"(*Tractatus*, 6423).

family we are part of, to the friendships we form, and to the stories informing our lives together. For many believers, that nexus of relationships itself is in a relationship with the divine being. Even in its non-theistic form, however, the view of spirituality that results yields a rich (and complex) ontology of human identity that is linked to our ethical and spiritual thinking in a number of ways. It also reveals why the hope that a new scientific theory of causality could illuminate ethics and religious thought by relating them to "brain states" is misplaced and philosophically naïve (Koch, 2004, 326).

## Theological thinking after Lacan and post-structuralism

Lacan's influence on the humanities has been widely felt and theology after Lacan looks very different from that found in standard texts on apologetics. It departs from modernist metaphysics with its apparatus of objects, causes (in the physicalist sense),[3] durations, absolute positions determinable in space, and so on to entangle us in a world of meaning. Resurrection identity makes vivid the fact that quasi-scientific thinking about any theological issue fairly quickly gets into similar impasses (think, for instance, of the personality and omnipresence of a God who acts in history).[4]

The structuralist entree directs us to the connections and content of the terms and phrases articulating our beliefs. Philosophers have, traditionally, regarded beliefs as pictures or representations of the world positing a fairly direct relationship between the content of a true belief and the way the world is ("a vertical relation" tying the word directly to the world or a bit of it). This is problematic the moment one tries to spell out just what the resemblance or linkage is.[5] For instance when I believe that a wolf is a type of dog a certain picture of the world comes to mind, but when I say to a friend, "Watch out, that's a wolf not a dog!" *what* (if any) picture comes to mind?[6] Disharmony or incompatibility of beliefs arises not only from downright contradiction ("God is both omnibenevolent and

---

[3] A sense which is now acknowledged to be inadequate to the kinds of thoughts we need to do contemporary physics.

[4] These are discussed and mercilessly exposed by D.Z. Phillips in his recent work (2004).

[5] A problem for philosophical semantics that is so radical that the early Wittgenstein formulated the doctrine of saying and showing to deal with it and ultimately rejected any such account. See appendix F for a discussion of reference.

[6] If correct I should validly infer that some wolves are not dogs which contradicts the belief that a wolf is a type of dog or that any member of the subclass *wolf* is also a member of the inclusive class *dog*.

nasty"), or incoherence ("God is omniscient and omnipotent but he doesn't always know and can't do a lot about what happens next door"), but also from incomprehensibility ("God is not omnipotent because he cannot ride a bicycle"). But the dog/wolf example suggests that not all contradictions are created equal. So what kind of inconsistency haunts the religious beliefs that cannot be affirmed because they do not withstand intellectually rigorous scrutiny?

We ought next to be clear that physical conformity to laws of nature as we understand them is not required, in that the common affirmation of belief in miracles should not be ruled out *a priori* as part of a rationally defensible faith. We might, after Wittgenstein, also have reservations about intuitive imaginability.

> There is a lack of clarity about the role of imaginability in our investigation. Namely about the extent to which it ensures that a proposition makes sense (*PI*, #395).

He has a point. Can I imagine steam coming out of an empty kettle? (Is the stuff I imagine vapourised water? Is it coming out or just materialising at the tip of the spout? How is it coming into being? And so on.) Can I imagine a totally disembodied being? (What makes this a *being*, rather than a *nothing* mistakenly ascribed existence? Is my imagined thought only contrasting an object with bodies of the solid kind with which I am familiar? Is the imagined being anywhere and, if so, in what sense is it there rather than somewhere else? And so on.) Can I imagine its being 5 o'clock on the sun?[7] These knotty imponderables are just the beginning because, for theology, the tensions concerned are not merely of logic but also concern the spirit. For instance, the thought that a robot could fix you with a cruel and steely gaze is coherent, but the thought that a saint could is not (saints are not machine like). The connections and resonances (perhaps unconscious) of our beliefs should support and strengthen the claims concerned so that they feel convincing rather than just preserve some kind of logical consistency. Logical consistency may offer us "clever-sticks" answers to theological questions but do nothing to deepen spiritual thinking.[8] Spiritual thinking should help articulate and clarify matters of the spirit (to do with human worth, how life should be lived, and our place in the scheme of things) and a

---

[7] Wittgenstein's own example, that raises all the knotty questions.
[8] Logically consistent theodicies are always within parameters constructed in a tendentious way and often buy into systems of thought that are not theologically sound.

theological claim should respect core connections and resonances of the constituent meanings forming its content. We might, for instance, think about a divine law of love and compare it with natural laws or governmental laws but this is problematic in that the natural world (in which we live and move and have our being) works in ways to which our mind is attuned by an intuitive knowledge of space, time, and causality.[9] We have no assurance that the world of the spirit obeys similar laws so that to ask whether God must love human beings as a psychological or legislative aspect of God's being might be a kind of idolatry—making the divine in our own image. We might expect deeper meanings to inform key theological insights concerning grace, moral and personal relationships, and the ultimate nature of things in the scheme of creation-redemption than claims framed in terms of the behaviour of "middle sized dry goods"(to use Austin's phrase) or their animate counterparts.

We might also impose emotive and moral constraints such that the thought concerned should be meaningful in ways that go beyond merely offering closure in an abstract argument. For instance, some find it deeply meaningful to say that the Christian God completed the creation of humankind in the knowledge that it would result in the death of his only begotten son. Such a story of faith enlists our assent in a way that feels right or satisfies us when we confront the problem of evil. A creation in which there is both suffering and redemption speaks to the deeper levels of our being and does not gloss over the emotive enormity of that suffering or cruel things such as the death of children. If we are entangled in a cruel world (that disturbs, provokes and unsettles us) but also one that is a source of (human all too human) joy, then it is no wonder that the many traditions linking both good and evil together in the being of God while rejecting the thought that God plays with us (as wanton boys with flies) get a grip on us. These general hints as to where to find spiritual truths about ourselves frame a post-metaphysical inquiry into resurrection life and human identity.

## Orthodoxy

Orthodox Christians believe something like the following.

---

[9] In this vein, Kant discusses the relative surety which we can have about our rational deliberations in the world of nature—to which the human mind is well adapted, and the speculative and quite possibly nonsensical nature of pronouncements beyond that (*Pure Reason*).

A. Resurrection life is a continuation of the actual life of the redeemed person.
B. A person's body returns to dust at death.
C. Resurrection life is by grace not law.

There is a more intellectually tractable view that eternal life is human life lived in a godly or spiritual way. That view also addresses important spiritual insights, and is relevant to a discussion of identity and spirituality in that it locates the human spirit in a context that goes beyond scientific descriptions, but it is not my immediate focus.

*The objections*

AntiR1: If B is true then a new body must be created to live in whatever realm is the medium of the afterlife.

AntiR2: Normal criteria of identity would make this a new individual rather than a continuation of the "ancestor" person (or original living human being).

AntiR3: The new individual is a copy of the person who died (*The replica objection*).

Addendum: The new person/copy/replica may believe he or she is the original person (*The deluded replica case*).

In fact this objection applies wherever death really is destruction of the individual and some shadow, echo, likeness, or set of characteristics is preserved so as to recreate an apparently derivative individual (like a ghost or disembodied spirit). Thus, even though the discourse of human identity includes the ending of a human life in death, a metaphysics of substances and properties[10] requires a substance that persists and sustains identity in a way sufficient to defeat *the replica objection*. The substance (the *hypokeimenon* or that which is the bearer of a set of determinable properties) most apt for metaphysical continuity is the human body, but claim B — a person's body returns to dust at death — constitutes a fatal (pun intended) objection to that view. We are left with only three candidate views underpinning a metaphysical solution to the problem.

1. We could "dig in our toes" after Reid and Butler, Locke's contemporaries, and say that personal identity is not dependent or supervenient on any other thing but is primitive in our notion of persons.

---

[10] See Appendix B on essence and identity noting that a substance is a self-contained individual thing of a determinate type and not just matter.

This amounts to a credo backed by the intuition that any supporting theses adduced to argue that a human subject is the same numerical individual as a former self are less certain than the brute fact we are seeking to establish. Reid and Butler argued in this vein against Locke's rendition of identity in terms of psychological criteria. The present discussion grounds the primacy of individual human identity on the fact that a human subject becomes a self through a complex of relationships and formative influences (which, for a theist, might include a unique relationship with God).[11]

2. We could argue for a *spiritual body* existing in parallel with the physical body but that survives its dissolution.[12]

There are two problems with this view. The first was expressed by Locke when he considered the possibility of a soul (thought of as a spiritual substance) as the bearer of personal identity. He remarked that the fate of a thing with no essential connection to the properties of mind and personality that make me *me*, would be of no more concern to me than any part of my body that was incidental to my ongoing existence as a continuing thinking and intelligent thing. And to claim that the properties of the soul (as psyche) reside in this immaterial substance is to take on the metaphysical problems of Cartesian Dualism.[13] Locke's solution was to stress first person criteria of identity — if my resurrection self thinks he is me then he is me. But this claim is vulnerable to the thought that the *new-heaven-and-earth-Me* could be deluded.

One might object, in a Cartesian vein, and argue that one thing I surely cannot be wrong about is that identifying myself as myself seems, in the jargon, to be "immune to error through misidentification".[14] But there are significant constraints on the referential implications of the token reflexive use of "I" on a particular occasion such that 'I' cannot be taken to indicate anything other than that I am aware of myself as the present subject of certain cognitions. What is in question, however, is whether I, as present subject of certain cognitions, am also the I who existed at another time (e.g. on earth

---

[11] Which, for Aquinas, is the only basis on which resurrection life is available.
[12] Peter Geach notes this view in *God and the Soul* (1969, 18)
[13] Geach mentions some of these and they are often rehearsed in the literature. They predominantly concern the many body-involving characteristics of the soul (such as perception, pain, memory, emotion, mortality and vulnerability, intimate relationships, and so on).
[14] See Shoemaker (1984, 10ff); Williams (1973); Nagel (1979) and others.

before my death) or whether it merely seems to me that I am (I think/it seems to me that G's memories are mine, I think?... G's relationships are mine, etc.). The truth of the claim is normally taken to require some actual (and natural) basis apart from my conviction that it is so (perhaps in terms of causal relations between current cognitions and past experiences or whatever) but, in the case of resurrection, such natural continuity has been disrupted by death so the subjective intuition has no objective correlative.[15] A naturalistic reading of the present view is that continuity of identity reflects the natural conditions for the possibility of cognitive and narrative unity and the embeddedness in a nexus of relationships that create forensic identity.[16]

The sceptical worry in the face of a first person intuition that one is the same being as one's living (pre-mortem) counterpart is both intensified and defused by the work of Lacan.

Lacan argues that the self is a construct on the basis of the reflection or image of self derived from the reactions, responses, and discourse of others so that, "the ego is always and as such a meconnaissance" (Lear, 2003, 140). We could read this in two ways.

(i) If the self is a "fiction" then concern about one's own persistence or survival is a concern about a fiction and should be exploded as such (as in a Buddhist ontology); there are no actual selves only the images of selves that are part of the world of illusion. That concession defuses the worry about life after death because the self, as a creation of a currently situated historical subjectivity coeval with and dependent on worldly discourse, is without any robust existence at all.

(ii) On the other hand the worry is defused because if the self that I experience as myself here and now is "always and as such" a construct of the type envisaged, then that is "as good as it gets" and the relational and other experiences that seem to transcend one's present life are a kind of non-mortal life.

But these thoughts do not speak to the life-after-death believer who wants something more intuitively substantial to believe in.

---

[15] Evans is perhaps the most careful about this and links his assertions about the self of self-reference to the cognitive equipment and skills that allow us to keep track of ourselves as objects in a domain of objects (1982, 243).

[16] The basis of moral accountability, including praise and blame, responsibility for certain things, other-involving commitments and promises etc. Aquinas can, of course, help himself to the objective correlative of one's being in God by grace through faith.

3. The straight response to *the replica objection* aims to provide some defining or constitutive attribute of the individual that reassures us that we are talking about the same actual person in the after-life. A promising candidate is the Aristotelian idea of *the form* giving an individual his or her essential identity as the thing he or she is (Polkinghorne, 2002).

We have already struck this view and noted that the human form is a principle of organisation of the living body and psyche as a longitudinally extended pattern and the indwelling principle of a changing aggregation of matter over time. In the post-Lacanian spirit, we ought to do some post-structuralist work locating this view in the Aristotelian and metaphysical context of Locke's discussion and in the light of the many discourses — biological, personal, moral, and theological — that articulate our understanding of human identity. The human form exhibits characteristic features and realises norms of synchronic and diachronic integrity applicable to critters of our kind. One aspect of this form is a characteristic mental life that takes on coherence and unity over time and under the influence of discourse with others. But notice the implicit reliance (as pointed out by Reid and Butler) on the fact that my memories (of being the person to whom this that or the other happened at some point in my past) are genuinely mine. But this cannot simply be assumed if autobiographical memory, as we have seen, is itself problematic. In fact, the replica objection also applies to the tele-transportation thought experiment that has many features in common with the idea of death and resurrection.[17] In the tele-transporter I am vapourized, my (ex-)molecules dispersed and then I am recreated at my destination out of matching raw materials. But, Schechtman notes, "to many, teletransportation is not transportation but execution and replacement by a replica" (1996, 22). Which is the right view of the two cases? Am I recreated in both by a process that preserves my identity or am I, in fact, destroyed and a deluded replica — who thinks he is me — created? Our intuitions are divided but the present view is somewhat more helpful, and in an instructive way.

I have noted the many ways in which I am kept true to myself by sustaining relationships with those around me as a key aspect of my situated being as an embodied subjectivity and therefore of my individuality and coherence. Depending on the nature of the people and animals concerned, I have diverse relationships with them that are

---

[17] This has been popularised by Parfit (1986, esp ch 5).

more or less central to the self I take myself to be. The changing complex of relationships has a pattern over time and may or may not outlast my death, depending on the extent to which a lasting link is picked up by the living. But we should not slip too easily into a view of the after-life based on my "just living on in other people's memories". The ideas and memories of others are, after all, just aspects of their psyche and do not constitute a living being.

But there is another for whom to think of something can be to confer being on that thing. Polkinghorne has suggested that the form of a human being is a unique pattern or configuration of matter that is created and sustained by God and constitutes the essential life of me as me. He therefore echoes Aquinas and supplements Locke's Aristotelianism by invoking the sustaining work of God holding a human being's form in existence through death and into the afterlife. We can reconstruct the argument as follows.

*The argument*

1. Identity is determined by realised form and not constituent matter.
2. The identity of an intentional object is not given by physical likeness.
3. A human soul has the form of a contingent extended historical existent.
   3a. A human soul essentially has a developmental history.
4. God has created me and sustains me and God does not have false beliefs.
5. God both discerns and determines the identity of any object he thinks of.
6. The identity of a resurrected being is known and guaranteed by God.

The human soul as the form of a human being encompasses the internal dynamic (that from which movements and processes arise), the purpose (that for the sake of which it exists), and the pattern (the formal configuration) of the human body. The human form, as for that of any living thing, changes over time while being part of one unfolding reality (implied by the narrative shape to human life). Polkinghorne argues that the form of an individual is held in existence through death (dissolution into dust) so that as the recreated individual I have my own genuine memories and correctly think of myself as me. But is that believable or just rationally persuasive?

Notice that this view contextualizes human identity in two ways:

(i) A human life develops from conception as a result of a number of factors shaping the life as the individual gradually comes into being.[18]

(ii) A human individual is a product of his or her earthly span (as a being-in-the-world-with-others).

Ultimately this complex of influences produces a characteristic life and personality that is historically distinct and metaphysically unique. But does that survive death?

Polkinghorne argues that it does. On his view, the human being comes into existence "as my character forms and I acquire new insights and memories" so there is "an unchanging component in the information carried by the soul, constituting the personal signature that guarantees continuity of identity" (Polkinghorne, 2004, 59). Although this embodied pattern dissolves at death, a quasi-Cartesian move (invoking the grace of God in re-creating a resurrection me)[19] allows him to set aside the replica objection. Thus a credo in which one is divinely held in existence can have a conception of life after death, in that the holding guarantees continuity; but the picture does not bear too much scrutiny. One could say this relationship is that of a God with a thought in the mind of God — perhaps with a moment of delusion or self-forgetfulness that has become possessed by the delusion that it is separate from the God in whose mind it subsists. Faced with the replica objection, that belief may seem inadequate unless one's experience of being held is quite compelling.

The form view secures the conclusion that a human being is an individual with a certain place in the human world, who is then somebody in the mind of God, a being foreseen but not predetermined.[20] But the replica objection retains its intuitive force if all I am is "an information bearing pattern in the mind or memory of God" that evokes images of blueprints (not actual beings) with an interactive life among their fellows (Polkinghorne, 2004).

---

[18] As I have argued in Chapters 2 & 3 above and is explained in Copland & Gillett (2003).

[19] A move that closely follows Aquinas.

[20] The problem of my foreseen but not predetermined nature (which is necessary to ground our sense of justice and moral desert) is another thorny issue for billiard ball (object-space-time-causality) metaphysics; but it is not the central topic of the present discussion, so I will leave it for now even though the post- Nietzschean life skills or will-to-power view does provide a fairly good idea of how that might work.

The metaphysics of form and matter, a legacy of traditional metaphysics, is therefore unsatisfying because, despite its intellectual elegance, a fundamental problem dogs its account of life after death. *The replica objection* unsettles any *attribute-and-instance* conception of a human being because it resonates or draws on thoughts in which a pattern or attribute is "stamped on", "realised in", or "instanced by" an actual existent occupying a location in space and time. On this view, the recreated being who seems to be me (even to himself) is no more than a reproduction taking my place, with memories and attributes ensuring that he and my resurrected friends and associates mistake him for me. But if a human self is of this type then the best that can be done is that a new (deluded) instance of a once-realised attribute "me-ness" is found in a new heaven and a new earth.

Thus the major objection is untouched:

Anti R3: This new individual is at best a copy of the person who died.

"But," one might say, "that is because we have not fully absorbed the form account, on which I am a pattern and the matter making me up is progressively or successively absorbed into the one continuing identity. Besides that, God thinks the new me (call that individual Me$_R$) is me and if God is omniscient then that belief cannot be wrong, *ergo* Me$_R$ is me. In fact, any of my acquaintances who mistakenly identify me with my body might first see me as I really am in a new heaven and a new earth and might, as they recognise me, realise that they have not ever really known me before."

The omniscience of God does entail (in a clever-sticks way) that Me$_R$ is me and the note about my acquaintances may carry valuable spiritual lessons, but one is left with a nagging feeling that our thinking and knowledge in general (insofar as it reflects how we feel things are "in our waters", so to speak) demands an identity that is actual, relational, able to love and be loved, that embeds true being-with-others, rather than merely notional (even if the notions are in the mind of God).

## Escaping mechanistic metaphysics

Kant would not be surprised at the impasse we find ourselves in and nor would the phenomenologists, existentialists, structuralists and post-structuralists who follow him. They would decry the attempt to assimilate all our thinking to the structures and modes of understanding adapted to *res extensa*, a world of "middle sized dry goods". Kant warns of the temptation (to which we often succumb) to extend our mechanistic metaphysics beyond nature and into the realm of spiritual or ontological thought.[21]

In such an impasse, a post-structuralist (like Lacan) turns to the texts, looking not for points of logical agreement securing the disputed view as orthodox within a metaphysical order of things, but for ways of "fleshing out"(the metaphor is telling) the story so that it satisfies us "in our waters". When we do so we find material that evades analyses of the type valorised by contemporary metaphysics (and a systematic theology in thrall to it). We get something for the mind to grasp hold of, stories and pictures that show us something that cannot be said without distorting our thinking about things of eternal significance so that they fit the language of natural science.

Plato probably deserves to be the first thinker called to this conversation, in that in the *Phaedo* he argues that at death the soul is separated from the body, released from slavery to the distractions of the senses and appetites, and can properly engage with the domain of pure thought. Plato's arguments based on the doctrine that what things truly are is actually revealed by their form (as apprehended by the mind) do not help us, but his insight that the soul is inspir(it)ed by Truth can serve as a useful clue in an inquiry into the human spirit. Aristotle follows that clue while noting that a human being is a rational, social animal (*Nicomachean Ethics*, 1.7) and concludes that philosophy or the pursuit of truth in its most wide ranging and pure form — the life of exercising and cultivating reason — is the key to the well-being of the human soul (ibid. X.8). Aquinas takes us further. He defends the resurrection promise of Christianity and, accepting that the essence of the human form is the life of reason,[22] considers mortality to be an accident and therefore inessential to human identity. He argues that mortality is defeated in the redeeming work of Christ so that the identity of the redeemed one is numerically preserved in resurrection (or life after death).[23] Aquinas therefore affirms that divine grace and power can supply what nature cannot and restore the corrupted to integrity. Here the Aristotelian idea of form as a particularised animating and informing principle that gives an individual the distinctive life that that it has — not merely a type of life — is a key notion. Therefore perhaps Polkinghorne as

---

[21] In his purple passage at the outset of the discussion of phenomena and noumena (*Pure Reason*, B294-5)

[22] Which for Aristotle is clearly an activity carried on with enthusiasm and joy.

[23] Even though it cannot be so naturally, as incorruptibility is over and above its natural principles.

Thomist has more to say than the replica objection allows in that it is through an actual relationship between a creature and the divine intellect (seen in redemptive terms) that continuity is achieved. But this view can only be of comfort to the orthodox Christian believer. Life after death as a general possibility still suffers from the the replica objection (+/- delusion of identity) as well as a further problem of the mode of existence of a pure *res cogitans*.[24]

What is essential to the existence of the thinking subject, if to exist thinking is the essence of a rational social being? And can an existence of that type survive death? The orthodox have the reassurance that Aquinas gives about existence after death—through the grace and power of a redeemer God. But that is not a metaphysical claim. Such claims about resurrection life are often coy. St Paul, for instance, is too wise to be drawn on the problem of the mode of survival and, apart from celebrating the new heaven and new earth and lauding our resurrection bodies, he only hints at the relation between present earthly life and resurrection life: "we shall not all sleep but we shall be changed"(I Cor 15.51); "awake sleeper, rise from the dead, and Christ will shine in you"(Eph 5.14); "you have died and your life is hidden with Christ in God"(Col 3.3). Other writers are similarly guarded. "In the resurrection they neither marry nor are given in marriage but are like angels in heaven. ... God is not the God of the dead but of the living"(Matt 22.31); "I saw underneath the altar the souls of those who had been slain because of the word of God ... and they cried out with a loud voice, saying 'How long ...'"(Rev 6.9-10). In each case we are told that the dead are real existents in a state of not-quite-presence held close to God but alive in some sense. They are not patterns on God's "DVD disc" or the divine "hard drive" but people who witness what is happening, who cry out, and who are morally concerned.

St Paul also remarks "we shall also be in the likeness of his resurrection", an intriguing image because of the presence (but not mundane fleshliness) of Christ in the resurrection accounts. The resurrected Christ was among them but not subject to their limitations, a state hinted at in the phrase, "It is sown a perishable (corruptible) body, it is raised an imperishable body"(I Cor 15.42). Christ stood beside and talked to a woman who loved him, walked with others on the Emmaus Road, and became manifest to them when he chose to

---

[24] The problem was noted by Heidegger in his critique of Descartes' neglect of the *sum* of *cogito ergo sum* (*Being & Time*, H 46), but was also the subject of Kant's paralogisms.

be even though "their hearts burned within them as he spoke to them" (Luke 24.13-35). He appeared among them as a bodily presence (*avec* wounds) in a locked room. Believers are told they have died in him and will be like him such that resurrection life is awakening and is as continuous with mortal life as the waking self is with the self who was awake the day before who slept through the night.

There are other stories such as the summoning of the spirit of Samuel by the witch of Endor at Saul's behest (I Samuel 28). In each case the dead are represented as being in a deferred present but capable, in some form, of coming among us.

These stories and images do not yield a metaphysics of space- time, causality, and conditions of survival in the terms suited to understanding the natural world but they provide narrative attachment, a structure of meaning, in which the dead are real, and can be released from whatever exclusion applies to them as a consequence of the fact that their bodies have been "returned to dust" or "corrupted".

None of these images or narratives supports the replica view and each engages us with a transcendent reality outstripping mortality as part of the world of the Creator of the universe, persistent although in a quite different way from the way that a mortal is engaged with the world. This way of being and what it means, beyond indicating a spiritual reality in which we are included as thinking subjects or inhabitants of the world of thought, cannot readily be articulated. The images of being held, relatedness and within-ness connect to thoughts of a cleft in the living rock, of never being lost, and the everlasting arms which enclose the individual that one is in life on earth and do not let one be torn away by death.[25]

The imagery of the resurrection body also includes themes of light, glory, and spirituality, so that the heavenly is quite unlike the earthly. This is a Platonic view focusing on human subjects as essentially beings of reason. But even this claim poses problems for the form view, in that the particular form shown by a wooden chair, for instance, cannot be the same particular form shown by a bronze chair no matter how similar they are. The form is not, in that, sense totally independent of the package of matter of which it is made. Thus formal identity seen qualitatively cannot be what underpins resurrection life and the hacceity (or bare numerical identity) of

---

[25] Notice the theistic tone and personal reality of these images which are quite removed from the exalted tone of the pure spirit or Platonic form and its world of sun and light.

being a certain individual is indispensable if we wish to derive a workable (even though inadequate) conception of life after death.

Perhaps here we find the same elusive kind of truth that is found when we try to intellectualise or conceptualise love. Why do I love my lover? Do I love him or her because of his or her looks, because of his name, because of anything about him or her, any quality? Would someone else whom I could not tell apart from him or her do? No, Merleau Ponty has the rights of it when he remarks:

> We weigh the hardihood of the love which promises beyond what it knows, which claims to be eternal when a sickness, perhaps an accident will destroy it ... but it is true, at the moment of this promise that love extends beyond qualities, beyond the body, beyond time, even though we could not love without qualities, bodies, and time (1964, 27).

No matter how imaginative one is, the fact of love which is so basic to our social and personal world is not a matter of any subsidiary, contributing other facts which add up to love (or not according to my ways of reckoning what goes on in the world). I love my lover as a numerical individual with a name and identity. That love transcends qualities or any complex of features that constitute the person that I love and if some of them are changed, I only want to be assured that the individual I am engaged with is still the person I love.[26] No substitute will do even though the needs that my lover fulfils might be fulfilled, or even fulfilled better, by some other.

This particularity, unanalysable as it is, is a recurring theme in our dealings with people and their relationships. The relationship between lover and beloved is all about identity with all the contingency that that implies. If spiritual experience of God is articulated in terms of relationship then it embodies a similar irreducibility to the lover-beloved dyad and is distanced from a metaphysics of objects and their material relationships because the individuality of the object merely distracts us from the abstract general or mechanical truths governing the relevant area of our thought. It is no wonder that such a metaphysics cannot comprehend a life that transcends death but only deals with images and likenesses.

### A different thread: religion and the brain

I have argued that in trying to understand the spiritual aspect of human identity we should not accept the terms offered by standard

---

[26] As we saw in the discussion of cyborgs, a fact that makes certain radical changes of character after brain injury so distressing for those concerned.

metaphysics (suited to material relations between "middle sized dry goods") because they deny the centrality of language that has traditionally been taken to speak to us (at least analogically) about the relationship between humankind and something greater (which is essentially spiritual and not quasi-physical at all). Kant's quote ("the starry skies above and the moral law within") reminds us that there is an aspect of our being that responds to an apprehension of our place in the order of things and also a moral law that resides within and embraces all humankind. These are traditional loci for beginning the exploration of spirituality so, in the neuroethics of spirituality and human identity we should look to the world of images and symbols that reach beyond nature or biology to disclose truths about human beings. When we do so, we find that much is wrong in contemporary work relating religion to human brain function.

I have mentioned Christof Koch's claim that the metaphysics of ethics and religion, for a scientist, wait on an elucidation of causation and not just correlation:

> Science seeks a causal chain of events that leads from neural activity to subjective percept ... what organisms under what conditions generate subjective feelings, what purpose these serve and how they come about. If such a theory can be formulated ... this is bound to have significant consequences for ethics including a new conception of humans (Koch, 2004, 326).

Writers such as Koch and Ramachandran (see Ramachandran & Blakeslee, 1998) notice the correlations between spirituality (or religious experience) and activity in certain parts of the brain and speculate about the causal links between them, but such questions might miss the mark entirely. When creatures like us have experiences and think about them, the brain is where those are inscribed. But just as a trace or set of traces in the brain says nothing about the reality of an aspersion or insult that has deeply affected one, so it tells us nothing about the kind of truth discerned in the connectedness of all things or my links to my ancestors or the indwelling or haunting of the world by sources of meaning that transcend everyday creaturely realities. Our appreciation of art (and not just as a depiction of valued objects like sexual targets or desirable foods for instance) could be taken to indicate that we recognise genuine aesthetic values. My relatedness to an ancestor who stood for decency towards others and saw human beings as each being unique and of worth neither mitigates nor explains my commitments to those insights even though, at times, they might disturb my pursuit of what seem desirable life goals.

The issue of human spirituality touches our thinking both in ethics and concerning religious belief, whether or not we link an absolute conception of ethics to a context of divine law emanating from our common law-giving father.[27] Such a context, that of an eternal word that embodies truth about human life (no matter which religious tradition it emerges from) and articulates goodness (comprising purpose and worthwhile meaning) in terms of demands conditional only upon the fact that one is a human being, may or may not deserve our respect. Should such demands be heeded? Studying the brain and how it enables us to articulate and interrogate such questions does not help us answer such questions.

MacIntyre makes the disquieting suggestion that our moral discourse draws on "fragments of a conceptual system" that once structured our knowledge of the world and our place in it. So moral thought is part of a context that subtends certain attitudes and grounds a sense of belonging according to which "oughts" and "shoulds" have a place. These words stand as signposts based on ties of family or kinship to every other human being because of ancient progenitors (such as sky father and earth mother) and underpin expectations of one another and dues to each other. There is a sense in which we are all children of the earth and sky (dust and breath), but what significance should this have in our lives and how is it to be applied (or not applied) in our understanding of ourselves? The relation between such thoughts and our moral convictions is not a matter of deduction but of one's mind orienting itself within a framework of meaning. Acknowledging another as a soul grounds certain ways of regarding and addressing him or her and eschewing certain kinds of conduct.

The fragments of meaning that move us (as they moved our ancestors and can move our children) provide a context transcending the mundane, petty, and contingent (or economic, self-oriented) concerns delineating the horizons of life and focuses on "ontological" truths (pertaining to our being). Ethical thought sustainable within an ontology can, as Kant says, inspire, awe, and create reverence in us, thereby providing a basis to articulate, debate, and explore our self conceptions and values. Notice that there is no immediate connection between ontology and goal-directed action; yet if the man or women before me has a place in the order of things that makes him

---

[27] Lacan makes use of the idea of the name of the father.

or her unique, then paying him or her for work performed or suggesting a sexual relation with him or her is framed in a certain kind of way that transcends my own views.

Such ontological ground for our lives enlightens and enriches them in that it brings out features otherwise overlooked. It would be wrong to use such possibilities to sneak a "master narrative" into the discussion that enshrines a certain order of things, but a conception of spirituality in terms of our historical situation in a certain human group (richly criss-crossed by kinship relations that function as our roots and supports in a very obvious sense) and with images and icons (conveying and embedding mythologies and cosmologies) of special relevance to that group gives one plenty to work with. In such a context one's subjectivity is developed so that one's connections to others are formed both in an articulate (meaningful, psychic, or ideational) sense and in a more responsive or relational sense (as some-body among others who tend and care for each other). Appreciating those aspects of our being-in-the-world-with-others engages us with rich understandings of the beginning and ending of life and of the names and self-constructions each of us can "wear" (or apply to him or herself). The stories, myths and symbols that human beings in different settings use, to try to help them cope with the crises and encounters that occasion ethical texts, are ways of articulating our being (in terms of structures of significance that go beyond the mechanical or functional). These sources of illumination transcend economic conceptions of life and may disrupt or even overturn the "demands" of the ordinary. If life has meaning, this is where it must be sought, and therefore whether it does or not, an understanding of spirituality in this sense appears in the texts of liberation that are increasingly important in an age of reductive biomedicine and its commercialization. The point is well made in Barry Lopez's *Crow & Weasel* by the character Badger:

> The stories people tell have a way of taking care of them. If stories come to you, care for them. And learn to give them away where they are needed. Sometimes a person needs a story more than food to stay alive. That is why we put these stories in each other's memory. This is how people care for themselves. One day you will be good storytellers. Never forget these obligations (Lopez, 1990).

I have already rehearsed how stories of identity and relatedness can "take care of us" when we contemplate death by telling us that we are held, that we persist, and that there is a significance to our mortal

## Connectedness and the inner self

Two prominent themes in spiritual life are our connectedness with others and the idea of a self that is inner and may, with discipline and diligence, be discerned and developed. If the *hypokeimenon* of human subjectivity is not individualistic, then these facets of spirituality may be deeply (even internally)[28] related. The themes of connectedness and the inner self (or one's authentic identity) appear in different traditions in different ways but the myths and symbols used are very revealing.

Spirit as distinct from both body and mind often shares etymology with the idea of breath or wind moving in and through the individual to create ideals or sources of aspiration and inspiration (thus pneuma, noumenal, noemata, norms). We are inspired by taking into the body that non-material component of the source of one's energy and the basis of one's voice. The air we breathe is the present and immediate sign of life itself such that fasting is a traditional means of communing with (or living only by) the spirit and the chakras are exercises focusing on breath as spirit. The air I breathe out, you breathe in, it is the medium of life uniting us.

Spirit reaches beyond time and space and connects us with our beginnings so that the rhythm we see in our own breathing is echoed everywhere (for instance in the waves and in the cycle of night and day). The earth and all living things emerge from the void and share life. In Maori myth, *Tane* the father of all living things creates the space between earth mother and sky father for life to develop and, like the God of Judaism, Islam and Christianity, is personal and omni-present with those who live: "If you go to the ends of the earth I am there",[29] and (in Maori mythology) the queen of the dead has to create/descend into the realm of the dead in order to escape him. We who live share with each other in a way that death effaces so that Achilles, when he meets Odysseus in the land of the dead remarks that he would rather be a landless field hand, and alive, than be the king of the dead.

---

[28] Internally — through a conceptual connection — they are tied up in each other's meaning.

[29] Compare: "If I take the wings of the morning, and remain in the uttermost parts of the sea; even there also shall thy hand lead me, and thy right hand shall hold me" (Psalm 139.8-9).

In all traditions Spirit adds moral significance or purpose and meaning to human life by providing a context of order and belonging within which the moments of life take on a supra-mundane significance and are connected with the transcendent. For Plato, the spirit or soul contemplates the forms and uses them to reveal the nature of earthly things, themselves only imperfect and corruptible instances of their divine correlates. But a step back into philosophy locates the discussion more readily in traditions of scholarship that inform secular bioethics.

### The philosophical spirit: Kant, Heidegger and Levinas

Kant, as we have seen, pointed out that our representations (or significations) of the world are not the world itself but merely ways of rendering our dynamic being-in-the-world tractable for thought. He also has laid before us the thought that an individual is free to act when he or she enacts a way of being which stands under a conception of the order of things and the moral law. That conception ought to inspire reverence and it reminds one of one's membership in a kingdom of ends where each member has his or her own dignity and is framed by the same context. Therefore our being-there or thrownness into being-in-the-world-with-others (understood by using techniques that history and language give to us through the care of others) can be illuminated through the categories of spirit inherited from some tradition or other. It would be silly to think that what those traditions tell us about our significance can be grasped by relating them to brain events. Kant noticed this when he noted that to try to use causal (scientific) thinking to answer the question "Why is there something rather than nothing?" (a question about ontology or "first cause") is futile.

The idea of a ground of our being, that we are rooted in a reality with an order of its own and that we are entangled in that reality, is common to a number of spiritual traditions. Christians speak of God the creator and sustainer of all life; Buddhists and Hindus of human beings as "moments of God's self forgetfulness" who, like drops of water rising from the surface of the ocean, forming clouds in the heavens, falling as rain on the earth, coalescing into streams, rivers and lakes or frozen into glaciers and icefields, think of themselves in each of these states as having definition and finality. In reality the essence remains unchanged, the same in all its configurations. The origin and centre of life from which all life emanates is, for Maori, found in *Tane* who brings forth from *Papatuanuki*—earth mother—

children of men each with an indwelling and distinctive life or *mauri* as a legacy of their birth.

Emmanuel Levinas follows and extends Heidegger's notion of being-in-the-world-with-others so as to underscore the fact that to engage with another human being allows something radically other to irrupt into one's world with its egocentric order of things, something that is indicated by the human face. The face presents an enigma because our representations of the other do not "capture" that other so that we find ourselves "face to face" with the core of ethics — the fact that the world is a shared world and those sharing it with us have their own ways of representing it that answer to their own standing in being and not our representations of it. That disrupts the egocentric picture and the dominance of one's own psychic economy in constructing the world. For instance, Levinas reminds us from within a Jewish tradition that the face of God is to be encountered in the face of every human being and writes indelibly there the commandment "Thou shalt not murder!" As a result, one is engaged in a series of open-ended encounters which may be transformative in unexpected ways.

But the phenomenology of being-with-others is, necessarily, inarticulate as Derrida shows in exploring Heidegger's claim that one's historicity is inescapable, so that self-understandings must be articulated and are manifest through our utterances, inscriptions, postures, and relationships. Each of us is some-body, in fact, an embodied intersection of multiple texts (derived from icons, myths, images, and stories) that lie at the heart of the culture that has inscribed us and drawn us into its disciplines. But where does this leave the inner, authentic self?

The "inner self" discovered by dispelling the "fog of unknowing"(world of illusion) surrounding us is a recurrent theme in spiritual texts. Christian mysticism and the mantras of self renunciation both try to strip away illusions and reveal the indwelling of the divine in a human being. If we pursue our intertextuality (as beings multiply inscribed by different traditions linking us and our ancestors to powerful symbols and motifs), the self is revealed as a living or inspir(it)ed node of resonance of being-in-the-world, given meaning (and energy) by the narratives that generate it.

The energy arises, *inter alia*, from the significance to be found in mythologies, iconographies and symbolism, that offered us ways of understanding our mortality, singularity, contingency and existence. As we enact them we enact significance by narratively locating our current experience and what we find in it. We are shown our place within an order of things laid out and mapped by generations that have gone before discerning patterns in the world that would not be evident to any one of us in isolation. The theme of an all-encompassing Word, imparting order and life to human beings and securing their place in the world, is widespread — the *logos* of the stoics, the way of Confucius, the paths of life, are all portrayed as written into us and connecting with the human spirit so as to map our life-journeys, record them, and provide guidance or consolation when we are lost.

The unique and eternal value of each being is captured, for instance, by texts referring to the fall of the sparrow, or the death of an ant. Such texts become vital as we try to understand, with a young couple, the death of their hopelessly premature infant. The thought that this scrap of humanity is a being marked out as clearly in the great scheme of things as any "great event", allows the grieving couple to articulate their grief for this huge and awful thing, and cry out from the depths of their spirit in a way that cannot be articulated in a scheme that sees the death of a human being less that three months old as being of almost no consequence in the moral balance of life.

A vision of things deeper than or transcendent of the everyday or material is sometimes needed for us to understand what is happening to us. The sixteen year old girl, dead as a result of cerebral anoxia after aspiration and respiratory arrest in the context of a teenage party is visited by her father who cannot come to terms with the monstrous absurdity of her death. The loss is made even more painful as she lingers in a persistent vegetative state and no-one wants to broach the possibility of withdrawal of nutrition and hydration. A wise woman articulates her state as one of being held back from her journey to the land of the spirits that wait for her. Her tube restrains her among the living where she no longer has a real place. The pain is just as bad, but the loss can be understood as more than a mere cessation of function in a body — her death is engaged with the world of spirit — given depth and meaning along with all the "brief candles" that are human lives. Is the story of spirit the truth? It shows her life as something bringing together, in a unique way, two human lineages, it places her among those who have gone before, it adjusts our thinking to a sense of what makes us alive, something to be valued rather than just preserved. These are truths that need to find articulation but cannot do so in the imagery and language of biomedicine.

The ineffable, the holy, that which the mind cannot encompass by using its tools for limning the ordinary objects that surround us and opening their workings to a technological gaze, captures our attention in a different way. To shrink this into a point of inner contemplation is to take from the holy its all embracing significance in relation to the world around us, its beauty and wonder. To allow our minds to be touched by the spirit that enlivens or gives significance to all things is to re-expand the boundaries of our being so that we re-affirm the uniqueness of each of us and yet also acknowledge the deep affinity we should or can find with each other when we look past the many differences and details that can preoccupy us. To see the spirit of life in the "dosser" whose eyebrow we are stitching after his drunken fall in the street is to transform a chore into a potentially redemptive act, whether it is recognized as such by the patient or not.

These broad brush thoughts about the human spirit and our place in the realm of spirit are given form by stories and motifs that illuminate our clinical work in ways that transform it.

Thus in Norse mythology the Gods so loved Baldur that they sought promises from all things in heaven and earth that they would never harm him. So they played a game in which every one of the Gods would cast missiles or try to wound Baldur knowing that he would be unscathed. But Loki, who was jealous of Baldur, fashioned a dart out of mistletoe, overlooked in the oath taking. He gave it to Baldur's brother Hodur to throw and as the missile struck, Baldur fell down dead.

Nobody blamed Hodur, who had after all only wanted to join in the rejoicing over Baldur's invulnerability. But nevertheless the most beautiful of the Gods was dead and, as it turned out, nothing could bring him back.

We often wonder how the spirit of a young person can cope with the tragedy that follows an accident in which one of their friends has died. But do we have the stories that equip us for such moments or are our spirits are so undeveloped that the stories we need are "only stories" and not woven into the fabric of our being? Each tradition offers us stories where life is at its nadir and all seems bleak but something arises that is unprecedented, transformed and given significance by what has gone before. Christ rises from the dead, Te Rauparaha leaps from the Kumara pit, Gandalf rides again after the

Balrog, and young people survive severe injuries to refashion lives that are sometimes richer and more full of good things than the lives they would otherwise have had. But facile reassurances that "something good will come of it" do not catch the spirit of these stories — they are psychological reductions of the real story.

The visitation appears in many stories of the spirit — the coming among us of glory humble and unrecognized until our eyes are opened. There are many story-tellers who shuffle about making remarks usually construed as meaningless in psycho-geriatric wards. These stories are vanishing before our eyes but they represent a historical treasure that is unrecoverable. In stories of the spirit we are told to look closely so as not to miss something of great value which otherwise we would pass by (the pearl of great price, the Sam Gamgee). Stories of the spirit transcend historically situated consciousness and connect us with the wit and wisdom of other ages and their human quests to find meaning, to fashion lives worth living and to find the grace to face death with dignity. Stories of the spirit disclose forgiveness where, by rights, we have only the language of contract, restitution, dues, harms, and entitlements, so that an aspect of our being together is rendered invisible and unthinkable. For that reason among others, stories of the spirit are liberating.

## Freedom and contesting mores

Spirituality lifts our eyes from the possibilities defined by the everyday and economic. The divine wind recalls the breath that gives us life and the cleansing water that allows healing and refreshment in the arid wastes of suffering is a figure with meaning that goes beyond the material. In the most unlikely places we find loving and transformative touches, that are the things of the spirit in that they are ways of not only understanding but also beatifying what we do, however bloody, messy and unromantic it is. We are beset by directives and discourses that reduce, demean, and obscure our humanity, that are not noble, uplifting, inspiring, and fulfilling. We can render life in operational (or narrowly functional) terms and make it tolerable through escapism and pleasure but there is another way. We live and love in a world where real tragedies happen, real joy is found, and real connections are forged through time and across barriers of culture and position. In those things we discover the resonance in ourselves of inscriptions, utterances, and works that deepen our understanding.

### Care of the soul as spirit work and the crafting of flesh

Foucault's *cura sui* recalls that the Greeks regarded philosophy as therapy for maladies of the soul. Wittgenstein strikes the same chord, claiming that ethics is absolute, disinterested and concerned with "the health of the soul"(1994, 93–4). He also refers to ethics as "supernatural"(beyond the scientific descriptions that deliver a certain kind of knowledge). Foucault's care of the self comprises: *a critical function*, the dynamic of *a struggle, a therapeutic function*, and *a disciplinary function*, aspects of fitting oneself to fulfil the good inherent in one's own being.

A *critical function* reminds us that ethical thought requires appraisal and reflection upon oneself and what one has (literally) become so that the inscriptions of culture can be evaluated.

The *dynamic of a struggle* is informed by ontology in that one's standing in relation to others and one's place of belonging may be in conflict with selfish needs and interests and may need to be moderated by mutual recognition and a sense of one's membership in a kingdom of ends. This is not the traditional struggle of the flesh against the spirit, but rather a struggle between ways of engaging with the world that allow desire (with its will o' the wisp nature) to eclipse the presence, vulnerability and needs of others, and ways of being that open the soul to the other so that the effects of my actions on the other becomes an intrinsic part of my motivations.

A *therapeutic function* is exercised in the company of another who models, reflects, reacts and engages with one, so as to help articulate and contextualise one's own feelings through a conversation showing integrity in its moral, personal and relational characteristics (these are more or less of a piece).

A *set of disciplinary functions* developes one's ability to enact criticism and the therapeutic function. Foucault follows the Greeks in likening these to the routines and regimen of an athlete preparing him or herself for the games. The disciplines are diverse: some general such as listening and writing; others quite specific such as the meditation on future ills, practices of abstinence and privation, the control of thought, and the meditation on death. Heidegger famously regards the last as essential to authentic life in the face of our own mortality, and a reminder to use our moments well. This ethical work *connects oneself to the truth* and therefore connects me beyond my self (narrowly conceived).

Wittgenstein remarks that such truth is not subjective but part of a meaningful discourse that reveals aspects of the world not investigable by the scientific method (*Culture & Value*, 3e): "the good is also divine, the good is outside the space of facts" — an awareness lacking in those who make a common neuro-ethical mistake.

## A neuroethical mistake

It should now be evident why it would be mistaken to identify spiritual or ethical aspects of our being with any complex of neurological functions arising from or caused by structures associated with the temporal and limbic systems. The ethical and spiritual aspects of my identity make me aware of, and give a certain significance to, my actual connectedness to those who predate me in my culture and lineage and to the order of things considered as a whole. These are not fictions or mere experiences. And, given that thinking about them closely involves my emotions — feelings of awe and wonder, relationships with others and the things around me, and a sense of who I am in myself as a named and embodied being — they involve the areas of the brain integrating memory, the influences of socialization, and my inner bodily states. The temporal and limbic lobes are the areas that provide the informational substrate for this material, so that abnormal activity in them would evoke the complex thoughts and images that one might find emerging from our history of experience in which these aspects of our being-in-the-world-with-others are shaped.

Nevertheless the icons, symbols, images and meanings active in this area of our symbolic and shared being do have a significance that different individuals relate to in their own way (and therefore they have an objective being in the world independent of the individual subject who thinks about them). They entangle us with such widely connected historico-cultural realities that they move us (in our bowels, so to speak) in ways about which neurobiology can tell us only certain things. It can tell us the means the nervous system uses to process and record things with the relevant associations, and may even prompt us to look at areas of our function we would not otherwise have realised as being so closely involved (although good phenomenology will usually give that away), but it does not tell us about the significances animating our dealings with them. That is not a question for neuroscience but for ethics and metaphysics, that deal with the more things in heaven and earth than are dreamed of in neurophilosophy.

The tendency of many scientists is to a reductive view, according to which the neural mechanisms underlying our cognitive abilities are identified with features of what we come to know about: Ramachandran and Blakeslee, for instance, write:

> But does this syndrome imply that our brains contain some sort of circuitry that is actually specialized for religious experience? Is there a "God module" in our heads? And if such a circuit exists, where did it come from? Could it be a product of natural selection, a human trait as natural in the biological sense as language or stereoscopic vision? Or is there a deeper mystery at play, as a philosopher, epistemologist or theologian might argue? (Ramachandran & Blakeslee, 1998, 175)

This short remark implies that either the neural mechanisms are a product of evolution or that they indicate a deeper mystery but why not both? It is possible that everything about us is evolved, but also that our cognitive systems have evolved to track the truth and that therefore things that they tell us about are, in some sense or another, true of our being-in-the-world. If that were so, then the spiritual aspects of our identity, such as the use of stories to make sense of our lives and value them, might be as much a part of ourselves as our ability to exploit natural resources so as to adapt to widely diverse ecological contexts. Malcolm Jeeves makes the point as follows.

> Since each of us is a complex system, simultaneously part of a larger social system and composed of smaller systems which in turn are composed of ever smaller subsystems, any aspect of human behaviour and cognition chosen for investigation may be analyzed at different levels. Each level entails its own questions and appropriate methods for answering them. While the account given at each level may be complete within itself that does not mean that by itself it constitutes a full account of the phenomenon under investigation. Each level complements the others (Jeeves, 1997, 237).

The current work implies that neuroethics may be part of ethics as first philosophy (as Levinas would have it) if it retains its recognition of whole human beings as beings from whose discourses all philosophical inquiry springs (Levinas, 1996, 1–10).

It remains to spell out the implications of these and the preceding thoughts for our policies and sketch a guiding framework of socio-political life that acknowledges our standing beneath "the starry skies above and the moral law within" following the decade of the brain.

Chapter 10

# The Expulsion of Humanity

## The Reductive Society and its Friends

> The first sign that an animal has become human is that his behaviour is no longer directed to his momentary comfort but rather to his enduring comfort, that is, when man becomes useful, expedient: then for the first time the free rule of reason breaks forth.
>
> (Nietzsche, *Human All Too Human*)

Are we part of a reductive society and, if so, how so? Aristotle claims that the essence of a human being is to be a rational and social animal, through intellect able to participate in a world of truth not driven solely by physical needs. A reductive view of human beings takes properties considered to be quintessentially human (such as criticism, taste or affection) and equates them with something less than human — the outworking of our animal nature through acquired tricks designed to serve our animal needs and without any other significance. A reductive society, therefore, ignores the fact that a human desire is "montage in a surrealist collage" (to use Lacan's phrase — 1979, 169) structured not only by bodily or physiological economy and its elements but also by myth, symbol, and the icons of hope or creativity that inspire us. The colours and contours of the montage are fascinating and elusive — not quite real and yet more than real in their psychic power and they are produced according to a conception of what it is that one wants (itself a production of self and situation in the way one might expect from the structure of the present account). Taylor has linked the tensions and conflicts in contemporary society to what he calls "the malaise of modernity", where I have used the ideological characterisation of the reductive

## The Expulsion of Humanity                                    223

society, but both approaches grapple with the same problem — an expulsion of the human and uniquely valuable in favour of unreal ways of understanding ourselves designed to order our sociopolitical relations. I will examine the case of Alzheimer's Disease to explore the more holistic and enigmatic[1] elements of human identity and set up a discussion of what a reductive society denies to those living within it.

### You always were a bastard: a case study

> You always were a bastard. Bastard is as bastard does, not as he says. You screwed me and you screwed up my life. Bugger! bugger! Bugger! You would bugger anyone if it gave you what you want.

Imagine these remarks coming from a refined looking older woman, directed at her husband, in the middle of a medical interview about her problems with memory and cognition. This brief disturbing episode erupts but is soon over and the interview carries on. What, we might ask, does it mean? Does it indicate "bottled-up" feelings previously suppressed but finally released or is it an anomaly, an expression of stress produced by a failing brain in a difficult situation?

Alzheimer's disease (AD), often associated with paranoia, contrariness, and waywardness of thought, is frequently the context for events of this kind: out-of-character attacks on those closest to the patient who then become deeply distressed by what the patient has said. Their distress often prompts them to ask whether their relative has harboured these thoughts and attitudes but, for various reasons, inhibited them so that their relationship has been founded on lies. But do the aggressive remarks of a person with dementia express his or her real feelings or are they merely an effect of a disease throwing up random thoughts and comments not authentically reflecting the person who utters them?

The gradual and subtle alteration in the self, characteristic of AD, and the allowances made by others compound the problem.

> Things began to happen that I just couldn't understand. There were times I addressed friends by the wrong name. Comprehending conversations seemed quite impossible. My attention span became quite short. Notes were needed to remind me of things to be done and how to do them. I would slur my speech,

---

[1]   The term comes from Levinas' discussion of enigma and phenomena (1996).

use inappropriate words, or simply eliminate one from a sentence. This caused me not only frustration but embarrassment. Then came the times I honestly could not remember how to plan a meal or shop for groceries (Post, 2000, 83).

This passage graphically illustrates the disabling of cognition that undermines the subject's grip on her lived story the subjective "basis for talk and action, a point of departure for telling stories about experience, and for rendering those stories intelligible" (Gubrium, 2000). I will argue that understanding the narrative skills involved in being who I am is, in fact, the key to the question of pathology and authenticity.

### *In vino veritas* and the civilized veneer

Two beliefs inform our understanding of interpersonal discourse: first, *in vino veritas* — the idea that disinhibition allows the expression of aspects of oneself that one would normally keep from others and, second, the idea of self as a presented or constructed persona. The *civilized veneer* stereotype combines the two with the "presentation self" as a kind of mask concealing, to some extent, who one really is.[2]

The civilized veneer is, in part, a romantic image arising in an era when colonial expansion and the valorization of empire (evident in fictional works such as *Lord of the Flies* and *Heart of Darkness*) pictured the forces of morality and decency pitted against the activity of savages and barbarians. The wildness, innocence, vigour, and violence "found" in "savages" could be likened to a "Mr Hyde" (or Medea) in each of us and the thought that primitive instincts and real feelings lie beneath the polite and properly socialized psyche covering the inner self (as clothes cover the body) suggests that disinhibition reveals the reality within.

The current account paints a more complex and importantly different picture and can usefully draw on Jaspers' distinction between causal and meaningful connections in life history (Jaspers, 1913 [1974]). Jaspers argues that causal effects on the subject are not integrated in a meaningful (narratively structured) way to the life events of a person and in mental disorder can be manifest as pathology because they influence cognition perhaps by acting at a neuronal level (e.g. toxic delirium, habituation) or perhaps at a macro-level (e.g. stroke or a brain tumour). The brain functions most vulnerable

---

[2] Like many popular ideas this one is the offspring of a certain kind of noble savage romanticism and a degenerate kind of Freudianism. I have discussed it in Gillett (1999a).

## The Expulsion of Humanity

to such influences are those implicated in higher order cognitive activities such as fine tuning of the motor system to, say, a moving target or of cognition to subtle social constraints.[3] Thus both complex cerebellar activity and complex psycho-social skills can be affected as is seen in the motor incoordination and social ineptitude evident in toxic states (for instance in a pub on a Saturday night).

*In vino veritas* succinctly captures the idea that the skills needed for self control, can be disabled by intoxication to reveal authentic feelings striving for expression in all of us. But perhaps the link between fine motor skills and cognitive-social skills should more prominently inform our model of the mind in a way that helps us understand character and identity. In the nervous system, ontogenetic (and perhaps evolutionary) processes of inclusive transformation allow integrated brain processes to take up, modify, and interact with more primitive brain functions. In that way the more primitive activity becomes engaged with highly adaptive information-gathering and strategy-forming processes to produce the complex behaviour of a developed (not primordial) ego. The interconnections and moderations of function thereby possible are not always beneficial, for instance a basic function such as the ingestion of nourishment or the elimination of wastes can become the focus of complex attitudes leading to ill health.[4]

A significant aspect of Freud's legacy is the idea that there are layers of the psyche containing material that may or may not appear in consciousness. This view, or a closely related conception of the contents of the mind, is widespread in the post-Freudian era and plays a pivotal role in the belief that a person with dementia may be voicing thoughts that they have long harboured but not previously expressed.

Perhaps we ought not think of the mind as a container with a variety of contents some of which are conscious and some not,[5] but the model persists because the idea that the real self may be hidden beneath one's public face concurs with many common ideas of authenticity and sincerity. Searle's critique of the post-Freudian claims that non-conscious mental states are just like conscious states despite being "inaccessible to consciousness" does not touch eco-

---

[3] The high cognitive demands of social intelligence are widely recognised.
[4] Thus we have anorexia and other self-damaging psychopathologies.
[5] We could call this a Cartesian realist view of the unconscious except that Descartes was committed to the unity of the mind rather than its division into strata or other functional sub-parts.

nomic and moral theories of human nature and reductive accounts of the psyche (Searle, 1992, 152). Saul, Nietzsche, and Levinas all attack the implicit subversion of human dignity and nobility, and Lacan and Foucault the naivety of the concept of intentionality and human desire involved in such accounts. But if this is not how the mind should be construed, then what is the alternative?

If we pursue the claim that consciousness comprises a many-faceted complex of skills of human intentionality (the use of concepts to characterize and respond intelligently to conditions presented to the subject), then the significance of any event or situation to a subject is articulated in terms of the features that human beings have learned to conceptualize. A moment of experience is invested with significance by the subject and things that merely evoke a reaction, absent clear definition of the way that one thinks of that thing, are therefore indistinct (for instance, did I jump because I saw a shape suddenly appear or because I realized that my nemesis had just arrived?).

In a more lyrical vein, the narrative trajectory of life forms (and informs) a stream of significant events comprising an autobiography that is both culturally and historically situated. The narrative is unique to, and also (to some extent) crafted (or at least edited) by its author.[6] It is from within that narrative that I react to others and that my reactions and conversation with them become significant for me.

## Life as narrative

I have argued that a person is the cumulative result of a life story, though some of the episodes and feelings inscribed in the subject are neither fully comprehensible nor comfortably integrated with other of the subject's life events.[7] One's life story may therefore have significant aspects that are not evident, even to oneself (without a very perceptive and reflective analysis) but nevertheless we should "recognize the narrative coherence, however obscured, of the patient's life" (Frank, 1996, 155).

So how does this help us with the eruptions of irrationality in AD? I have argued that one's story results from an actual history of interaction with the world and others that can be thought of in two quite different ways:

(i)   as a causal stream of brain/body/world events;

---

[6]   The present view is also, for instance, in Taylor (1989).
[7]   As is dramatically seen in MPD.

(ii) as a narrative involving and partly composed by the subject.

The first is a physical stream of activity in which the embodied brain does its thing—receiving and sampling the impingement of the world on the organism and initiating actions that are likely to be advantageous. But this stream by itself does not determine the narrative[8] or the story "fitted" to the brain-world stream by the whole person who uses the narrative resources available to her in that task. The second stream results from discursive work (on the brain-world interaction in the light of one's ongoing formation as a person) and the two streams interpenetrate in complex ways.[9]

One's personal history and one's immersion in the world produces a psyche jointly contributed to by the significance attached to things and their brute causal impact on oneself as a (subjective) body. For instance, if a person head-butts me at a football match its effect depends not just on the physical impact but also on the context, the nature of the person concerned, and so on, I could treat it merely as an unpleasant incident or develop a deep aversion to people like him. The world and the mind, we could say, are in a "dance" comprising the significations surrounding me woven together with the events inscribing me with my autobiography.

My autobiography makes me the person I am[10] and my thought life is filtered and censored by the sensibilities and standards of reason and goodness realised in that story. Taylor remarks; "making sense of my present action ... requires a narrative understanding of my life, a sense of what I have become which can only be given in a story" (1989, 41, 48) and it concerns "the issue of my place relative to the good" a negotiation within a socio-cultural context. My autobiographical activity results in an inclusive and ongoing editorial transformation of the episodes in my life central to my auto-biographical work and my development as a person[11] and (disorganized and unstable as it might be) it shapes my identity (as somebody).

Being somebody just is an ongoing process of being inscribed in this way (by the world and the significations surrounding me) and living out the psychic effects of that cumulative inscription under the shaping influence of (possibly haphazard) self-creation. The self

---

[8] As I have argued on the basis of work by Dennett and others.
[9] I have discussed this in Gillett (2000).
[10] As in Gillett (1997).
[11] This became evident in Schechtman's study of autobiographical memory (discussed in Chapter 5 above).

results neither from outside impingements (plus alien or causal influences from inside) nor from existential creation radically contingent upon the subject's conscious choices; the real story is more subtle and shifting so that contingency, bodily trajectory, and the subject jointly produce a narrative.

## The real me

Who am I, the embodied subject? I am the creature who presents myself to others and my self-presentation reflects many choices that are constrained (but not determined) by my pre-existent nature and historical contingencies. Inevitably I express myself in a myriad ways that betray who I am and do not merely display a veneer even though that genuine self may be a chaotic or somewhat "Topsy"-like reflection of my narrative choices and values.[12] Carson remarks:

> To make sense of ourselves and our world to ourselves and others, we tell tales — tales of truth, tall tales, tales of wisdom and woe — and listen to tales told by others. Stories, with their beginnings, middles, and ends, redeem life from contingency and make it something other than a meaningless succession of events (1997, 233).

Most of us, whether through *phronesis* (Aristotelian "skill in living" or practical wisdom) or (less admirably) existential inertia, adopt, compose, or drift into a life that evinces who we are so as to "live openly and in good faith with ... neighbours"[13] without constant pretence and dissembling, and that counts as a "good enough" identity.

In each of us there is a struggle between what could be broadly construed as good and evil, opposing qualities evident in life lived by human beings-in-the-process-of-becoming-among-others. Some tendencies conduce to living a good-enough life with good-enough relationships and are consonant with *eudaimonia* as a rational and social creature, a responsible member of a kingdom of ends (or moral community). This approach accommodates a wide diversity of meta-ethical positions (from that of Nietzsche to that of Aquinas, or, if you prefer, from that of Mill, at his best, to that of Kant). In general there are ways of living that cut one out of certain kinds of reciprocity and participation with others and the satisfactions that result, and other ways that enhance relationships opening up new satisfac-

---

[12] When asked, "Do you know who made you?" Topsy, a black American child of, presumably, slave parents said, "I 'spect I growed" (*Uncle Tom's Cabin*, Ch. XX)

[13] Discussed by Philippa Foot (1978).

# The Expulsion of Humanity

tions and possibilities for growth. And the good-enough moral life evinces a reflective concern for one's own well-being and the good of one's human group.

In fact there are "bastard" and oppositional moments in each of us but, for the most part, they are overwritten by more humane and reasonable tendencies. Harmony with others and harmony within oneself smooth out the more loutish and self-indulgent tendencies in each of us and result in a mode of living that allows us to appreciate what is worthwhile in the lives of others (even where those others may, in certain ways, be deeply disappointing or even repulsive). One could remark, with Aristotle, that to live in harmony with one's fellows is necessary for living in harmony with oneself (for critters like us).

## The finely crafted self and its decay

The overwriting of loutishness and insensitivity by congenial relationships with others (and the satisfactions that follow) is a complex piece of self-shaping. The finely tuned constructions arising from it are therefore vulnerable to random causes of (neuro-cognitive) destruction such as Alzheimer Disease or head injury. When such evils befall us, the self one has shaped in line with one's values and commitments (and in the face of many temptations and influences inclining us in more base directions) can begin to unravel just as would an intricate tapestry.

I have noted the metaphor of a tapestry in relation to the moral life and it is an image that greatly enhances the current approach to self and personal identity (Murray, 1996). A tapestry is woven from coloured threads that contribute to an emergent pattern. The weaver makes use of traditional cultural designs and combinations of form and colour just as the author and narrator of a lived autobiography uses a certain temperament (or palette of colours) and a treasury of narratives available within their cultural setting to in-form a self. The tapestry is a life, replete with relationships, actions, commitments, myths, reminiscences, and so on and is influenced by one's place of belonging but also by an individual trajectory so that it is unique (and one's own) in a myriad, perhaps non-salient (and even unintentional) ways.

Imagine that the tapestry is attacked by a moth or a process that randomly obliterates, corrupts, and tangles it so as to obscure the pattern. Then the (tapestry) self becomes degraded or ravaged and the pattern may no longer have the rich meanings it once revealed to the sympathetic or empathic viewer.

But the true self is no more the degraded self than the true artwork or tapestry is the complex of damaged threads and fragments of weaving.

> Mrs F. would rather be seen as someone possessing the positive attributes of her past, in the role of a teacher, than as someone who is seen primarily as an AD sufferer and a participant in an adult day care center. The latter places more emphasis on her deficits, which cause her much frustration and sadness (Sabat & Collins, 1999).

So what is a right view of the disturbing and hurtful remarks of some sufferers of Alzheimer Disease? Should their relatives reevaluate past shared moments in the light of these "previously hidden" thoughts or should they understand them as, in some way, a product of the disease? And should we treat the sufferers as human beings who have lost the intact function definitive of human autonomy and dignity and become pathetic shadows of themselves, mere biological organisms who are subhuman and need custodial care or curation? The two styles of museum curation are revealing here: older style of curation preserves the exhibits so that they do not crumble away; the newer style allows the exhibits to speak to those who encounter them and make them as alive as they can be for folk who do not share their history. The shift in styles, one might argue, could usefully be reflected in contemporary institutions for the elderly and "cognitively impaired".

## Word demons, significations and the broken psyche

The "you" being called a bastard *might* indeed have always been a bastard or at least have had certain areas of insensitivity that damaged his wife. But the vice in play here, while reprehensible, is often a sin more venial than mortal; it may, for instance, be particularly prevalent in ambitious and high achieving men and perhaps especially in their treatment of their wives.[14] In the normal course of events it would not, perhaps, justify the degree of hostility shown. Disturbing outbursts from a person with cognitive impairment is, therefore, problematic in various ways. None of us are completely exempt from the tendencies at issue and we often admire in each other the extent to which the relevant dispositions (or any of the

---

[14] As, perhaps, an unthinking reflection of a social discourse.

undesirable traits arising in such soil) get transformed by personal moral development through "self-making" that makes any person the character that he or she becomes.

The trajectory of self-making expresses what one values and (perhaps very inadequately) expresses the person one wants to be. When I lose the capacity to conduct myself in accordance with my values, I might well make remarks or express opinions that have arisen in a vulnerable psyche and that I do not really "own". "You always were a bastard" and similar ejaculations can drop out of the damaged tapestry of the mind or even result from threads or snatches of discourse that I, as editor, would never deploy if I was "in my perfect mind". But I can lose control of the skilled processes that structure my autobiography and, in such a case have to rely on the charity that I would show were I only able to use it to moderate the thoughts that take up residence, in my disintegrating psyche.

What can one do with the woman who attacks "the bastard"? Perhaps she is a person who has suffered much and has borne it with great dignity. If so we can witness her statement and consider it sympathetically in the light of her life and times, see her as somebody whose words are not to be explained away, whose individuality is to be affirmed, and who should be treated in accordance with the values that we have "volunteered" to uphold.[15] But there are wider lessons to be learnt in relation to "the reductive society".

## Learning the lessons: the reductive society and what it lacks

Lacan argues that both identity and desire are constructed within "networks of constitution of the subject" so that they arise neither from the primal or archaic nor from stimulations exterior to the psyche, including the biological "interior" of the body (1979, 177, 162, 166). Human motivation—the drive—is like "a surreal collage" reflecting the "play" in the subject of many discursive influences that may have inscribed him or her and with which he or she is in a dynamic, reflexive, and creative relationship. This feature of human subjectivity problematizes a reductive view (in which human desires are equated with instincts or basic needs collectively expressed as a selfish or self-centred orientation) amenable to capture by interested parties.

John Ralston Saul, describing the role of self-knowledge and the questioning of the human condition associated with the Delphic

---

[15] Philippa Foot regards us as volunteers in a human collective with a common moral cause to uphold (1978).

injunction to "Know thyself", has little doubt that we are part of a reductive society.

> Nowhere in all this questioning ... was the individual seen as a single ambulatory centre of selfishness. That idea of individualism, dominant today, represents a narrow and superficial deformation of the Western idea. A hijacking of the term and — since individualism is a central term — a hijacking of Western civilization (Saul, 1996, 2).

Once one has a picture of the human as a system of cognitively organised self-serving routines, it is possible, through rationally designed structures and institutions, to eclipse the view that we are self-questioning individuals (thereby capable of care of the self) and to idolise individual choice and make "appeals to authenticity that justify ignoring whatever transcends the self ... rejecting our past as irrelevant ... denying the demands of citizenship, or the duties of solidarity, or the needs of the natural environment" (Taylor, 1991, 22).

> "Miracles in the world are many," Sophocles wrote in the fifth century B.C. "There is no greater miracle than man." Suddenly, at the end of the twentieth century, we discover that no, after all, it isn't true. Historical inevitability is a greater miracle than man. As is the dialectic. As is the superiority of various groups according to blood type. As is the genius of an abstract mechanism called the market. As is the leadership of inanimate objects — called technology — which worker bees create and then, inevitably, are led by (Saul, 1996, 54).

This passage, both provocative and rhetorical, rewards philosophical examination because if it is true, we have diminished ourselves in a way that we should be aware of and the genealogy of which we should trace and critique so as to know the truth about ourselves. But a further question remains in the context of the current inquiry. If we are part of a reductive society, to what extent does neuroethics share the same spirit and play a part in that attitude towards human beings?

The role of neuroethics in reducing our image of ourselves is not direct and can hardly be part of the cultural history of rational consumerism and corporatism; but it stands at the culmination of a tradition in which we conceive of subjectivity as a functional mechanism designed to maximise our self-centred needs. This view has arisen in discussing action, freedom, and identity and pictures the subject as causally ruled by economic and interpersonal regularities[16] all designed to harmonise every person's needs and wants to those of others. This, for Saul, is socially coordinated selfishness and it yields, according to Nietzsche, the morality of the "Darwinists",

> with their principle of the smallest possible effort and the greatest possible stupidity ... certainly a different imperative from the Platonic, but for an uncouth industrious race of machinists and bridge builders of the future (*Beyond Good & Evil*, #14, p. 27).
>
> So long as the utility which dominates moral value-judgements is solely that which is useful to the herd, so long as the object is solely the preservation of the community and the immoral is sought precisely and exclusively in that which seems to imperil the existence of the community; so long as that is the case there can be no morality of love of one's neighbour (*Beyond Good & Evil*, #201, p. 104).

It is dangerous to over-romanticize Nietzsche's individualism, anti-conformity, and his admiration of robust and vigorous human excellence to conceal or diminish the fact that he seemed to deride virtuous compassion as an outworking of *ressentiment* and part of the ideological campaign of the weak against the strong so as to produce an inversion of the values that made humankind great. Philippa Foot tellingly remarks that Nietzsche was "in some ways a most humane man" and finds in his thought strands that deserve careful consideration. But she tempers her regard with a caution: "There is no reason to suppose that we really are in the dilemma that he insists on—that we either sacrifice the weak or else deform the strong" (Foot, 1978, 94).

The crucial move towards "the morality of the herd"(in the bad sense) accepts that we are preference-ordering utility consuming systems, numerically individual but otherwise fairly uniform, whose actions should be coordinated by a socio-political mechanism (aided perhaps by culture) that configures us in accordance with approved ends (encoded in the wetware device we each carry in our heads). Once that move is made, the human subject is treated as a socio-biological entity working for its own satisfaction, exactly the theoretical reduction that economic theory trades in and that Taylor finds in the modern malaise—"a point where our major remaining value is choice itself" (Taylor, 1991, 69); it finds a willing ally in the brand of neuroethics under discussion.

---

[16] Notice that it is not only thinking which is ruled here but the environment itself which is constructed as an encompassing artifact from our thoughts about ourselves.

The general conception (as in the discussion of action explanation) begins with the Millean[17] picture of mind as machine (a Victorian idea that depicts the human subject in impersonal or functional terms apt for a *res extensa*) but with compensatory tendencies to sentimentality, moralism, and woolly thinking.[18]

> Science seeks a causal chain of events that leads from neural activity to subjective percept; a theory that accounts for what organisms under what conditions generate subjective feelings, what purposes these serve and how they come about (Koch, 2004, 326).

This passage about subjectivity gives expression to the search for consciousness, ethics and religion in causally analysed brain function that is also seen in the reduction of psychiatry to neuropsychiatry or biological psychiatry. It is symptomatic of technocreep (the intrusion of mechanistic thought) without regard for a clear view of the nature of morality and the discursive domain of human relationships.

> ... as behavioural disorders are transformed into neurological disorders caused by biochemical problems, they naturally become the province of medicine (Blank, 1999, 174).

When we recall that the Greeks regarded argument as therapy for the soul, we glimpse how far we are in danger of falling in this ideological *glissando*. Glannon, assessing the implications of brain science for bioethics, sounds a warning note: "neuroscience can inform ethical judgment. But ethics is not just a function of neuroscience" (Glannon, 2007, 180).

The current work is a dissenting voice inspired by post-Kantian naturalism. A human being is not a mere object but is also a centre of subjectivity whose existence precedes its essence and creatively generates its own (perpetually becoming and therefore unfinished) way of being-in-the-world-with-others.[19] The human subject transcends a functional characterisation of the *psyche* and is therefore dimin-

---

[17] The Mill, that is, of *System of Logic* not the Mill of political philosophy.

[18] In the sense that many authors believe that there is a magic stuff called consciousness that will suddenly emerge from looking ever more closely at the workings of neurones (as they might believe that one could understand sight by looking closely at the eyeball).

[19] The view is post-Kantian in its distinction between the noumenal (things as we understand them to be when we consider them through the lens of clear philosophical thought) and phenomena (things that can straightforwardly be

ished in so far as he or she must be fitted into a standardised mode of collective living that (in Taylor's words) flattens the spirit and negates value by substituting for those things which make demands of us mere preference satisfaction and individual choice.

### Edgework and counterculture — enchantment

Many people live through taking risks of one kind or another (Goffman, 1959), engaging in activities at the edge of their "comfort zone". Even more read stories of this kind. Harry Potter takes us beyond the secure, functional, and comfortable world to which, as civilized human beings we are so well adapted, to meet a darker, more dangerous and exciting place. He falls within a long tradition of "edgy" stories (both hi-brow and lo-) where normal constraints are disrupted and we stand at the abyss or fault line of the human world — war adventures; *The Lord of the Rings*; *Clockwork Orange*; James Bond; the "Bourne" saga; fantasy, and science fiction spring immediately to mind. Virtual games engaging the player in conflict and vicarious danger or plunging him or her into instability and chaos to be endured, triumphed over, or navigated through abound not only in amusement arcades but in "ordinary" sheltered (at least at a superficial level) suburban homes. Does all this merely answer primeval urges that used to prepare us for the hunt or is there something more to this "surreal" montage that deserves deconstruction? If so we should own it rather than explain it away in terms of outmoded genetic endowments.

Empirical studies reveal that the motivations are intrinsic, holistic, and internal to the activity concerned (Lyng, 2005). Sociologists of "edgework" relate it to the flattening effect of rationality, conceived in a narrow, economic and functional sense, in every area of contemporary life. The concept of disenchantment (Weber) is invoked:

> enchantment in the form of the mystical qualities associated with religious practice and intimate connections with nature ... are lost in a rationalizing social world moving inexorably toward the "iron cage" of bureaucratic domination ... The disenchanted world of formally rational social institutions offers little possibility for the vibrant experience of unexpected and unimagined sensual realities (Lyng, 2005, 21).

The edge offers an antidote to the secure existence of the herd and its institutions.

---

studied by science) but it also quite evidently draws on existentially influenced post-structuralism.

> Standing alone on the wheel strut of a skydiving plane waiting for the signal to jump is a breathtaking experience even though it may be an entirely personal one. The experience of negotiating the edge typically results in a narrowing of the perceptual field in which participants become highly focused on those elements that determine success or failure. ... Alterations of time and space and the hyperreal quality of edgework lifts participants out of the mundane reality or rational mediations and transports them to a world of sensual immediacy (Lyng, 2005, 23, 24).

An unpredictable but edgy world where success or failure depends on all the senses being attuned to the environment is also valorised in martial arts and its cultural products: *Kill Bill*, "Die hard" series, and the quasi-magical east of *Crouching Tiger, Hidden Dragon*, all with enough human realism to engage a suburbanized self and enough magic to transport it beyond itself. This is a very visible (but often merely distracting or diverting) response to Taylor's "malaise of modernity".

Lyng extends his analysis to high risk business enterprises and criminality:

> we find perpetrators confronting highly fluid situations of unfolding suspense and uncertainty ...
>
> In a world of increasing economic exploitation, technological deskilling, rationalization, and individualization and the resulting injuries of alienation, self-estrangement, and disenchantment, the risk experience offers an escape to a sensual universe of emotional intensity and self-determination. This, the source of the seductive appeal of edgework can be found in the contrast between the institutional constraints of modern societies and the intense emotions and spontaneity of high-risk situations (Lyng, 2005, 27, 30–31).

The sensual thrills of edgework as an antidote or corrective to the reductive society are not my current focus but rather its edginess and its problematisation of the criteria of worth or a well-ordered human life in the world of the herd. For Lyng, Foucault is a kindred spirit in analysing the ontological significance of "edgework";

> the exploration of limits or "edges" between sanity and insanity, consciousness and unconsciousness, or life and death provides a way to break free of the rigidified subjective categories created by the disciplinary technologies that circumscribe almost every aspect of human experience.

## The Expulsion of Humanity

Lyng's analysis is conducted in the midst of "the continued growth of the human sciences and popular discourses of improvement" and therefore concerns the *imagos* presenting themselves as forms of identity in contemporary society. It exposes the serious flaw that constructions of that type conceal within them.

### The human spirit and a sense of life

An *imago* is a construction, made out of signifiers and given substance by the significations they bring in their wake. I am "a man of the world", "a winner", a "shark in the commercial sea", a "good time girl", an "intellectual". Each of these captures a way of being that structures a possible life story and therefore serves as a representational framework for *a sense of life*, the sense of being a living subject who experiences life as valuable, as worth valuing, and is alert to traces of value that one's delving in the earth of experience might uncover.[20] A sense of life enters into *reflective equilibrium* (in John Rawls' sense), the melding of ethical intuition with ethical principles in forming an ethical judgment. Ethical intuitions and principles are, famously, linked to conceptions of the good life (or orthodoxies) often held to be irreconcilable and competing (and beyond rational argumentation) in a fragmented moral landscape (MacIntyre, 1984; Engelhardt, 1986) but a sense of life seems otherwise. Nussbaum remarks,

> ... we notice and clearly describe the tensions among the views we find. Where there is inconsistency or irreconcilable tension ... we aim to revise the overall picture so as to bring it into harmony with itself, preserving, as Aristotle says, "the greatest number and the most basic" of the original judgments and perceptions. There is no rule about how to do this. Individuals simply ask what looks deepest, what they can least live without — guided by their sense of life, and by their standing interest in consistency and community (Nussbaum, 1990, 174).

She illustrates using the case of Strether (in Henry James' *The Ambassadors*), sent to Europe to "check up" on the scion of a New England family in Paris for "finishing". Strether finds himself "at sea" in respect of the values and duties sanctioned by New England society as he encounters the ways of being permeating The Old World. He finds himself at the edge, in Nussbaum's words, "marked by a

---

[20] The term is drawn from Martha Nussbaum.

child's fresh delight in seeing and an undirected openness to the new concrete thing".

> This sense that life is an adventure, and that part of its joy precisely is the confrontation with the new — this is a sense of life already far removed from that where dignity is preserved by keeping down the new, acknowledging it only insofar as it exemplifies some law whose sense is already understood. ... heroically untouched by any horrible or wonderful aspect of life (Nussbaum, 1990, 179).

She distances herself from a morality "solidly grounded" in a set of allegiances and duties defined by a socio-political framework that defines the good for those "like me"(my herd), a conception that may seem irreconcilable with others of its ilk so that it leads to a crisis in the virtues (Macintyre) or an ethic of liberal tolerance.[21]

Immediately we can say something that a sense of life is not — it is not wedded to absolutes defined in advance so as to order ways of doing things in the decent governance of society. The sanctity of each human life or a duty to opt for quality of life are often contrasted as moral bases for social agendas but, if Nussbaum is right, perhaps the relevant value should be more fluid and engaging.

Jean Paul Sartre identifies a "spirit of seriousness" (1958, 626) that "considers values as transcendent givens independent of human subjectivity", aspects of our being that constrain human morality and provide a stable framework reflecting "the order of things" that is not subject to human creativity and argument. By contrast, a sense of life captures the idea that ethics should be developed in the light of a finely attuned sensibility to the human condition and a nuanced view of contested situations. There is no ethical truth laid down in an extra-human domain immutable and unresponsive to the particularities of human life. Perhaps such a sensibility generates a framework and a set of dues that should inform our action and out of which we can critique certain ways of going on but, importantly, that would engage us within the wider and deeper resonances of our being-in-the-world-with-others

A sense of life gives us a sense of life's value and what it is that makes a life valuable, that can only be appreciated as one lives and encounters other living human beings whose lives are both distinct from my own and yet full of things that make them worth living.

---

[21] MacIntyre traces the fragmentation of the good and Engelhardt argues that rational tolerance is the only credible recourse in the face of Taylor's "flattening" or "equalizing" of values.

Will Munny in *Unforgiven* observes: "It's a helluva thing you do when you kill a man, you take away everything he has and everything he's gonna have." In a sense, the value of a human life is incalculable (despite the fact that the Talmud is prepared to fix the price of the life of a person taken by bandits at the equivalent of two year's crops) because it is irreplaceable.[22]

Levinas' "Thou shalt not kill" as the principle of discourse and spiritual life now takes on further substance: the mere thought of ending a human life should give us pause,[23] even where we have a sufficiency of powerful considerations in favour of that decision. A sense of life is an essential qualification for ethicists involved in such decisions and related policies and procedures. And if, as ethicists, we need a sense of life, then ethical thinking has certain dimensions that evade codification but should inform all our doings including the education of the young.

First, we ought to be finely attuned to others in that it is in discourse and inter-subjectivity that we get a sense of what is at stake in matters of life and death. Such attunement also is important in relation to those human beings that get categorized as disabled. MacIntyre remarks that the recognition creating and sustaining respect for such individuals and fostering self-respect as a general attribute in a society reflects the conviction "that each member of the community is someone from whom we may learn and may have to learn about our common good and our own good, and who always may have lessons to teach us about those goods that we will not be able to learn elsewhere" (MacIntyre, 1999, 135). Nick (not)-trapped in a Locked in State confirms that lesson: we must recognize him for what he is before we can encounter him. We are all subjects who are born of women, live entangled with the world, and exhibit a being-towards-life and death with more or less resolve. A sense of life and the uniqueness of each individual attunes us to whole beings of that sort.

As subjects attuned to our own (and others) being-in-the-world we should find in discourse, not merely what others are saying out there, nor merely echoes of our own (or the herd's) "take", but care (or mindfulness) about the life-worlds of others and the stories and inspir(it)ations they have to share.

Attentive or attuned awareness of and responsiveness to others embodies recognition and responsiveness to mortality, even as instanced in "the widow, the cripple, and the orphan" (who are not

---

[22] I have argued this in Gillett (1996).
[23] I have explored "the pause" in several pieces of work (see e.g. 2004, ch 12).

mere exemplars of types but) particular subjects each one of whom is a unique (and perhaps unquiet) dweller in the spirit world that encompasses us all (in which we are "in proximity" with one another).[24]

As these thoughts and attitudes inform our ethics and medical law, they are infected by a developed sense of life that alerts us to the freshness of life, the beauty of the moment, the fragility of goodness as lived by mortals, the true value of desire, and the need for care of the self so as to foster the health of the soul through conversation with others in the light of spirit and truth.

These dimensions of human life are intrinsically transformative with the result that our understanding of life, death and human nature reaches beyond the daily grind of mundane functionality and re-introduces enchantment into our lives and lifts our eyes from the grass upon which we are munching. Some of us live in constant proximity to mortality, but, sadly that can make us *less* rather than *more* alive to the lives of others (in the clinic and elsewhere).

## The *imago* and its falsities

Lacan remarks that *meconnaissance* is a basic feature of the ego.[25] Even the (barely self-conscious) primordial human ego produces images of what it sees in the external world (including its own bodily reflection in a mirror) "subtended" by public discourse:

> a transformation takes place in the subject when he assumes an image ... indicated by the use, in analytic theory of the ancient term *imago*. ... this Gestalt symbolizes the mental permanency of the I, at the same time as it prefigures its alienating destination (1977, 3).

As the child comes to "see" itself as a unified gestalt, he or she begins to use this as the basis on which self and world of others come into relation. The gestalt presented by the mirror (a type of the mirror of discourse or conversation wherein one appears as a unitary being referred to by others who use one's name) generates an *imago*, self-as-distinct-from-other-with-a-bounded-existence-of-one's-own (1977, 4). The apparently self-sufficient and contained existence implicit in this conception, gives rise to an idea of agency or "an alienating identity" according to which a living human subject is self-understood as a being containing the basis of explanations of its

---

[24] To use Diamantides' phrase.
[25] He particularly develops this in his essay "The mirror stage".

activity in the world. This is a denial of (inter)dependence, the coming to be of the self through the other (Husserl, Vth Cartesian meditation), and the fact that the *hypokeimenon* or (what supports) the identifiable human subject is necessarily situated, derivative, and connected.

Only after one has deconstructed the *imago*, can one derive a conception of society and human community that is apt "to link together truth and the subject" and "to arm the subject with a truth it did not know" as the basis of ethics (Foucault, 1994, 101-2). The holistic reality beneath the illusion (the *hypokeimenon*) demands an antireductive approach.

## The uniqueness of the human subject

Emmanuel Levinas, indelibly inscribed by the events of the holocaust, reminds us of the primacy of the ethical subject encountered in discourse. He directs us to the human face as the mode of presentation of other subjects each of whom indwells a world that is not my world. For that reason they are different from anything else such that I can see the back or non-evident side of an object by changing my position but I cannot see the "inside" (other side/transcendental side) — or subjectivity — of another (Merleau Ponty, 1964, 14-17). The other calls to me or reaches out to me and, in a sense, escapes my categories or descriptions because s/he transcends my conception of him/her as an object in my world.[26] Any other person can show me that my story of the world is only one among many so that there are "different worlds" into which one can be introduced if the people who live and make those worlds are gracious enough. Generosity and grace reveal these differently inspir[it]ed worlds, not mine and yet able to enrich me in ways not otherwise possible. Levinas remarks, after the enormity of the Holocaust, "'You shall not kill' is ... the principle of discourse itself and of spiritual life". We can broaden the point: "Ethics, of course, is not simply law, either in theory or practice. But justice and law surely *proceed* from the ethical relation found in proximity" (Diamantides, 2000, 13).

The uniqueness of each human being has another implication, often overlooked at the level of policy or socio-political ethics: the work of women is, importantly, production or co-creation and not just reproduction. Women may reproduce in a narrow biological sense but child-bearing and nurturing is much more. Reproduction renders invisible the extent to which humanity relies on women (traditionally)

---

[26] Discussed in Levinas (1996) ch 1, 3 and 5.

doing creative, indefinable, and unbounded work involving care, engagement, affirmation, nurturing, and education unequalled by any other (in terms of emotional inclusion and the taking on of vulnerability and suffering). This work, discounted or ignored through the fact that the male child tends to distance himself from his mother and find a role outside the sphere of womenfolk,[27] is the foundation of any society that refuses to equate any individual with any other and therefore values in an unquantifiable way the life of each beyond their general properties or characteristics. "Only his mother could love him" should give us pause when we realize that whatever one does there is somebody in the world who is condemned to love one just for who one is.

Wittgenstein talks of the world of spirit when he discusses ethics (as does Levinas). Ethics is ontological and indicates the inadequacy of all our categories and the totalisations they offer. Acquaintance with another potentially opens a "pore"/"door" from one's own world to a differently inspir(it)ed world. This is a glimpse into the world of spirit which we could think of as the set of all inspir(it)ed worlds full of diverse stories, each of which is created just by living a human life. Mothers, one could say, have insights into the world of spirit and the vulnerability of inhabiting it that others may lack. The world of spirit loses something when the story that is a life is cut off in an untimely way even though, as finite or mortal individuals, all our stories end (in a way that is tragically unfitting in cases such as the suicide of a young person).

## Intersubjectivity and goodness

I have critiqued "the order of things" and "values as transcendent givens", so it seems Quixotic to introduce Simone Weil to this discussion. Nevertheless the current account indicates a Good that is not a matter for private determination and embraces all of us, something that becomes apparent through the words of the human spirit.[28] Weil remarks, "One can really be fully conscious only in so far as one is virtuous. ... For a reasonable being, there can only be one end: reason itself" (1978, 173). To understand the neo-Kantianism here, we must connect virtue and reason in a way indicated when Weil veers close to Foucault's aphorism about ethics: "The need for truth is more sacred than any other need" (Weil, 1952, 35). She notes

---

[27] Nancy Chodorow has written a great deal about this.
[28] Hence it deserves a big "G". I have discussed the human spirit and the world of spirit as a world in which stories meet and are appreciated in themselves for what they bring of meaning and insight.

that we investigate things and come to an apprehension of the truth about them so as to reveal masquerades and images for what they are, inescapable features of persons (or *per-sonae*—modes of self-presentation through which one speaks). A person is a creation of life and the word, the mixture of meaning and embodiment that is lived human subjectivity. We are alive and therefore need those things requisite for critters like us and our dealings (or associations) give us access to them.[29] But the words that form us should also nourish our capacities to explore and interrogate our associations with things (in thought and action) so that our dwelling among them brings us riches of enjoyment and growth.

The intersubjective order where that happens is replete with expectations and interpersonal associations in which evocations and imperatives proliferate; "the psychoanalytic experience has discovered in man the imperative of the Word as the law that has formed him in its image" (Lacan, 1977, 106). The order of things is a domain of touches where subjective bodies affect one another and make commitments connecting each of them to others in two contrasting ways: (i) life affirming ways or (ii) ultimately stultifying and destructive ways. The latter disconnect us from the truth, detracting both from a person's knowledge of themselves and their ability to recognise others. Reason, by contrast, is nourished by argument and recognition whereby words and their meanings in-form us and provide us with tools that we can use to fashion ourselves in ways that, when examined, are good.

The fact that one is open to the discursive milieu in which one finds roots among those to whom one belongs, and who are entrusted with the task of helping one grow, is nowhere more evident than when the strands of subjective being begin to fall apart, the scenario of the severely cognitively impaired with which we began this last chapter.

Some implications and corollaries of the anti-reductive view are as follows.

1. *Each individual needs recognition as the living author/narrator/ subject of a unique story with its own indwelling of spirit and truth.*

This strand of thought is developed by Macintyre in his *Dependent Rational Animals* where he argues that giving and receiving from each other as members of a human group, acknowledging each

---

[29] Heidegger uses *umgang*—going among, ways of behaving, or associations—to indicate our dealings with things that set up their signification for the subject.

others' individual worth and mutual interdependence, is the basis of a healthy society (MacIntyre, 1999).

2. *A society that is totalising and functional creates a reaction through edgework and counter-culture to attempt to recover the enchantment that we need in a liveable world.*

Lyng recalls Nietzsche's polemic against "the herd mentality" and the mind-set of "unthinking Darwinists" or self-satisfied human organisms, arguing that the growth of "edgework" (risk taking and criminality) in contemporary society, indicates the deep unhappiness and triviality of the reductive society and its (non-)aspirations for human being-in-the-world.[30]

3. *We need to create the capacity among us for people to harmonize the demons that enliven them — that is the function of education — worked out in argument, critique and struggle not by training as functionaries.*

Eudaimonia (a harmony of the demons) rather than hedonistic pleasure is dependent on a lively energy infecting what a person does so as to give them a sense of life and that one's individual life is meaningful. Finding a sense of life that energizes us in a way that appeals to an individual as an individual is, in Nietzsche's terms, a step away from "the herd"(as herd).

4. *We are bombarded with imago-fragments and we do not develop the skills to assess them for their worth.*

Lacan's claim that each of us develops an *imago* — a constructed self informing our conduct among others and giving meaning to what one does so as to create a sense of integrity in a life — reveals the openness of one's being to interrogation and enrichment from contact with the worlds of others. The *imago* is formed under the influence of socially mediated forces but, in an age of sound bites and slogans, the techniques of criticism essential to the examined life and invaluable in crafting a life-story that is sustainably liveable are not fostered whereas ethics fosters and in-forms those narrative skills so as, in Foucault's terms, to connect the subject to the truth in a certain way. As one touches and is touched by other ways of being one's resources in this task are extended so that the self does become a thing worth caring about.

---

[30] "Triviality" is Taylor's term for one of the roots of the malaise of modernity.

5. As we discover self-worth and dignity as subjects in an intersubjective world, we become witnesses who recognise others for what they are.

Recognition and witness are not functional terms but human beings need them as the basis of the dignity proper to being-in-the-world-with-others. One can see how being recognised for who one is might be vital to a collectively adapted creature such as early hominids probably were, but the dimensions of recognition and witness have, in the contemporary human world, taken on dimensions foreign to any hierarchy of biological needs. From the moment of birth, when we are "still sunk in ... motor incapacity and nursling dependence" and must be helped to survive by those who care for us,[31] to the moment of death when many fear that they will be abandoned, we inhabit the contested (and contextual) space of intersubjective being. Although we might be, in some sense, "volunteers banded together to fight for liberty and justice and against inhumanity" (Foot, 1978, 167), the (self reflexive) way of morality is not in any way an optional extra to our *eudaimonia*.

## A naturalistic structure for antireductive ethics

Those who believe there is a naturalistic basis for morality (whether or not it is an *analogia entis*) related to our well-being embrace certain (neo-Aristotelian) axioms.

1. Human beings share a biological form or nature.
2. We are all members of an interactive community.
3. Different individuals have different perspectives on human situations.
4. Each perspective arises in a discourse that positions the subject in the human world and attaches value to the things that happen.
5. Much is gained by sharing our inherently individual knowledges of our world.

These naturalistic propositions suggest certain responses grounded in practical reason as a connection with the truth of our being because they generate desiderata or dicta that plausibly conduce to human flourishing. Those dicta fall into two groups, the first concerning our interactions with one another and our collective

---

[31] Lacan uses this to explore why the way that we are mirrored in the eyes (and hearts and minds) of others is so important to us.

flourishing, the second concerning the individual human being and his or her flourishing.

*Two theorems:*

a. A human being must belong somewhere or have a place to stand.

b. A human being is a unique individual.

These first dicta tell us that we thrive through being brought to being by others in such a way that each of us is encouraged to develop his or her own way of being entangled with and independent of those others. The resulting creative tension undercuts simplistic theories about our associations and our nature because through our cooperative diversity we become, individually and collectively, much more than would otherwise be possible.

*Corollaries:*

(i) We should appreciate the diverse knowledges that different individuals bring to our situation.

(ii) We should attend to silences and discern why they are happening.

(iii) We should be wary of moral "truth" held by a privileged few.

(iv) We should give special attention to those who are experienced participants in a moral situation and to those who are vulnerable or marginal.

The structure as a whole emerges from an analysis of what a human life is and must be for a human being concerned to survive, grow, and develop into adulthood.

We are slowly learning that a sense of one's roots and attending to the health of those (biological, cultural and spiritual) roots is essential for the health and psychological well-being of any person and that a failure to attend to this need is a powerful source of discontent (evident in all kinds of social pathology such as substance abuse, gambling, unstable and violent family relationships, and criminality). The society that neglects roots and emphasizes only functional goals is therefore likely to cripple itself through creating endemic alienation in its members and thereby denying them the sources of strength and identity needed to make life meaningful and provide resilience in the face of adversity.

Belonging is, however, only one foundation for the human journey towards being somebody; the second is the room to develop as an individual who is unique and therefore irreplaceable so that one can truly be valued for who one is (and not merely as a charitable concession). Placing value on the human subject as an individual (*somebody* rather than *some body*) means that we must see the work of families (or kin) in bio-political terms as more than reproduction—it is production or creation of something unique, the like of which will never be seen again in quite the same way.

The corollaries recommend moral responses such as learning from open discourse with others (including those whose cognitive impairment renders them immune to popular and well-marketed illusions), a spirit of humility, listening to the voice of the oppressed, overcoming serious injustices which blight the development of individuals, the sharing of cultural and moral perspectives, deriding the exploitation of any human being and opposing economic or political discourses tending to reduce the individual to a functionary in a rationally ordered socio-political system of relations. What each of us ought to do and be as somebody is, on the one hand, to celebrate both belonging (which imparts depth, horizons of value, crafted traditional forms of human expression, and knowledge which transcends the evanescent present) and individuality (which encourages each of us to make what we will of those shared resources in a way that evinces integrity and creativity) and, on the other, to resist, through ironic and (if necessary) destructive critique, the demeaning of human beings by treating them as mere consumers or manipulable things.

"It ain't necessarily so" sings Sportin' Life, opposing attitudes and intuitions that arise from totalizing views and hallowed metanarratives of the human condition. The complexities of identity as it applies to self-transforming agents each of whom only becomes somebody by negotiations and permissions exchanged between self and others, undermine reductive answers (in terms of a type of circumscribed and self-contained thing that a human being is) as simplistic and ultimately oppressive because they expel the human spirit from the world.

For each of us, this means providing a place for people to belong and a space for their individuality but also the graciousness to understand when preserving a life is no longer consistent with the values of the "somebody" being cared for. Such an orientation yields an ethics founded in a sense of life and the need of each one of us to become and be recognized as somebody when, at the beginning of our lives, as at their ends, one may be little more than some body.

# Chapter 11

# *Retrospective and Conclusion*

## *Problematising the Subject*

> To the extent that he believed over long periods of time in the concepts and names of things as if they were *aeternae veritates*, man has acquired that pride by which he has raised himself above the animals : he really did believe that in language he had knowledge of the world.
>
> (Nietzsche, *Human All Too Human*)

> The body is the inscribed surface of events (traced by language and dissolved by ideas), the locus of a dissociated self (adopting the illusion of a substantial unity), and a volume in perpetual disintegration.
>
> The relationship of domination ... establishes marks of its power and engraves memories on things and even within bodies.
>
> (Michel Foucault)

I have suggested that the human subject as an embodied subjectivity is the site of five successive (or layers of) conceptual problematizations.

The *first* disrupts our tendency to see the human subject as an object with a fixed nature. The illusion is that we can fix the subject in a "basilisk" like gaze which freezes him or her in time and allows us, in principle, to do an inventory of his/her essential characteristics or properties. But this is not the case; the subject not only is a dynamic being whose properties are changing (as s/he grows for instance) but is also an unstable complex of subjective activities in relation to the world of objects. As a complex subjectivity, one is not able to be examined, even as a dynamically changing object. What is more, aspects of a human being (as of anything) are either revealed or obscured by our mode of investigating them. Looking through a biological lens, one might see, for instance, oxygen consumption in different areas of the brain but not a sense that one has allowed oneself to be consumed by trivialities or that the system of meaning (such as a success culture, or a political crusade, or a religious faith) to which one is committed is one that involves a fundamental distortion of human life.

Each of us is a being-in-the process-of-becoming, whose essence (a tricky term) is to live a narrative and is therefore not logically determinate and unchanging through the contingencies of life and situation. As somebody, one cannot be plucked out of the continuity within which one is somebody and expect one's being somebody to be evident from the atemporal (narratively disarticulated) body that is then made available as the object of study. We see this writ large as we trace the origin and evolving identity of an embryo into a human being who is somebody, a being with aspects to their identity that span and integrate the days of their lives.

*Second*, the subject (acknowledged to be subjective, dynamic, and changing) is not easily located and bounded but rather is a relational being configuring him/herself as a node in a discursive milieu: I am the surgeon, who acts decisively and can be relied on to distil a problem into the elements needed to formulate a plan of action, but I am also a family man who finds it difficult, in the complex of family tensions that are sometimes caused by a demanding surgical life, to say anything decisive and well considered about any issue that is raised. But an inventory of the body and its physical relations is not what we need in trying to understand being somebody, as can be seen when we note that the identity of a human being from the time of their life's beginning is a relational identity. Most human groups have names reflecting our relationships and many have rituals, however perfunctory and informal, that place us in the relational domain of the moral community when we first meet somebody else.

A human being is therefore a being-in-the-process-of-becoming-among-others where those others that one develops among bring out facets of one's own identity dependent for their expression or articulation on the being-among that supports them. In this sense each of us is incomplete, in some ways like an enzyme which is only seen for what it is when the appropriate substrate is there for it to act upon.

*Third*, the subject as a relational and quasi-stable (dynamically evolving) being-in-relation is not amenable to a mere documentation or conceptualisation of their own being as an objective individual plus an inventory of those relationships in which they are embedded, because the relationships themselves are importantly mediated and moderated by the subject. A young man, for instance, may see himself as a janitor, with no real interest in the institution he is cleaning and maintaining and a person of no real distinction, until an encounter with a difficult maths problem reveals him to himself and others as a gifted mathematician.[1]

*Fourth*, the multiple inscriptions that arise from the subject's being-in-relation are not only cross-grained with respect to each other but interfere with each other in diverse ways. We are beings-in-relation but each of one's relationships affects many of the others. Somebody might call a flower shop to order flowers for a woman he is smitten by but, on announcing that he is the President of the United States, may not be taken seriously. Interactions between discursive relationships can pose problems in that one might find oneself having to act towards a friend in a way that seems, on the surface of it, quite inconsistent with friendship (as, for instance, as a professional censor required to investigate irregularities in that friend's conduct). In that sense being somebody may cause cross-currents of commitment, disposition, attitude and knowledge that seem to partially efface and disrupt one another so that one's own psyche and effectiveness become unbalanced and threaten to fall apart at certain points in one's life.

We could say that the human subject is a dispersed and fragmented subject were it not that the inscriptions which create the subject as somebody all arise from events involving some body (as the surface to be inscribed), a body with a fleshly nature, sensitivities, and vulnerabilities, and the body traces (and carries the traces — including explicit memories — of) a trajectory through a world in which it is a being-in-relation-to-others. The body so inscribed is socio-politico-historico-culturally situated so that it must combine within itself the accumulated inscriptions it carries and it reflects those as it enacts its being in the life events in which it is caught up. These life events might seem to dominate the person and inscribe on them marks of power or it might seem that the person forges a course through tossing and stormy seas. Which metaphor is more apt largely depends upon the (discursive, narrative) skills of the subject-as-agent in enacting her/his identity, and, as is readily evident, makes a difference to that person's way of being.

---

[1] A brief précis of the film *Good Will Hunting*.

*Fifth*, all these aspects of the self-as-embodied-subjectivity in the midst of others are subject to misconception and illusory reification by the subject in ways that mediate and moderate each aspect. I might see myself as an edgy and yet tolerated young rebel until it occurs to me that I am at an age of maturity and responsibility and such a persona is no longer fitting. A medical student might see his or her instructor as an aloof, uncaring, and somewhat cruel figure who despises her and all the other students and resents their intrusion on his time. She might feel loath to approach him or reveal her deficiencies to him fearing to be the target of even further scorn and disapproval. But the instructor, brought up in the old school, might see himself as preparing the students for the unforgiving world they are about to enter where they will need a certain toughness and mental resilience. He may not consciously wish to seem impatient or resentful toward the students and would hate to think that he was intolerant or abusive in the way that he treats them. He may not recognise in himself a less-than-conscious attitude that they are beneath him nor be aware of the hostility and resentment produced in his own psyche by the ways he has been treated. He might be proud that he has not allowed himself to be affected by his treatment in the past. Perhaps the students respond to this inner malaise even though they could not articulate it in that way and he would not recognise it in himself if it was articulated. He might protest that he is only doing what is best for them and, when he thinks about it, he may realise that actually he considers that the students, by and large, are good young people and begin to question the fact that he sometimes does feel resentment towards them. He may still not believe it helpful to change too much and he may read his own behaviour, quite sincerely, at the level where he consciously intends it—i.e. as enacting for them a preparatory version of "the school of hard knocks".

In this example there are multiple levels of *meconnaissence*. The students misread the instructor's real conscious attitude but perhaps sense his unconscious attitude. They think of themselves as despised and perhaps internalise some of the negative self-directed attitudes that are implied. The instructor misconstrues his own behaviour, failing to realise that it has motivations that are not evident to him, he misconstrues the students' response by regarding them as slightly soft and self-indulgent or even sulky so that they do deserve the sharp end of his tongue. One could go on, but this is not an exercise in higher educational practice supervision so I will not. The point is clear — the somebody-that-one-is is sometimes hard to know even for oneself and subject to deceptions, pretences, misconceptions, misdirected reactions and responses, so that identity — being somebody — is complex and negotiated in the unfolding fabric of life and relationships in ways that may lead to multiple disconnections and misdirections. As somebody, one becomes, through a critique of the production of the subject, not adrift but in fact empowered to see what is being done to and through oneself and able to join in the struggle against domination and reduction of the self to some manageable caricature of human subjectivity. Therefore Foucault's claim that the human subject adopts "the illusion of substantial unity" whereas it is actually "a volume in perpetual disintegration" is, perhaps, a little one-sided. The body that is inscribed through the tracing on it of ideas and the critical acid of conversation (the deployment of language) is, after all, a body with an origin in history. It is a result of a biological conception with a spatio-temporal trajectory in the world-among-others during which one's subjectivity is configured by history and culture through relationships, so that one takes on substance as an identity more real than that of "any spider in my garden".

Through appreciating this complexity, we realise that the human subject, construed according to Aristotle's dictum that *the soul is to the body as sight is to the eye*, is not amenable to simple or reductive theses about its essence or nature. If, as somebody, one has a real essence it is to exist and be open to all the contingencies of life and, in the many ways characteristic of a self-making and self-knowing thing, to be able to transform those contingencies in various ways — even as one is affected by them. It is as if the quantum particle could knowingly and demonically play with the light that reveals it, a prospect that would send shivers down the spine of any self-respecting realistic scientist but that, like it or not, is the lot of those who seek to limn the soul and, through that exercise, to understand the human subject and his or her identity as a being-in-the-process-of-becoming-in-the-world-amidst-others. Only when one has glimpsed the subtlety, nuances, and resonances of that investigation, and the ironic yet authentic care of the self that results, does one begin to see why being somebody is not just a matter of being some body.

# *Appendices*

**Appendix A: On method in moral science**

In philosophical discussions we need to distinguish epistemic from metaphysical claims. Epistemic claims concern our ways of gaining knowledge of a thing and take the form that we can only know the thing in thus and so respects, whereas the metaphysical claim would be that the thing really is thus and so. Thus, for instance, we might claim that the colour red is only known by colour vision but in reality is a certain configuration of reflectance etc. conditions on the surface of an object. This is a classical route taken by those (such as Locke) who believe in *res extensa* and the metaphysical primacy of primary qualities. Others, however, would argue that the colour red is an abstraction from a set of S–O relations involving colour vision so that it makes no sense to talk about colour apart from sensory relations. On that view, the reality of certain things is underpinned by some feature of human being-in-the-world rather than a feature of the world *simpliciter* or considered in abstraction from the reality of sensory relations and their signification in thought.

The second approach problematizes claims that certain features of the world are mind-independent in that minds construct the concepts in which they are understood to be that way. Thus mind-independence is a conflation of two ideas: (1) that a feature is dependent on a subjectively conditioned way of thinking of things, and (2) that a feature is as it would appear to any creature minded in such a way as to be able to have the relevant thoughts. The first is something we might want to escape the clutches of in the interest of open intersubjective discourse but the latter is something we cannot escape and is innocuous provided only that being minded in a certain kind of way does not import the threatening and prejudicial kind of subjectivity that hinders clarity of thought and communication.

Following this vein we might want to distinguish **Realism$_M$** from **realism**, where **Realism$_M$** is metaphysical and entails that there is a determinate single canonical or to-be-preferred way, that the world is in its fundamental nature, and **realism** understands us as adjusting what we think in the light of our dealings with things but does not commit itself on the issue of whether a single determinate characterisation is uniquely appropriate to the world as it is in itself (independent of all our ways of thinking about it). **Realists$_M$** make a sharp distinction between ways of thinking or representation which are a series of glosses or understandings of reality subject to all the vicissitudes of any epistemic endeavour and the way things actually are, the real topic of metaphysics. Most current thinkers of this type are critical scientific realists who claim that the world really is the way our mature science represents it as being. More common sense or down to earth (deflationary) **realists** concede that we are always limited by our modes of inquiry and derive answers somewhat conditioned by them, but aim to make these as open to reflection, revision and the deliverance of experience as thought can be (given broad requirements for logical consistency, expressibility in natural language, determinacy of judgment about the applicability of categories, and so on). Real dyed-in-the-wool **Realists$_M$** regard deflationary realism as making far too many concessions to epistemology. The current work is realistic in the (down to earth) realistic spirit of Cora Diamond's work, not in the (**Realism$_M$**) sense of "**Real** as they **Really** are and not just as our dealings with them have them as being"; this latter view, I, with Diamond and Wittgenstein, regard as an illusory ideal.

I will however preserve a distinction between psychologism and naturalism, whereby the former establishes what we are right to think by trying to ascertain the way the human mind happens to work or what most people find psychologically suasive, while the latter relates our thinking to our broadest and most inclusive rationally sustainable understandings of the natural world. The latter ideal is meant to wean us away from narrow criteria of logical consistency or non-contradiction and direct us toward the sum total of our dealings with things as the basis of our thought. Heidegger calls the latter "circumspection" and notices, with Wittgenstein (early and late), that the sum total of our thoughts about the world is an abstraction from and idealisation of our actual dealings with things in the forms of life that form us and give meaning to our lives. In this manner a realistic spirit can aim to do justice to our diverse understandings and ways of thinking about things and try to achieve some balance which most preserves those things of epistemic and human value within them (what some call "saving the appearances").

Radical disagreement versus cultural disagreement is one further opposition worth noting. A radical disagreement is one that cannot be solved by reason, for instance a fundamental moral disagreement over whether it is wrong to murder the innocent. A cultural disagreement is a disagreement that hinges on some cultural contingency, such as the view that an anencephalic child is a monster rather than a human being so that killing such a child is not a case of killing an innocent human being at all but of dealing appropriately with an abject monstrosity. Either kind of disagreement can lead to moral conflict but distinguishing them allows a more inclusive understanding of the world (that can defuse one but, perhaps, not the other).

Consider for example the cases of Winch and Vere faced by the same facts about Billy Budd, in the film of that name. There is no disagreement as to the facts nor how they should be understood and yet Winch and Vere come to different conclusions about the right action in the circumstances, while sharing the same moral intuitions and values. This is a radical disagreement without a cultural overlay at its heart.

The notion of *whakapapa* and that of genetics give rise to a different problem. A Maori thinker may appeal to *whakapapa* in justifying a refusal to countenance genetic splicing from one species to another. A non-Maori thinker may equate *whakapapa* with genetic lineage and say that one is not interfering with a lineage or pattern of inheritance when one splices genes across species, merely modifying the biochemistry of the individual so treated. But the Maori thinker may come back and say that if you understood what she meant by *whakapapa* you would see it in a different light and then may begin to talk about patterns of connectedness and the nature of things that cannot with impunity be meddled with. Now it may be true that, thought of in that way, genetic splicing looks as if it crosses a boundary and should be *tapu* or forbidden for spiritual reasons and not just looked at as a biochemical intervention using certain tools to do a molecular biological job for some apparently laudable purpose. But there is a breakdown in understanding here in that the two ways of looking at what is going on are not easily commensurable.

A different kind of disagreement may result in the concepts of *Whakapapa*, *tapu* (sacred), and *noa* (workaday) being invoked differently in an ethical discussion where there is no culturally mediated loss of communication. Take for instance a Maori scientist who agrees that genetics concerns *whakapapa* and that genetic splicing is infringing an area that might be *tapu* and acting as if it were *noa*. But, she argues, the gods of the Maori are also tricksters who infringe the old order of things when there is a greater good to be gained and therefore, if there is a greater good, *tapu* can be made *noa* (using, of course, the correct protocol or *tikanga*). A more traditional Maori might, however, say, "No, this is too much! No good can ultimately come from this kind of violation of the sacred!" So here the two have a dispute similar to that of Vere and Winch: there is no lack of cultural understanding but there is a profound moral disagreement. Note that it is possible that further discussion, but not the mere deployment of rational argument, may bring them closer together even though it may not resolve their disagreement (or it may).

## Appendix B: Essence and identity

Metaphysical essence is an attempt to answer the question "what is it about an X that makes it an X?" The question is very old and famously illustrated by noting that the statue of Apollo ($S_A$) is clearly a distinct thing and it cannot be identified with the bronze that makes it up ($Br'$). The non-identification proceeds because the same bronze may be present in a statue of Diana ($S_D$) and yet that would not be identical with the statue of Apollo. Therefore the following is the logical result of identifying the statue (in either case) with the bronze.

1. $S_A = Br'$ &
2. $S_D = Br'$ therefore
3. $S_A = S_D$ (False)

This will not do; something has to go and there is no reason for simultaneously affirming either 1 or 2 and denying the other, so it looks like they must both be false. The normal response is to invoke the form of any given thing as that which essentially fixes its identity. On that basis $S_D$, $Br'$, and $S_A$ are all different objects even though they have material substrate in common and at any given time two of them may occupy the same volume of space.

Notice that this means that when we talk of a substance we are talking of a thing with a certain form and then we can regard some of its properties as being essential to its being a thing of that type and some being incidental. For instance it might be essential to my being me that I am a human being and incidental whether I am wearing blue or red clothes, or whether my hair is short or long. One might then get into a debate about whether, for instance, my gender or biological sex is an essential or incidental part of my being me given that so much else from birth onward is predicated on gender.

The question (when asked of individuals in virtue of their being examples or tokens of a given type or their membership of a set) focuses on what is it to have a distinct or numerically singular token of a given type, and it blurs into the question about what properties an entity must have to count as being of the relevant type. So, for instance, we might debate what it is for a tree to be a tree. We might conclude that trees in general have to have root systems, a trunk or trunks with a common root system, and branches. In general the relevant metaphysical distinctions relate to our conception of the real essence, so that the relevant branch of science then becomes determinative for the judgment. On that basis a sample of water must be a sample of $H_2O$ and a modern human being must be a member of the species *Homo sapiens*. If we then ask, "What is a species?" we are led into debates about biological theory and some kind of neo-Darwinian essence tends to capture the current consensus. Given that this is cladistic (concerns lineages and patterns of interbreeding) and historical in relation to geological or evolutionary time (broadly speaking), then genetics are part of the story; but recent advances in developmental effects and dynamic systems theory in biology make a purely genetic essence problematic.

The difficulties in this area are evident when we notice our intuitive acceptance of the principle of identity of indiscernibles (or Leibniz's law) which states that if A and B are identical then every property of A is also a property of B.

For the present purposes we need not get into complex questions about possible worlds, rigid designators, and so forth; but we ought to notice that this principle raises a problem which is different from but related to the problem of form and material constitution. The traditional problem of Hesperus (the Evening Star), Phosphorus (the Morning Star), and the planet Venus (discussed by Frege, 1980; Quine, 1953; Kripke, 1971; and others) arises because these three terms designate the same heavenly object even though one may know what each is, in some sense (forgive the pun), without knowing that they are the same thing. When we made the astronomical discovery that they were the same what, exactly did we discover? We obviously discovered something other than the trivial truth that the planet Venus is the planet Venus, and more significant than the truth that one object has two different names, but did we discover something about the names (merely a fact about language) or something about the world itself?

This kind of problem lurks behind many of the issues we talk about in relation to what it is that makes a given individual the same individual as one identified by other means (e.g. John Digger the second son of Rex and Judy and the product of a conception event involving sperm RD21-10-1987_5295741xkgt and egg JD20-10-1987)?

Wittgenstein in his early philosophy considered the whole idea of the relation of identity a nonsense as he could not, to his satisfaction, answer the question as to what was said to be identical to what. Was an object of thought (appearing in the logico-mathematical domain of thought) said to be the same as another object of thought? That could not be true because the logical grounds and entailments of "This is the Morning Star" are distinct from and could possibly come apart from those of "This is the Evening Star". But otherwise what is one saying? It seems to be like holding a thing in your hand and shaking it once when you say "This" and then again and saying "is this" (perhaps forcefully because a really basic truth is at stake here). Wittgenstein thought that we can discuss the way an individual is locked into a particular definable location in our structure of thought (so that it has determinate grounds and entailments required to establish its truth and its relation to a range of thoughts) and we can indicate which thing in the world we are talking about, but we ought not to equate the one type of procedure with the other because they invoke different domains (in Frege's terms, such statements violate a fundamental distinction between "what can only occur as an object, and everything else", something we are frustrated in discussing because of "the awkwardness of language" or, in Armstrong's [2004] terms, because statements of that type are "cross-categorial").

In any event what we have here is a problem concerning our ability to pick out an individual and say things about it as the thing that it is, not just as in another mode of thinking which obscures its reality. Heidegger invokes the Greek *hypokeimenon* to indicate that which is revealed in a phenomenon (i.e. representation or in ideational clothing as we try to specify it in language). This reality, which lies beneath and which language or thought gives us an ideational grip on for the purposes of reflection, is not the representation or logical form that it is given. However the error of metaphysics is to regard the logical clothing or forms of thought that we use to specify or define something as capturing the real nature of the thing, such that we can base our dealings with it in the ways of thinking to which some preferred representation gives rise (for instance in terms of the fundamental components of a thing or "the metaphysical simples" that are combined to give it its distinctive form). This view is one of the principal targets of Wittgenstein's remarks in *Philosophical Investigations*: "Essence is expressed in grammar" (*PI*, #371).

### Appendix C: On possible worlds and metaphysics

A possible world is a way things might have been.[1] It is a way of speaking about what exists, or is possible, if things were different from what they in fact are. The possibilities concerned are settled by appeal to intuition (and here be dragons). Thus we need to be sure that the relevant intuitions are as firm as they need to be to support the weight of the metaphysics they carry and are as clear as they need to be to make the metaphysical conclusions unambiguous. Some of the thought experiments, as it seems to many scholars, are not quite of the required standard.[2]

A possible world which seems exactly the same as the actual world in which we are present is Twin-earth. Thus we might posit that, in twin earth, creatures seemingly exactly like us (apart from the fact they have Twater in their bodies not water) speak a language Twenglish (that is isomorphic with earth English) and call Twater (a substance qualitatively indistinguishable from water) "water". In fact Twater is XYZ not $H_2O$, so that one could argue that the meanings of our words are world-involving and depend on what they actually refer to in the actual world (a thesis akin to Locke's distinction between real and nominal essence).

The test on whether something is actually possible then becomes whether there is a possible world in which the phenomenon exists. Kripke (1971) exploits the device in arguing that what is essential to the existence of an identifiable human being is not any achievement of the person concerned but something more basic about him or her. He acknowledges that we might pick a person out by some characteristic that is contingently true of her, such as whether she wrote some work or invented some device, but that there are possible worlds in which that person did not do that thing. His argument depends however on there being a way of picking out an individual that is (a) unique to that individual (thus individuates them) and (b) that captures a feature of them essential to them being the person

---

[1] The major contemporary source is David Lewis (e.g. 2001).
[2] Donagan (1990) for example, or Wilkes (1988).

that they are. The present analysis suggests that (a) is something to do with the entry of that person into the world of human beings and (b) is a complex of a set of determinants. Parfit's Origin is, in principle, (except in cases of ICSI [Intra-Cytoplasmic Sperm Injection] or some comparable technique) indeterminate and may not be essential because a person indistinguishable from you (therefore making the you that is you a function of which possible world we are in) might have come about through any one of a number of such pairings. But perhaps the terms have shifted to an epistemic rather than a metaphysical basis — what we can know rather than what is in fact the case?

Let us say that Immanuel Kant in World 1 ($W_1$) comes about through the pairing of sperm JGK14-07-1723 n5493xk' and ovum ARK07-1723u and in World 2 ($W_2$) through the pairing of JGK04-08-1723 and ovum ARK08-1723t. There is no other difference between $W_1$ and $W_2$ so that it is quite unclear which world is the actual world. But that surely does not affect who Immanuel Kant is, he is the philosopher from Konigsberg born to Anna Regina and Johann Georg at 5am on the 22nd of April 1724. Which egg and sperm he actually came from is indeterminate and irrelevant to who he is; that depends on a complex cluster of other things. Imagine that some subset of these are known to a transworld historian called Wilfred (a different but commensurate subset from those known to Johann and Anna) but it is the critical or essential cluster that we ought to be concerned with rather than the irrelevant pairing. One might want to protest that the *actual* pairing is necessary to the *actual* Kant. In fact it is only that some pairing has occurred that is necessary and exactly which pairing pales into insignificance compared with what then unfolds (according to the arguments of ch 2 & 3 above), so that the actual pairing, in relation to the individual in whom we are interested, is immaterial.

Notice that, if Kant is rigidly designated by his naming in the actual world, then it is still not clear that any particular originary pairing is necessary, because the designation proceeds by picking out the Kant who lives among us; which early events are thereby picked out remains indeterminate because we do not know which (possible) world is the actual world in which the reference has been fixed in the preferred way.

The Immanuel Kant/Georg Kant problem is an example of the problem of Transworld identity (TWI) noticed by Chisholm (1967). Chisholm imagines an individual changing one property after another as we move through possible worlds until he is completely unlike the individual he is in $W_1$ and, in fact, exactly like another individual in $W_1$, by the time we get to $W_n$. Imagine, for instance, that in the actual world (W) Georg Kant is an individual born roughly at the same time as Immanuel Kant (but is, as noted, severely impaired). As we move through possible worlds we reach a world $W_{263}$ where the individual who is Immanuel in the actual world has transmuted and been renamed "Georg" so that he exactly resembles Georg in the actual world. Now who is whom and in virtue of what is Immanuel in $W_{263}$ the same individual as Immanuel (in W)? If you are like me then the notion of human identity has now lost any bite it might have had,[3] but it is in any event clear that any intuition being appealed to here is insufficiently robust to rule that Wilfred's joy at finding his friend, Immanuel, involves a mistaken identity judgment. If we were to go with Lewis' counterpart theory, we might say that Wilfred re-baptised and adopted as Immanuel Kant is Immanuel Kant's counterpart in the relevant possible world.

We could even intensify the scrutiny of possible world arguments by imagining that Wilfred, on discovering Georg Kant in $W_{263}$ and re-creating himself as "Immanuel Kant", becomes so conversant with the works of the actual Immanuel Kant and his ways of thinking that at a certain point he has a transfiguration experience (within the context of his pietist worship and private devotions) as a result of which he declares, "The spirit of Immanuel has come upon me!" When giving witness to this event he claims that the irrepressible and numerically identical spirit of analysis and creativity animating Immanuel Kant in the actual world has found expression in him in $W_{263}$ where, until his transfiguration, that profound, energetic and enlightened spirit was frustrated in its coming to be. So, is he wrong?

In any event I want to be a bit more realistic about this issue and not allow a shaky set of intuitions to push us into an equally shaky set of conclusions.

## Appendix D: Kant's I and the refutation of idealism

Kant's philosophy of mind is individualistic in the sense that each individual has a cognitive apparatus (of the categories, the schematism, and so on) enabling true judgments about experience to be made. Cognition uses synthesis to put together the deliverances of sense and the structures of the understanding to ground anticipations of experience and thereby traverses "a single subjective experiential route … through the same objective world" (Strawson, 1966,

---

[3] Why, for instance, should I care at all about the fate of Immanuel in $W_{263}$?

104). The subject has to be attuned to the environment (an objective rather than subjective determination) and Kant invokes the Aristotelian idea of training (and exposure to correction)[4] as the means of that attunement. Human cognition is structured by the use of rules governing concepts and, after Wittgenstein, my kind of neo-Kantian[5] thinks of concept mastery as a set of shared techniques entwined with language as it is used around here.

If that is true, the discursive environment is of crucial importance in Kant's account of right thinking or the proper functioning of the understanding (contra Strawson).[6] According to this "discursive naturalist" interpretation of Kant, a subject develops epistemic virtue as s/he latches on to the subtleties and nuances of the discourse but remains tied to the logical entailments and dependencies inherent in his or her cognitive structures to make sense of his/her activity in the natural world. These networks of logical connections are revealed by "a mere analytic of the pure understanding"(*Pure Reason*, B303) or a set of "principles of the exposition of appearances" according to which we understand what we encounter.[7] Given that we are constantly finding new phenomena and ways of classifying them, the "exposition of appearances" may change our understanding of self and world.[8]

In "The refutation of idealism"(B274ff) Kant explicitly rejects the metaphysics arising from "dogmatic idealism" which "declares things in space to be merely imaginary"(B274). Given that any appeal to intersubjectivity (as in the present work) as the basis of human knowledge implies that the rational subject discursively interacts with other thinkers and with the natural world – one can infer an ontological conclusion about the accessibility of that world to multiple subjects (rather than merely subjective or "as-if" conclu-

---

[4] *The Critique of Pure Reason*, B172 ff. Notice that this is a prescriptive and normative condition on the possibility of experience in general and therefore defeats any crass naturalism of a reductive sort.

[5] As outlined in Chapter 4.

[6] Strawson remarks "We should remember that all Kant's treatment of objectivity is managed under a considerable limitation, almost, it might be said, a handicap. He nowhere depends upon, or even refers to the factor on which Wittgenstein, for example, insists so strongly: the social character of our concepts, the links between thought and speech, speech and communication, communication and social communities" (1966, 151).

[7] A claim which provides a direct link between Kant and structuralism.

[8] As Jaspers points out in defusing the objections to Kant based on the displacement of Euclidean geometry (Jaspers, 1975, 22 note 18).

sion about the world as it appears to those subjects [Westphal, 2004]). The conclusion is secured because absent the relevant engagement with others in relation to co-referentially available objects and events, any claims about training and the distinctive marks of objective knowledge (as distinct from opinion and belief), provide nothing more than further corroboration at a subjective or representational level and the idea of correction by others becomes logically incoherent (as argued in Chapter 4).

That Kant saw himself as drawing out the implications of addressing the epistemic dilemma of the subject in the actual world (requiring justification for theses about its objective existence) seems plausible from three sources:

(i) a plausible (but contested) interpretation of Kant's refutation of idealism;

(ii) Kant's rejection of the idea of a purely mental substance in the paralogisms (Bird, 2000);

(iii) remarks about *sensus communis* and intersubjectivity found in *Anthropology from a Pragmatic Point of View* (Kant, 1798 [1974]).

Kant argues that the possibility of a subject with inner experience depends on the subject having "outer experience" of a world with which it has genuine contact rather than just ideational experience. The argument builds on his treatment (B218-65) of objects, causality, and the community of interactions that defines a domain of objective changes and substances undergoing them (such as the natural world).[9] A thinking subject (as a denizen of the natural world) therefore exists, like nature itself, in time; and thinking of human beings as being affected by and acting on other things, entails that a human subject is an occupant of some causal domain (Matthews, 1969). The present interpretation then follows.

(i) I am an existent in time so that I undergo changes evident in, but not reducible to, the changing representations that arise in my inner experiences.

(ii) Therefore I am an actual empirical substance with objective existence and not just a flux of *sensa* (or variations of subjective affect).

---

[9] All commentators agree on this but then divide over whether Kant establishes that we have actual dealings with an objective world or mere "as if" dealings with a world that we take to be that way. See, e.g. Walker (1978), Bennett (1966) and arguably Strawson (1966) on one side and Bird (2000), Westphal (2004), and Matthews (1969) on the other.

(iii) As an empirical substance I must be a natural object among others in the world of time, space, causality, and change.

(iv) As a natural object I interact with others through my perceptions and actions both of which are structured by reason.

(v) These perceptions and actions embed an immediate consciousness of my being affected by things (as things about which I and others make judgments).

Notice that this interpretation embeds a kind of naturalism antithetic to dualism or "noumenalism"[10] and draws together preceding arguments establishing that my consciousness of my own existence reveals that I am an object among others in relation to which I move, perceive, and act.[11]

We can detail the argument as follows.

(i) I am a subject who apparently comes into contact with things which persist and may appear and re-appear in my experience in a way that distinguishes them from the inherently unstable and shifting flux of subjective appearances. Kant claims that he has here turned the game of the idealist against itself in conceding the shifting and unstable flux of inner impressions but then rejecting the claim that our only experience of the outer (or perceived rather than imagined) is mediate and inferred from that flux. He argues that in the midst of this subjective flux we are directly struck by some appearances that do not covary with subjective shifts of attention and interest but whose relation to time and space is fixed by something external — they reveal a happening in which the order of succession is necessitated by something objective or transcendent of my own subjective impressions — so that I must distinguish "the subjective succession of apprehension from the objective succession of appearances" to capture this fact. The crucial appearances evince a succession and stability not subject, for instance, to vagaries of apprehension and attention (even though the imagination is active in all experience — as he remarks in his footnote)[12] and, as objective successions (discerned and not imagined), they implicate the subject

---

[10] Bird and others have applied this name to the idea that *noumena* are objects in a suprasensible and atemporal realm. Strawson calls the relation between *noumena* so conceived and the world "the A relation". The kind of naturalism is best described by Robert Hanna (2006).

[11] An interpretation similar to that of Quassim Cassam (1997).

[12] Strawson discusses the distinction between the appearance of succession and a succession of appearances but he does not sufficiently relate this to the immediacy of receptivity that is the basis of the strong anti-idealist argument.

in a determinate and stable relation to time. The subject is not adrift in a subjective and imaginary world because the (relative) permanence and discernible change pervading my experience proves that inner experience in general carries the trace of something objective. But what of the experiencing subject? Is that also a being in the world looked at in a certain way — a natural being — or is it something quite other (noumenal in the "spooky" sense) than the things with which it is in contact, so that it has no community of nature with them?[13]

(ii) Time and change implies that our conception of reality rests on the normative or regulative idea that there are stable objects in the world, evident by their persistence in perception (or relative permanence securing the stability of that which undergoes alteration — as argued in the first analogy). But if the subject undergoes change, as it does if it experiences a flux of appearances, then it too must be a persistent thing. Kant argues (Note 2) that the relevant stability is not that of a mere representation, so that I (considered as a mere representation of subjectivity) cannot be its basis. The <I think>, despite its transcendental necessity for the synthesis of the manifold, is (as Kant argues in the paralogisms but here merely notes) not an object and therefore does not instance predicates of objectivity.[14] But if the subject is a persistent thing, then the only plausible candidate for that thing is a human being (a corporeal object) pursuing a subjective trajectory through an objective world.

(iii) The relative permanence of "a corporeal object among corporeal objects" (Strawson, 1966, 102) undergoing changes, according to the third analogy, implies not only that the subject is "an empirical referent" but also that it is in community with the objects affecting it (through receptivity). Therefore my permanence and the changes I find determined in me by outer experience jointly require the actual existence of things undergoing the objective successions of appearance given to me by my immediate and determinate (time ordered) experience of the actual world (an ontological necessity) around me as distinct from the imaginary or subjectively negotiable play of the "inner" world. This point is strengthened greatly by the appeal to training in judgment as a formative feature for concept-using

---

[13] As Russell claims. Matthews, Westphal and Bird take Kant to be addressing this point in the Refutation of idealism and McDowell would like him to be doing so rather than losing himself in the darker realms of noumenalism (1994).

[14] Walsh, (1982); Walsh e;sewhere states that Kant "says little or nothing about the relevance of bodily identity to personal identity"(1975, 181) but then notes that "it might be the case that a body was needed to supply the latter"(182). If we follow Matthews it is the case as the current argument avers.

subjects and in that light entails their existence in a shared (public, objective) world.

(iv) Because I am conscious of myself as an existing object (with a trajectory through an objective world), I could not act and perceive unless I was in contact with other objects and, in order to enter into the relevant interactions, am not merely an object (as established in the third analogy) but also an active cognitive subject, exercising my spontaneity as a player in the world of nature, my knowledge of which is structured for me according to norms of objectivity and right thinking (imparted by training).

(v) Therefore perception and action place me as an object among other objects with which I am interacting or being affected and reason reveals to me the underlying order to be found there but also reveals that, unlike mere objects, I am a cognitive subject.

This interpretation of the refutation of idealism explains its placement in the *First Critique* (after both the Analogies and the transcendental doctrine of judgment which I have drawn on to flesh it out). It also provides a framework in the context of which I can justifiably believe that I learn to discriminate the objective succession of appearances from subjective succession of appearances (*Pure Reason*, B237-8). What is more the interpretation provides a *de juris* foundation for the sophisticated naturalistic orientation implicit in post-Kantian phenomenology, hermeneutics, existentialism, and structuralism. I construct my knowledge of the world in which I am situated on the twin bases formed by (i) the basic apprehension of things affecting me (rather than the mere subjective succession of appearances in me) and (ii) my ability to apply concepts to the objects and events with which I and others interact. Therefore consciousness of my existence as an object moving among other objects that I perceive as such and as a thinker who applies concepts consistently (and by and large correctly) are internally related (and mutually supporting) preconditions of my thought about the world. Thus all my conceptually structured conscious experience is only possible through experience of the outer, a law-like realm to which I am adapted (by nature or providence and training).[15]

I have already referred to Kant's notes (in "The Refutation of Idealism") but revisiting them strengthens the plausibility of this interpretation of the argument.

---

[15] Jaspers follows Kant in remaining agnostic, from a strictly philosophical point of view, between the naturalistic and theistic alternatives (1975, 33).

**Note 1.** Idealism assumed that the only immediate experience is inner experience but, when we attend to our phenomenology and what is entailed by it, we immediately recognise that receptivity (being struck or affected by an appearance) is not the same as spontaneity (conjuring up and reasoning about an appearance) and thus we have an immediate apprehension of the differences between the appearances of actual objects and events and mere subjective ideas-that-things-are-thus-and-so on whatever basis (e.g. imagination). That our experience of the world is immediate is shown by the clear and distinct nature of receptivity, whereby intuitions reveal that something has happened and that the relevant impressions occurred in a non-negotiable (non-subjective) way, constraining their content. Kant here reinforces a point he will later spell out in detail in the paralogisms: that the representation "I am" cannot be the basis of our intuition of the permanent because it contains no intuition of an object with the objectively fixed nature of outer experience.[16]

**Note 2.** Kant again reiterates the point that permanence or essential substantiality (through accidental change) is an *a priori* feature of the apprehension of change and cannot be given by the "I" of the "I think" which is not an intuitable object but a mere "intellectual representation of the self-activity of a thinking subject"(B278).[17]

**Note 3.** The existence of outer objects as a general condition for consciousness and therefore for that subset of it that is inner awareness does not imply that outer experience inherits the incorrigibility accorded by the empiricists to impressions and ideas or inner representations (as is often pointed out in critiques of externalism). Not all representations reveal an existing object and not all my judgments are correct, because imagination, dreams and delusions—even though my synthetic faculties are at work in all of them—depend on concepts honed in outer experience (through training) but employed in a different mode and, in fact, any skill can miscarry on a given occasion under certain subjective conditions. Therefore conscious experiences, even if necessarily they satisfy the constraints on content grounded in experience of actual objects and events detected by receptivity, fall under the epistemic constraints we imbibe with that experience (on the present account). On that basis we judge imagined events to be different from real events because they lack (i) the constraint of objective succession in time which

---

[16] Walsh (see note 14 above) and Bird (2000) both discuss this point at length.

[17] This is particularly important in view of the quasi-stable apprehension of the self and the *meconnaissance* to which it is subject.

arises from the natural order and to which I am attuned so that I am immediately aware of it[18] and (ii) the implicit intersubjective validity that I discern in veridical experience.

I have argued that the logical subject is subtended from a set of abstractions and is "located" in logical space or the space of reasons. This is a similar claim to that rehearsed by Cassam when he remarks: "I thoughts can only be grasped in the context of a range of other abilities. These abilities are such that they can only be possessed by persons or other subjects who are physical objects among physical objects" (Cassam, 1997, 197).

The relevant thoughts and other mental acts here are of the following kind: I think that tree is very old; I see the deer; I am walking away from you now. In all of these I am the subject and neither predicate nor object (a grammatical fact). "I" refers to the same individual as "you" or "s/he" when used by others speaking of me and these utterances are all part of a practice of the type in which language is taught and learnt (and in which my concepts take shape). That practice, from my subjective point of view as somebody in the world, is centred on me, a being-in-the-world-with-others.

Thus Kitcher's noumenal subject is a logical construct and, arguably, of no concern to anybody, but the terms denoting that construct also denote the human being—I, me, or myself—on the basis of whose doings the construction (by myself and others) occurs. The life of that being is of vital concern to me and every other subject who is a being-in-the-world-with-me.

## Soul and body

Wittgenstein (*PI* #398) makes some remarks related to the theory of types and directly relevant to the noumenal/phenomenal confusions Kant discusses in the paralogisms. Just as certain relations cannot be thought of according to any univocal sense of "being a member of" (which, logico-mathematically is quite different when it applies to a relation between sets and a relation between a set and an object) so having is not the same in relation to the soul and any object. Wittgenstein discusses such confusions in the *Tractatus* (3331-3) and in relation to the way that the visual room is in fact a feature of the subject and his/her cognitive mode of interaction with a room or a disposition of (actual) things in space. Any relation A-B (such as a person possessing an object) implies two metaphysically distinct

---

[18] This embeds a positive view of what Westphal and Kant both term the affinity of the manifold and its internal or conceptual relationship to human cognition.

individuals as the two relata. This is not satisfied because there is no "inner object" called the soul or noumenal self (just a mode of cognizing) and to think of the "I" as an inner object is to make the same mistake as is found in the theory of sense data i.e. to mistakenly hypostasize or reify (a move also used by Russell in "On the nature of acquaintance" against Brentano). That is the logical reason why I cannot have a soul (or sense data) and neither can anybody have a soul (or sense data) in that (metaphysically individual relata) sense of "have" that assimilates me and my psychic life to me and my handbag. After Aristotle, the relation between soul and body should be assimilated to the relation between the eye and sight (which, when pursued, tells us where to look to bring out the characteristics of mental life: our gaze should shift to the holistic relation between the human being and his or her context).

## Appendix E: On natural kinds

The philosophical idea of natural kinds can be traced to Locke's view that the real essence of anything is some principled basis in nature for its attributes, as detected by the mind, having the form and constancy that they do. In contemporary philosophy, the idea is most often linked to the work of Putnam (1973) and Kripke (1980) who argued that there are general terms that designate things naturally occurring in the actual world, such as gold, tigers, water, neutrinos, and white blood cells. These terms "carve nature at its joints" and underpin realist metaphysics. An object or type of thing really does belong to such a category if it appears in the best current scientific knowledge in the relevant area. The linguistic community defers to the scientific experts and therefore the category becomes *de facto* a product of orthodox scientific theory in the area in question. Science, on this view, reveals to us the real structure of the actual world and therefore identifies enduring categories in nature. But a radical and serious challenge to the scientific theory governing the phenomena in question therefore has metaphysical implications. Such a shift can affect even basic questions about when a certain scientific kind or phenomenon (such as oxygen) was discovered and by whom (Hudson, 2001).

There is a vigorous debate about whether diseases are natural kinds (in the sense defined) and represent objectively specifiable, dysfunctions of the organism they affect (Boorse, 1975). I and others have argued that defining diseases by reference only to aberrations in the natural or normal biological function of the human organism is problematic. Classifying something as a disease involves not just describing but evaluating a pattern of changes in an organism (Megone, 1998; Gillett, 1999a; Fulford, 1989). But the basic premise of biomedical science is that something like the objective metaphysical claim about human disease and dysfunction is true and ought — *sans phrase* — to underpin the taxonomy of biomedicine.

## Appendix F: The problem of reference

Reference is apparently one of the most straightforward relationships that can be set out, in that one has an object and a way of denoting that object as when one says "That frog is green" (and by so doing refers to a frog in the immediate vicinity). One could say that when you use a word and point, the word refers to the thing being pointed at. But as soon as we go beyond the obvious case things get difficult. How, to use Wittgenstein's example, do I refer to the colour of a piece of paper, rather than its shape?(*PI* #33) Quine famously used the word "gavagai" to make the problem vivid. He asked whether, were such a word to be uttered as a rabbit hove in view, it would refer to a rabbit or an undetached rabbit part. Wittgenstein explicitly connects words to a fragment of a language, the understanding of which enables one to appreciate what is being attended to as the thing denoted by the word (hence Wittgenstein's affinity to structuralism or limited linguistic holism).

The structuralist/holistic move is problematic because it seemingly severs the one-to-one link between a word and what it stands for but, as we have seen, this link may itself be quite illusory (as Frege notices when he discusses Phosphorus, Hesperus and Venus). The simple fact that language may give us many routes to a referent (the thing being referred to) gives rise to two problems which need resolution.

(i) How is language connected to the world?

(ii) How do we settle a basic set of connections between language and the world, on the basis of which a more interdependent set of significations can be elaborated (so as not to endlessly defer meaning by making the meaning of every term depend on contrasts and connections to the meaning of others)?

The first question is sometimes answered by invoking a causal connection between the subject's representational states and the world being represented but that thesis is deficient for the very simple reason that any given situation may connect to language in a myriad ways, as in the following case.

> That is a fox in the garden.
>
> The garden looks to be full of life this morning.
>
> What is that brown shape beside the scraps heap?
>
> The neighbour's dog is at the scraps again.
>
> Isn't a spring morning wonderful!
>
> Judging by the light in the garden, I would say it is 6 am.

Each remark is (*ex hypothesi*) provoked by the same situation and yet each has a different meaning and represents or refers to different aspects of the same (presented) set of conditions. Each, we could say, has a different truth-maker (Armstrong, 2004) for the embedded representational content (moderated of course by the relevant illocutionary force — interrogative, exclamatory, and so on). If that is so then each remark is equally caused by the same conditions and so to distinguish meanings (or their referents) we need to say which aspects of the conditions concerned are the relevant ones — a specification not available from an unelaborated causal connection.

The second problem motivates the thought that all signifiers slide over their signifieds and only holistically fix meaning. But this causes a nightmarish problem of incommensurability between differently nested knowledge claims (in that the content of the knowledge claim is yielded only by accepting the holistic system — or structure — which determines the meaning of any term). The most unattractive corollary of that claim is that two different scientific theories cannot ever be talking about the same things, and even that two so-called observation statements have different content depending on the system of observations they are nested in (this was made famous by Quine [1953] as the indeterminacy of reference or ontological relativity). Putnam (1981) then explored internalism (and mind-dependence) as the closest to realism that one could get by accepting that reference and representation both were a matter of connecting (indirectly) representational states in the heads of thinkers to the world in which the thinkers were functioning.

The current view does not begin with indirect representation as the route to the referent,[19] but with the thought that we are actually dealing with the things that get into our conversations, and that in

---

[19] Most versions of that view fall foul of the reification of sense data referred to in Appendix D (above) in the section "Soul and body".

these actual dealings we adopt ways of linking or relating (for their significance to us) conditions that give us a "grip" on the world. On this (Wittgensteinian) account, language is like a set of tools and words are woven into our dealings with things in diverse ways to make connections between us and the world, allowing us to differentially relate to different aspects of the world. Thus when I think of a person as an embodied brain, I think of the fact that the vehicle of their being-in-the-world-with-others is an embodied brain and its many connections to its context, informational relationships and interconnected functions. When, however, I think of a person as a fit target for praise and blame and attributions of responsibility, I locate them amongst others in ways that focus on their choices to act thus and so and express different aspects of their character (perhaps under diverse constraints and coercions). I then mobilize my ways of understanding people as agents like myself and respond appropriately in ways articulated by that kind of knowledge.[20]

I have suggested that knowledge (or signification), which unlocks the significance of what goes on around me, is subtended by all my dealings with things reactive, objective, emotive, and so on.[21] It follows that questions of the moral character of an individual are not accessible to detached or purely objective judgment, in that they importantly concern how the person concerned is impinged on or affected by others and the extent to which an understanding of that is evident in his or her dealings with those who are judging him. Therefore the jury needs to see the accused and register his reactions as the case unfolds, so that their intuitions about human beings can be fully engaged with the forensic judgments they have to make.

Reference is, therefore, not simple and it is entangled with the practices that give meanings to our words and our techniques of noticing, distinguishing, and comparing things so that we get a clear and distinct idea[22] of what (in the whole that is a situation in which one is participating) is being referred to.

---

[20] This roughly approximates Strawson's Objective and Reactive attitudes (1974).
[21] Heidegger's "circumspection" (*Being & Time*).
[22] The language is that of Brentano (1929 [1981]).

# Bibliography

Andorfer, J.C. (1985) Multiple personality in the human information-processor, *J Clinical Psychology* 41.3, 309-324.
American Psychiatric Association (1994) *Diagnostic and Statistical Manual of Mental Disorders* (4th Ed. DSM.IV) Washington, DC: APA publishers.
Aristotle (1986) *De Anima* (tr. H.Lawson Tancred) London: Penguin.
Aristotle (1925) *Nichomachean Ethics* (tr. D.Ross) Oxford: Oxford University Press.
Armstrong, D. (1981) *The Nature of Mind* Ithaca, NY: Cornell University Press.
Armstrong, D. (2004) *Truth and Truthmakers* Cambridge: Cambridge University Press.
Austin, J.L. (1970) *Philosophical Papers* Oxford: University Press.
Ayer, A.J. (1982) Freedom and necessity, in G. Watson (Ed.) *Free Will* Oxford: Oxfrod University Press.
Baer, S.L. *et al.* (1995) Cingulotomy for intractable obsessive-compulsive disorder: prospective long term follow up of 18 patients, *Archives of General Psychiatry* 52, 384-392.
Baier, A. (1985) *Postures of the Mind* London: Methuen.
Barsalou, L.W. (1988) The content and organization of autobiographical memories, in U. Neisser and E. Winograd (Ed.) *Remembering Reconsidered* Cambridge: Cambridge University Press.
Bennett, J. (1966) *Kant's Analytic* Cambridge: Cambridge University Press.
Bird, G. (1973) *Kant's Theory of Knowledge* New York: Humanities Press.
Bird, G. (2000) The paralogisms and Kant's account of psychology, *Kant Studien* 91, 129-145.
Bishop, J. (1989) *Natural Agency* Cambridge: Cambridge University Press.
Black,M. (1952) The identity of indiscernibles, *Mind* LXI 242, 157.
Blank, R. (1999) *Brain Policy* Washington, DC: Georgetown University Press.
Bohannon J. and Symons, V. (1992) Flashbulb memories: confidence, consistency and quantity, in E.Winograd and U. Neisser (Ed.) *Affect and Accuracy in Recall: The Problem of Flashbulb Memories* New York: Cambridge University Press.
Boorse, C. (1975) On the distinction between disease and illness, *Philosophy and Public Affairs* 5, 49-68.
Braisby N. and Gellatly A. (2005) *Cognitive Psychology* Oxford: Oxford University Press.
Braude, S. (1991) *First Person Plural* London: Routledge.

Braude, S. (1996) Multiple personality and moral responsibility, *Philosophy, Psychiatry and Psychology* 3.1, 37-54.

Brentano, F. (1929 [1981]) *Sensory and Noetic Consciousness* (Tr. M. Schattle & L. McAlister) London: Routledge and Kegan Paul.

Brock, D. (1998) Cloning human beings: an assessment of the ethical issues pro and con, in M. Nussbaum & C. Sunstein (Ed.) *Clones and Clones: Facts and Fantasies About Human Cloning* New York: Norton & Co.

Buber, M. (1970) *I and Thou* (Tr. W. Kaufmann) Edinburgh: T&T Clark.

Butler, J. (1989) Foucault and the paradox of bodily inscriptions, *The Journal of Philosophy* 86.11, 601-607.

Campbell, J. (1994) *Past, Space and Self* Cambridge, MA: MIT Press.

Campbell, J. (2002) *Reference and Consciousness* Oxford: Oxford University Press.

Carson, R. (1997) Medical ethics as reflective practice, in Carson, R. and C. Burns (Ed.) *Philosophy of Medicine and Bioethics* Dordrecht: Kluwer.

Cassam, Quassim (1997) *Self and World* Oxford: Oxford University Press.

Cavell, M. (1993) *The Psychoanalytic Mind* Cambridge, MA: Harvard University Press.

Chisholm, R. (1967) Identity through possible worlds: some questions, *Nous* 1, 1-8.

Church, J. (1987) Reasonable Irrationality, *Mind* 96.3, 354-366.

Church, J. (2005) Reasons of which reason knows not, *Philosophy Psychiatry and Psychology* 12.1, 31-42.

Churchland, P. (1986) *Matter and Consciousness* Cambridge, MA: MIT Press.

Clark, A. (1997) *Being There: Putting Brain Body and World Together Again* Cambridge, MA: MIT Press.

Clark, S (1996) Minds memes and multiples, *Philosophy, Psychiatry, and Psychology* 3.1, 21-28.

Confucius (1938) *The Analects* (Tr. Waley, A) New York: Random House.

Coope, C.M. (2006) Death Sentences, *Philosophy* 81, 5-32.

Copland, P. & Gillett, G. (2003) The bioethical structure of a human being, *Journal of Applied Philosophy* 20.2, 123-32

Conway, M. (2005) Memory and the self, *Journal of Memory and Language* 53.4, 594-628.

Conway M. and Holmes E. (2005) Autobiographical memory and the working self, in Braisby and Gellatly (Ed.) *Cognitive Psychology* Oxford: Oxford University Press.

Damasio, A. (1994) *Descartes' Error* New York: G.P.Putnam.

Danzer, G., Rose, M., Walter, M. & Klapp, B. (2002) On the theory of individual health, *Journal of Medical Ethics* 28, 17-19.

Davidson, D. (1980) *Essays on Actions and Events* Oxford: Clarendon.

Davidson, D. (1984) *Inquiries into Truth and Interpretation* Oxford: Clarendon.

Davidson, D. (1987), Knowing one's own mind, *Proceedings and Addresses of the American Philosophical Association* 60, 441–458.

Davidson,D. (2001) *Subjective, Intersubjective, Objective* Oxford: University Press.

De Grazia, D. (2003) Identity, killing, and the boundaries of our existence, *Philosophy and Public Affairs* 31.4, 413-442.

De Grazia, D. (2005) *Human Identity and Bioethics* Cambridge: Cambridge University Press.
Dennett, D. (1990) True believers: the intentional strategy and why it works, in Lycan, W.G. (Ed.) *Mind and Cognition* Oxford: Blackwell.
Dennett, D. (1991) *Consciousness Explained* Boston, MA: Little Brown.
Diamantides D. (2000) *The Ethics of Suffering* London: Ashgate.
Diamond, C. (1995) *The Realistic Spirit* Cambridge, MA: MIT Press.
Donagan, A. (1990) Real human persons, *Logos* 11, 1-16.
Duff, R.A. (1990) *Intention, Agency and Criminal Liability* Oxford: Blackwell.
Elliot, C. (2001) Attitudes, souls, and persons: children with severe neurological impairment, in *Slow Cures and Bad Philosophers* Durham, NC: Duke University Press.
Engelhardt, T. (1986) *The Foundations of Bioethics* Oxford: Oxford University Press.
Evans, G. (1982) *The Varieties of Reference* Oxford: Clarendon.
Foot, P. (1978) *Virtues and Vices* Oxford: Blackwell.
Foot, P. (2001) *Natural Goodness* Oxford: Oxford University Press.
Foucault, M. (1970) *The Order of Things* New York: Random House
Foucault, M. (1975) *Discipline and Punish: The Birth of the Prison* (Tr. A. Sheridan) London: Allen Lane.
Foucault, M. (1984) *The Foucault Reader* (ed. P.Rabinow) London: Penguin.
Foucault, M. (1994) *Ethics: Subjectivity and Truth* (ed. P. Rabinow) London: Penguin.
Frame, J. (1961) *Faces in the Water* London: The Women's Press.
Frank, A. (1996) *The Wounded Storyteller: Body, Illness and Ethics* Chicago: University of Chicago Press.
Frege, G. (1980) *Translations from the Philosophical Writings of Gottlob Frege* (ed. P. Geach & M. Black) Oxford: Blackwell.
Fulford, W. (1989) *Moral Theory and Medical Practice* Cambridge: Cambridge University Press.
Ganaway, G.K. (1989) Historical versus narrative truth: Clarifying the role of exogenous trauma in the etiology of MPD and its variants, *Dissociation* 2, 205-220.
Gardner H. (1974) *The Shattered Mind* New York: Vintage
Gazzaniga, M.S. (1970) *The Bisected Brain* New York: Appleton Century Crofts.
Geach, P. (1969) *God and the Soul* London: Routledge and Kegan Paul.
Gelder, M. Gath, D. and Mayou, R. (1983) *Oxford Textbook of Psychiatry* Oxford: Oxford University Press.
Gillett, G. (1986) Multiple personality and the concept of a person, *New Ideas in Psychology* 4, 173-184.
Gillett, G. (1991a) Language, social ecology and experience, *International Studies in the Philosophy of Science* 5, 1-9.
Gillett, G. (1991b) Multiple Personality and irrationality, *Philosophical Psychology* 4, 103-118.
Gillett, G. (1992) *Representation Meaning and Thought* Oxford: Clarendon.
Gillett, G. (1993a) Wittgenstein on the mind, *Inquiry* 36.4, 451-464.
Gillett, G. (1993b) Ought and well-being, *Inquiry* 36, 287-306.
Gillett, G. (1996) Young human beings: metaphysics and ethics, in Oderburg, D.S. & J.A. Laing (Ed.) *Human Lives* London: Macmillan.

Gillett, G. (1997a) Husserl, Wittgenstein and the Snark, *Philosophy and Phenomenological Research* LVII, 331-350.
Gillett, G. (1997b) A discursive account of multiple personality disorder, *Philosophy, Psychiatry and Psychology* 4.3, 213-229.
Gillett, G. (1998) Brain bisection and personal identity, in *The Mind* (Ed. D. Robinson) Oxford: Oxford University Press.
Gillett, G. (1999a) *The Mind and its Discontents* Oxford: Oxford University Press.
Gillett, G. (1999b) Consciousness and lesser states: the evolutionary foothills of the mind, *Philosophy* 74, 331-360.
Gillett, G. (2000) Moral authenticity and the unconscious, in *The Analytic Freud* (M. Levine ed.) London: Routledge.
Gillett, G. (2001) Wittgenstein's startling claim: consciousness and the persistent vegetative state, in Elliot C. (Ed.) *Slow Cures and Bad Philosophers* Durham, NC: Duke University Press.
Gillett, G. (2003) Freud and the neurological unconscious, in *The Nature of Psychoanalytic Knowledge* (Ed. Cheung & Feltham) Basingstoke: Palgrave.
Gillett, G. (2004) *Bioethics in the Clinic* Baltimore: Johns Hopkins University Press.
Gillett, G. (2005) The unwitting sacrifice problem, *Journal of Medical Ethics* 31, 327-332.
Gillett, G. (2006) Cyborgs and moral identity, *Journal of Medical Ethics* 32, 79-83.
Gillett, G. & McMillan, J. (2001) *Consciousness and Intentionality* Amsterdam: John Benjamins.
Glannon, W. (2007) *Bioethics and the Brain* New York: Oxford University Press.
Glass, A. and Holyoak, K. (1986) *Cognition* New York: Random House.
Gleitman, H. (1991) *Psychology (3rd Ed.)* New York: W.W.Norton & Co.
Goffman, E. (1959) *The Presentation of Self in Everyday Life* London: Penguin.
Green, C. & Gillett, G. (1992) Are mental events preceded by their physical causes? *Philosophical Psychology* 8, 333-340.
Gubrium, J. (2000) Narrative practice and the inner worlds of the Alzheimer disease experience, in *Concepts of Alzheimer Disease* (ed. Whitehouse, P, Maurer K, and Ballenger J.) Baltimore: Johns Hopkins University Press.
Hacking, I. (1994) The looping effect of human kinds, in *Causal Cognition* (ed. D. Sperber *et al.*) Oxford: Oxford University Press.
Hacking, I. (1995) *Rewriting the Soul* Princeton, NJ: Princeton University Press.
Haldane, J. and Lee, P. (2003) Aquinas on human ensoulment, abortion and the value of life, *Philosophy* 78, 255-278.
Hampshire, S. (1969) Some difficulties in knowing, in *Philosophy As It Is* (ed. Honderich and Burnyeat ) London: Penguin.
Hanna, R. (2006) *Kant Science and Human Nature* Oxford: Clarendon.
Harre, R. and Gillett, G. (1994) *The Discursive Mind* London: Sage.
Hegel, G. (1807 [1977]) *Phenomenology of Spirit* (Tr. A.V.Miller) Oxford: University Press.
Heidegger, M. (1953 [1996]) *Being and Time* (tr J.Stambaugh) New York: SUNY Press.
Hodges J. & McCarthy, R. (1988) Loss of remote memory, in Ellis & Young (eds) *Human Cognitive Neuropsychology* Hove: Psychology Press.

Hodgkiss, A.L. et al. (1995) Outcomes after the psychosurgical operation of stereotactic subcaudate tractotomy, *J. Neuropsychiatry Clin. Neurosci.* 7, 230-234.
Holland, A. (1990) A fortnight of my life is missing: a discussion of the human 'pre-embryo', *Journal of Applied Philosophy* 7.1, 25-37.
Honderich, T. & Burnyeat M. (1979) *Philosophy As It Is* London: Penguin.
Hudson, R. (2001) Discoveries, when and by whom? *British Journal of the Philosophy of Science* 52.1, 75-94.
Hume, D (1740 [1969]) *A Treatise of Human Nature* (ed. E.Mossner) London: Penguin.
Hurley, S. (1998) *Consciousness in Action* Cambridge, MA: MIT Press.
Hursthouse, R. (1999) *On Virtue Ethics* Oxford: University Press.
Husserl E. (1950) *Cartesian Meditations* (tr. D. Cairns) Dordrecht: Kluwer.
Husserl, E. (1958) *Ideas* (tr. W.R. Boyce Gibson*)* London: Allen and Unwin.
Jaspers, K. (1913 [1974]) Causal and meaningful connexions between life history and psychosis, in *Themes and Variations in European Psychiatry* (ed. S.R.Hirsch & M.Shepherd) Bristol: John Wright and Sons.
Jaspers K. (1975) *Kant* Munich: R. Piper & Co. Verlag.
Jeeves, M. (1997) *Human Nature at the Millenium* Grand Rapids: Baker Press.
Kant, I. (1788 [1956]) *The Critique of Practical Reason* (tr. Lewis White Beck) Indianapolis: Bobbs Merrill.
Kant, I. (1789 [1929]) *The Critique of Pure Reason* (tr. N.Kemp Smith) London: Macmillan (references are given by pagination in this B edition e.g. B562; at times I draw on the Guyer and Wood translation Cambridge UP [1997]).
Kant, I.(1798 [1974]): *Anthropology from a Pragmatic Point of View* (trans. M.J. Gregor) The Hague: Martinus Nijhoff.
Kant, I. (1948) *The Moral Law* (Tr. H.J. Paton) London: Hutchinson.
Kitcher, Patricia (1990) *Kant's Transcendental Psychology* Oxford: Oxford University Press.
Kleinig, J. (1985) *Ethical Issues in Psychosurgery* London: Allen and Unwin.
Koch, C. (2004) *The Quest for Consciousness* Englewood, CO: Roberts and Co.
Kolb, B. & Wishaw, I. (1990) *The Fundamentals of Human Neuropsychology* New York: W.H. Freeman & Co.
Korzenev, A.V., Shoustin, V.A., Anichkov, A.D., Polonskiy, J.Z., Nizkovolos, V.B. and Oblyapin, A.V. (1997) Differential approach to psychosurgery of obsessive disorders, *Stereotactic & Functional Neurosurgery* 68, 226-230.
Kripke, S. (1971) Identity and necessity, in M. Munitz (ed.) *Identity and Individuation* New Yoyk: NYU Press.
Kripke, S. (1980) *Naming and Necessity* Cambridge, MA: Harvard University Press.
Kristeva, J. (1995) *The New Maladies of the Soul* New York: Columbia University Press.
Lacan, J. (1977) *Ecrits* New York: Norton and Co.
Lacan, J. (1979) *The four Fundamental Concepts of Psycho-analysis* (Tr. A Sheridan) London: Penguin.
Lear, J. (2003) *Therapeutic Action* New York: Other Press.
Levinas, E. (1996) *Basic Philosophical Writings* Bloomington, IN: Indiana University Press.

Levinas, E. (1990) *Difficult Freedom: Essays on Judaism* Baltimore: Johns Hopkins University Press.
Lewis, D. (1969) Survival and identity, in A. Rorty (Ed.) *The Identities of Persons* Berkeley, CA: University of California Press.
Lewis, D. (2001) *On the Plurality of Worlds* Oxford: Blackwell.
Libet, B. (1985) Unconscious cerebral initiative and the role of conscious will in voluntary action, *The Behavioural and Brain Sciences* 8, 529-566.
Lloyd, G. (1978) *Hippocratic Writings* London: Penguin.
Locke, J. (1689 [1975]) *An Essay Concerning Human Understanding* (ed. P. Nidditch) Oxford: Clarendon. Cited as *Essay*.
Lockwood M. (1985, ed.) *Moral Dilemmas in Modern Medicine* Oxford: Oxford University Press.
Lockwood, M. (1985a) When does a life begin? in Lockwood (1985).
Lockwood, M. (1985b) The Warnock Report: a philosophical appraisal, in Lockwood (1985).
Loftus, E. (1993) The reality of repressed memories, *American Psychologist* 48.5, 518-537.
Lopez, B. (1990) *Crow and Weasel* Toronto: Random House.
Ludwig, A. Brandsma, J. Wibur, C. Benfeldt F. & Jameson, D. (1972) The objective study of a multiple personality, *Archives of General Psychiatry* 26, 298-310.
Luria, A.R. (1973) *The Working Brain* Harmondsworth: Penguin
Lyng, S. (2005) *Edgework: The Sociology of Risk Taking* Abingdon: Routledge.
McDowell, J. (1994) *Mind and World* Cambridge, MA: Harvard University Press.
McGuigan F.J. (1997) A neuromuscular model of mind with clinical and educational applications, *Journal of Mind and Behaviour* 18.4, 351-370.
MacIntyre, A. (1984) *After Virtue* Notre Dame, IN: University of Notre Dame Press.
Macintyre, A. (1999) *Dependent Rational Animals* Chicago and La Salle: Open Court.
Mackie. J. (1976) *Problems from Locke* Oxford: University Press.
Mackie, J. (1965) Causes and conditions, *American Philosophical Quarterly* 2, 245-255.
Macklin, R. (1999) The ethical problems with sham surgery in clinical research, *New England Journal of Medicine* 341, 992-995.
McMahan, J. (1998) Wrongful Life; paradoxes in the morality of causing people to exist, in *Rational Commitment and Social Justice* (ed. J. Coleman and C, Morris) Cambridge: Cambridge University Press.
McMahan, J. (2003) *The Ethics of Killing: Problems at the Margins of Life* Oxford: Oxford University Press.
Manshour, G.A., Walker, E.E. and Martuza, R.L. (2005) Psychosurgery: Past present and future, *Brain Research Reviews* 48, 409-419.
Marshall, J. III (2004) *The Journey of Crazy Horse* New York: Penguin.
Matthews, H. (1969) Strawson on transcendental idealism, *Philosophical Quarterly* 19, 204-220.
Megone, C. (1998) Aristotle's function argument and the concept of mental illness, *Philosophy Psychiatry and Psychology* 5, 187-201.
Mencius (1970) *Mencius* (Tr. Lau D) London: Penguin.

Merleau Ponty, M. (1964) *The Primacy of Perception* (ed K. Edie) Evanston, IL: Northwestern University Press.
Merskey, H. (1999) Ethical aspects of the physical manipulation of the brain, in S. Bloch, P. Chodoff & S. Green (Ed.) *Psychiatric Ethics* Oxford: Oxford University Press.
Millikan, R.G. (1990) Truth rules, hoverflies, and the Kripke-Wittgenstein Paradox, *The Philosophical Review* XCIX, 323-353.
Millikan, R.G. (1993) *White Queen Psychology and other Essays for Alice* Cambridge, MA: MIT Press.
Mill, J.S. (1874) *System of Logic: Ratiocinative and Inductive* New York: Harper & Sons.
Moscovitch, M. (1995) Confabulation, in D. Schachter (ed.) *Memory Distortion* Cambridge, MA: Harvard University Press.
Multi-society task force on PVS (1994) Medical aspects of the persistent vegetative state, *New Engl. J. Med*, 1499-1503.
Murdoch, Iris (1993) *Metaphysics as a Guide to Morals* London: Penguin.
Murray, T. (1996) *The Worth of a Child* Berkeley, CA: University of California Press.
Nagel, T. (1986) *The View from Nowhere* Oxford: Oxford University Press.
Nagel, T. (1979) Brain bisection and the unity of consciousness, in *Mortal Questions* Cambridge: Cambridge University Press.
Neisser, U. (1981) John Dean's memory: a case study, *Cognition* 16, 81-95.
Nietzsche, F. (1886 [1975]) *Beyond Good and Evil* (Tr. R.J.Hollingdale) London: Penguin.
Nietzsche, F. (1994 {1878]) *Human All Too Human* (Tr. M. Faber and S. Lehmann) London: Penguin.
Northoff, G. and Heinzel, A. (2006) First-person neuroscience: A new methodological approach for linking mental and neuronal states, *Philosophy, Ethics and Humanities in Medicine* 1.3.
Nussbaum, M. (1990) *Love's Knowledge* Oxford: Oxford University Press.
Nussbaum, M. (1994) *The Therapy of Desire* Princeton, NJ: University Press.
O'Keefe, J. and Nadel, L. (1978) *The Hippocampus as a Cognitive Map* Oxford: Clarendon.
Parfit, D. (1986) *Reasons and Persons* Oxford: Clarendon.
Parfit, D. (1979) Personal identity, in *Philosophy As It Is* (ed. T. Honderich and M. Burnyeat) London: Penguin.
Parkin, A. (1996) *Explorations in Cognitive Neuropsychology* Oxford: Blackwell.
Parkin, A. (2001) The structure and mechanisms of memory, in Rapp (Ed.) *Handbook of Cognitive Neuropsychology* Philadelphia, PA: Taylor and Francis.
Peacocke, A. and Gillett, G. (1987) *Persons and Personality* Oxford: Blackwell.
Phillips, D.Z. (2004) *The Problem of Evil and the Problem of God* London: SCM Press.
Piper, A. Jr. (1994) Multiple personality disorder: A critical review, *British Journal of Psychiatry* 164, 600-612.
Polkinghorne, J. (2002) *The God of Hope and the End of the World* London: SPCK Press.
Polkinghorne, J. (2004) The person, the soul, and genetic engineering, *Journal of Medical Ethics* 30, 593-597.

Post, S. (2000) *The Moral Challenge of Alzheimer Disease* (2nd Ed.) Baltimore: Johns Hopkins University Press.
Pressman, J. (1998) *The Last Resort: Psychosurgery and the Limits of Medicine* Cambridge: Cambridge University Press.
Putnam, H. (1973) Meaning and reference, *Journal of Philosophy* 70, 699-711.
Putnam, H. (1981) *Reason Truth and History* Cambridge: Cambridge University Press.
Putnam, F.W., Guroff, J.J., Silberman E.K., Barban, L. and Post, R.M. (1986) The clinical phenomenology of multiple personality disorder: review of 100 recent cases, *Journal of Clinical Psychiatry* 47, 285-293.
Quine, W.V.O. (1953) *From a Logical Point of View* New York: Harper.
Quinton, A. (1967) The problem of perception, in G. Warnock (ed.) *The Philosophy of Perception* Oxford: Clarendon Press.
Ramachandran, V.S. & Blakeslee, S. (1998) *Phantoms in the Brain* New York: William Morrow.
Ross, C.A. (1991) Epidemiology of Multiple personality disorder and dissociation, *Psychiatric Clinics of North America* 14, 503-517.
Rubin D. (1992) Constraints on memory, in *Affect and Accuracy in Recall* (ed. E. Winograd and U. Neisser) Cambridge: Cambridge University Press.
Russell B. (1988) On the nature of acquaintance (reprinted in *Logic and Knowledge* London: Unwin).
Sabat, S. & Collins, M. (1999) Intact social, cognitive ability, and selfhood: A case study of Alzheimer's disease, *American Journal of Alzheimer's Disease* Jan/Feb (1999), 11-19.
Sacks, O. (1995) *An Anthropologist on Mars* Sydney: McMillan.
St Thomas Aquinas (1945) *Introduction to St Thomas Aquinas* (ed. A.C. Pegis) New York: Random House.
Sartre, Jean Paul (1958) *Being and Nothingness* (Tr. H Barnes) London: Methuen & Co.
Saul, J.R. (1996) *The Unconscious Civilization* London: Penguin.
Schachter, D. (1989) Memory, in M. Posner (Ed.) *Foundations of Cognitive Science* Cambridge, MA: MIT Press.
Schachter D. et al. (1995 ed.) *Memory Distortion* Cambridge, MA: Harvard University Press.
Schechtman, M. (1994) The truth about memory, *Philosophical Psychology* 7, 3-20.
Schechtman, M. (1996) *The Constitution of Selves* Ithaca, NY: Cornell University Press.
Searle, J. (1992) *The Rediscovery of the Mind* Cambridge, MA: MIT Press.
Sellars, W. (1997) *Empiricism and the Philosophy of Mind* Cambridge, MA: Harvard University Press.
Shapiro D. (1999) *Neurotic Styles* New York: Basic Books.
Shoemaker, S. (1984) *Identity, Cause, and Mind* Cambridge: Cambridge University Press.
Singer, P. (1992) Embryo experimentation and the moral status of the embryo, in *Philosophy and Health Care* (ed. E. Matthews and M. Menlowe) Aldershot: Avebury.
Snowdon, P. (1990) Persons, animals and ourselves, in *The Person and the Human Mind* (ed. C. Gill) Oxford: Clarendon.

Spence, S. (1996) Free will in the light of neuropsychiatry, *Philosophy, Psychiatry, and Psychology* 3, 75-90.
Sprigge, T. (1996) Commentary on "Minds, memes and multiples", *Philosophy, Psychiatry and Psychology* 3, 31-36.
Squire, L.R. (1995) Biological foundations of accuracy and inaccuracy in memory in Schacter *et al.* (1995).
Squire, L. and Kosslyn, S. (Eds.) (1998) *Findings and Current Opinion in Cognitive Neuroscience* Cambridge, MA: MIT Press.
Stich, S. (1983) *From Folk Psychology to Cognitive Science* Cambridge MA: MIT Press.
Storr, A. (1987) Jung's concept of personality, in Peacocke and Gillett (1987).
Strawson, G. (1997) "The self", *Journal of Consciousness Studies* 4.5-6, 405-428.
Strawson, G. (2004) Against narrativity, *Ratio* (new series) XVII, 412-450.
Strawson, P. (1959) *Individuals* London: Methuen.
Strawson, P. (1966) *The Bounds of Sense* London: Methuen.
Strawson, P. (1974) Freedom and resentment, in *Freedom and Resentment and other Essays* London: Methuen.
Taylor, C. (1989) *Sources of the Self* Cambridge, MA: Harvard University Press.
Taylor, C. (1991) *The Malaise of Modernity* Toronto: Anansi.
Vallacher R.R. & Wegner, D.M. (1987) What do people think they're doing? Action identification and human behaviour, *Psychological Review* 94, 3-15.
Veatch, R. (1995) Abandoning informed consent, *Hastings Center Report* 25.2, 5-12.
Veatch, R. (1996) Letter in reply: Abandoning informed consent, *Hastings Center Report* 26.1, 2-4.
Walker, R. (1978) *Kant* London: Routledge.
Walsh, W. (1982) Self knowledge, in R. Walker (ed.) *Kant on Pure Reason* Oxford: Oxford University Press.
Walsh, W. (1975) *Kant's Criticism of Metaphysics* Chicago, IL: University of Chicago Press.
Warnock, Dame M. (1984) *Report of the Committee of Inquiry into Human Fertilisation and Embryology* London: HMSO, Cmnd. 9314.
Wegner, D. (2002) *The Illusion of the Conscious Will* Cambridge, MA: MIT Press.
Wegner, D. (2004) Précis of The illusion of the conscious will, *Behavioural and Brain Sciences* 27, 649-692.
Weil, S. (1952) *The Need for Roots* London: Routledge and Kegan Paul.
Weil, S. (1978) *Lectures on Philosophy* (Tr. H. Price) Cambridge: Cambridge University Press.
Weiscrantz, L. (1997) *Consciousness Lost and Found* Oxford: Oxford University Press.
Westphal, K. (2004) Epistemic reflection and cognitive reference in Kant's transcendental response to scepticism, *Kant Studien* 94.2, 135-171.
Wiggins, D. (1987) The person as object of science, as subject of experience and as locus of value, in *Persons and Personality* (ed. A. Peacocke, & G. Gillett) Oxford: Blackwell.
Wilkes, K. (1988) *Real People* Oxford: Clarendon Press.

Williams, B. (1973) *Problems of the Self* Cambridge: Cambridge University Press.
Williams B. (1985) *Ethics and the Limits of Philosophy* London: Fontana.
Winograd, E. and Neisser, U. (1992) *Affect and Accuracy in Recall* Cambridge: Cambridge University Press.
Wittgenstein, L. (1922/1961) *Tractatus Logico Philosophicus* (Tr. D. Pears & B. McGuiness) London: Routledge & Kegan Paul. Cited as *Tractatus*.
Wittgenstein, L. (1953) *Philosophical Investigations* (Tr. G.E.M. Anscombe) Oxford: Blackwell. Cited as *PI*.
Wittgenstein, L. (1965) Lecture on ethics, *Philosophical Review* 74, 3-26.
Wittgenstein L. (1967) *Zettel* (Tr & Ed: G.E.M. Anscombe & G.H. von Wright) Oxford: Basil Blackwell.
Wittgenstein, L. (1969-70), *On Certainty* (ed. G.E.M.Anscombe and G.H.von Wright; tr. Denis Paul and G.E.M.Anscombe) Oxford: Basil Blackwell.
Wittgenstein, L. (1980) *Remarks on the Philosophy of Psychology* I and II (Tr. & Ed. G. E. M. Anscombe & G. H. von Wright) Oxford: Basil Blackwell.
Wittgenstein, L. (1980) *Culture and Value* (Tr. P Winch) Oxford: Blackwell.

# Index

Action 2, 5, 107-35, 149, 227, 234, 266
  argument to physical priority 111-17
  basic actions 110-3
  causal view 107-9, 117, 129
  and character 119-20, 122-31
  deviant causal chains 116
  and embodiment 155
  identity structure account 117, 120-1, 124, 127
  neurophilosophy of 109-17, 129-30
  non-causal account 118-29, 130-1, 133-4
Adequacy requirement 20-21
Agency (see action)
Alien hand 148
Alzheimer disease (see dementia)
Amnesia 95, 98, 126, 171
Aquinas 8, 136, 200 n11, 201 n16, 206, 207
Aristotle 1-3, 8, 9, 10, 13, 16, 17, 42, 44, 62, 68, 83, 84, 121, 133, 149, 156, 167, 206, 222, 229, 237, 252, 262
Automatism, 119, 126-7

Bishop 109, 116
Brain bisection 75, 146-55
Buber 63n4

Care of the self 3, 180, 190, 219
Cause 17, 37 n13
Chimera 50
Church 81
Clark 154-5, 185

Cloning 48-9
*Cogito* 8, 9, 62, 63
Cognitive significance (see sense)
  unity 71, 73, 83, 85-6, 122, 151-3
  subject 100, 141
Commissurotomy (see brain bisection)
Concept 66, 71, 100-1, 121, 226, 262, 265-6
  and rule 68-9, 78, 85, 121-3, 129, 262
confabulation 126, 148
Confucius 7, 8, 32, 133
Consciousness 79, 127, 141, 185, 234 n18
  and the unconscious 79-80, 187, 224-6
Coope 52
Cyborgs, 160-8

*Dasein* 81, 82, 102, 104, 161
Davidson 36 n13, 72 n22, 76 n27, 116, 149-51
Dementia 223, 229-31, 243
Dennett 114, 120, 122, 125-6, 128, 154-5, 191
Descartes 8, 9, 64, 164, 177, 200, 225 n5
De Grazia 12, 52
*De re* conceptions 43 n27
Ding-an-sich 8, 9, 79-80, 81, 102
Disability 55
Discursive naturalism 51, 175, 186, 262
  psychology 175, 178-9
Disease 137, 177, 190-1, 269-70

Dissociation, 171-2
DNA essentialism (see genetic essentialism)
Donagan 42

Edgework 235-7, 244
Embodiment 2, 4, 5, 154-5
Embryo 9ff, 16, 17ff
Enigma (see also Levinas) 131-3, 215, 241
Epigenetics 13, 33, 41, 49
Essence 4, 9, 10, 12, 32, 43 n29, 48, 65, 73, 103, 249, 256, 259
   nominal 3, 8, 65
   real 3, 8, 9, 14, 64, 65, 68, 78, 100, 106, 252, 256, 269
   relational aspects 19
Eudaimonea 16, 137-8, 228, 244
Eugenics 54-6
Evans 10
Events 36-8

Foot (see also natural goodness) 114, 165 n35, 228 n13, 231 n15, 233, 245
Form 10ff, 22, 24-6, 42, 50, 73, 167, 206, 256
Formal cause 9, 17
Human form 15ff, 24-6, 73, 137, 203
   and identity 33, 73, 202, 208-9, 256
Foucault 3, 35, 83, 104, 133-4, 174 n8, 175, 180, 185-6, 219, 241, 244, 248, 252
Frege 39, 43 n29, 52 n47, 68, 257-8, 270
Freud 79-81, 102, 179, 225
Frontal lobotomy, 157-60

Genetics (or DNA essentialism) 11, 255, 256
   essentialism 11, 27, 33, 40
   genetic selection 54
God 206-8, 214, 215
Gradualism 20

Hacking 6, 61, 180 n17, 190
Hampshire 114

Heidegger 35 n8, 63, 66, 70, 81, 82, 83, 85 n2, 102, 104-5, 165, 207 n24, 215, 219, 243 n29, 254, 258
HLeF (Holistically Longitudinally-extended Form) view 12, 14-17, 21, 27, 29, 33, 41, 47, 50, 73
*Humambas* 11-12, 60 n61
   *Humamba* argument 12
Hume, 70, 73, 87, 89, 155
Husserl 14, 62, 241

Identity 2, 3, 14, 17, 32ff, 40, 148, 195, 256-8, 259-61
   and action 119, 124
   and the brain 49, 75-6
   and brain bisection 148-55
   and emergence 183-4
   fission and fusion 75-6
   personal 41, 42, 48, 51-2, 87-9, 100, 186, 195, 209, 227, 229
   psychological criterion 73, 101, 170, 177, 185
   reductive accounts 52, 73-5, 87-8, 101, 103, 185, 222, 231-2
   and relation R 48-9, 73, 249-50
   two aspects — belonging and individuality 105, 168, 202, 212-3, 219, 229, 246-7
*imago* 152, 175 n10, 183 n21, 188, 237, 240-1, 244
immortality of the soul 67, 199, 206
intention 108, 114, 116, 119, 120, 124-5, 127, 134
   and brain events (see action — neurophilosophy)
I think 63-4, 66-9, 77, 79, 261-9

Jaspers 224, 262 n8, 266 n15

Kant, 1, 2, 4, 9, 41-2, 43, 45, 63, 65-82, 100, 115, 121, 127-8, 131-3, 134, 149, 155, 172, 194, 198 n9, 205-6, 207, 210, 211, 214, 219, 259-69
Kitcher 72, 76-8, 269

# Index

Lacan, 81 n33, 103, 124 n22, 168, 187, 196, 201, 206, 211 n27, 222, 231, 240, 243, 245
Levinas 53, 81 n33, 102-3, 131-3, 134, 165, 174 n7, 215, 221, 223 n1, 239, 241
Libet 111-12, 114
Locke 3, 4, 8, 9, 10, 13-14, 42, 64-5, 73, 83-4, 87, 89, 100, 102, 200, 253
Locked in syndrome 138-46
   Nick's story 138-46
   ethics 142-4
Looping effect of human kinds 61, 89, 180 n17, 190
Luria 117

McDowell, 69, 149, 265 n13
McIntyre 211, 238 n21, 239, 243-4
McMahan 52
Memory 86-99, 102-3, 173
   q-memory 75, 98, 99
   semantic 92-3
   and personal identity 95, 98-100
*mens rea* (see intention)
Mental processes 94
Merleau-Ponty 209, 241
Metaphysics 3, 4, 10, 18-19, 32, 33, 35 n12, 35-8, 43 n29, 53, 172, 196, 197, 204, 208, 253-4, 256, 258-9, 269
   narrative metaphysics 32-40, 61
   and holism 44, 49, 52, 84, 196
Mind-independence 253
Mode of presentation (see sense)
Moral thinking 211
   moral subject 100-1, 164-8, 185
   moral value of human being 15, 19, 33, 42, 43, 53, 54, 162, 194
Mortality 30
Multiple personality disorder (MPD see also DID) 5, 170, 175-93
   alters 178, 179, 180, 192
   forensic problems 176-7
   therapeutic murder problem 172, 176-7
Murray 7, 8, 23, 229

Names 180-2, 249, 258
Narrative 34-5, 97, 123, 125, 127, 134, 144, 162, 170, 180, 212, 224, 226-7, 228
   theory of identity (see also narrative metaphysics) 33, 51, 61, 89, 178, 227
   subject 82, 95, 99, 162, 226
   and memory 95-6
   the anti-narrative stance 98-9
Natural goodness 16, 165, 245
Natural kinds 269
Naturalism 2, 226-7, 245, 254, 266
Neuroethics vii, 5, 137, 160, 162-, 192, 210, 220-21, 224, 232, 234
Neuroimplantation 160-
Nietzsche 222, 233, 244, 248
Non-identity problem 33, 44-6
Nussbaum 237-8

Objects 263-5
   individuation of 38-9
Origins
   and identity 33, 45-7, 56 n53, 249, 259-60

Parfit 33, 44-5, 47, 56 n53, 57 n58, 73-8, 87, 147, 202
Persistent vegetative state 140-1, 143-5, 216
Personal identity (see identity)
Plato 206, 208, 214
Polkinghorne 202-4
Possible worlds 45-7, 57, 259-61
Post-structuralism 3
Potential 20, 28
Primary process 103-4
*Principia individuationis* 13, 37, 102 n10
Problem of evil 198
Psyche (see also soul) 3, 10-11, 80, 103, 137, 169, 171, 172-3, 225, 227
   as palimpsest 104, 172
Psychosurgery 156-61
PVS (see Persistent vegetative state)

Quine 39, 40 n19

Ramachandran 155, 210, 221
Rawls 52 n49, 237
Reactive attitudes (see also Strawson, P.) 15, 54, 123, 156, 163, 180, 189
Realism 1, 253-4, 271
Recognition as an ethical response 17, 19, 28, 53, 54, 100, 133, 145-6, 243, 245
Reference 269-72
Replica objection 199, 204-5, 207
Responsibility 107-8, 118, 120, 127-8, 131-5
Resurrection 199, 206-8, 217-18
  body 208
Russell, 1, 2, 63, 269

St Paul 207
Sartre 5, 61, 125, 133-4, 238
Saul 231-3
Schechtman 50 n44, 65, 66 n9, 83, 87-9, 99, 202, 227 n11
Second nature 44, 69-70, 78, 89, 121, 127, 128, 149
Self (see also subject) 1, 62, 150, 158, 213, 215, 224, 227, 229-30, 240
  noumenal (see also *ding-an-sich*) 4, 9, 70, 72, 76, 78-9, 82, 213, 264, 269
Sellars 1
Sense 39, 43, 68, 102, 256, 271
Sense of life 237-40, 244, 247
Snowdon 43
Social constructivism 174
Sorites paradox 162
Soul (see also psyche) 1, 2, 3, 8, 10-11, 63, 79, 83, 102, 136, 156, 194, 200, 203, 206, 211
  scopic 100, 102, 106
Space of reasons 1, 2, 78
Spirit, Spirituality 6, 194, 197-8, 213-4, 215, 216, 218
  and the brain 209-11, 214
Split brain patients (see brain bisection)

Stem cells 23ff, 50, 160
  ethics 28-31
Stories (see narrative)
Strawson P. (see also reactive attitudes) 15 n13, 67 n12, 71 n19, 77 n28, 261, 262 n6, 264 n10 n12, 266, 272 n20
structuralism 196, 270-2
Subject (see also moral subject) 2, 8, 32, 63ff, 81, 82, 200, 234-5, 248, 261-5
Subjectivity 2, 232, 248, 253

Taylor, 24, 222, 227, 232, 233, 234-5
Tracking 43 n27, 71, 72
Trauma (see *tuche*)
Trajectory-based-moral essentialism 26, 28-9
Transcendental unity of apperception (see I think)
*Tuche* 81 n33, 102-3

Unconscious 5, 80, 127 n27, 171 n3, 187
Uniqueness of human life 55, 58-9, 193
Unwitting sacrifice problem 56
Utility 54, 56
  general impersonal utility (GIU) claim 54, 56-7

Wegner 118, 120
Weil, 242
Wiggins 42 n25, 43, 52 n49, 149
Will 4, 87, 107, 114, 118, 120, 133
  free will 120, 123, 128-9, 132-4
  to power 134, 204 n20
Williams 52 n49, 67 n12, 76 n27, 106
Wittgenstein 1, 2, 8, 32, 33, 35 n12, 39, 40 n19, 51, 62, 63, 69, 70, 72 n22, 86-7, 89-95, 107, 121, 122-3, 150-1, 164, 169, 195, 196 n5, 197, 219, 219-20, 242, 254, 258, 259, 262, 268, 270
Work-in-progress argument 20-21
Wrongful birth 54-5

www.ingramcontent.com/pod-product-compliance
Lightning Source LLC
Chambersburg PA
CBHW021137230426
43667CB00005B/152